The Black Kalendar of Scotland:
Records of Notable Scotish Trials

A.H. Millar

The Black Kalendar of Scotland: Records of Notable Scotish Trials

The Black Kalendar of Scotland. Records of Notable

A.H. Millar, Martin Anderson

NYB00046

Monograph

New York City Bar

Dundee; London; Edinburgh; Cupar Fife; Aberdeen: John Leng & Co., John Menzies & Co., Westwood & Son., W. & W. Lindsay, 1884

The Making of Modern Law collection of legal archives constitutes a genuine revolution in historical legal research because it opens up a wealth of rare and previously inaccessible sources in legal, constitutional, administrative, political, cultural, intellectual, and social history. This unique collection consists of three extensive archives that provide insight into more than 300 years of American and British history. These collections include:

Legal Treatises, 1800-1926: over 20,000 legal treatises provide a comprehensive collection in legal history, business and economics, politics and government.

Trials, 1600-1926: nearly 10,000 titles reveal the drama of famous, infamous, and obscure courtroom cases in America and the British Empire across three centuries.

Primary Sources, 1620-1926: includes reports, statutes and regulations in American history, including early state codes, municipal ordinances, constitutional conventions and compilations, and law dictionaries.

These archives provide a unique research tool for tracking the development of our modern legal system and how it has affected our culture, government, business – nearly every aspect of our everyday life. For the first time, these high-quality digital scans of original works are available via print-on-demand, making them readily accessible to libraries, students, independent scholars, and readers of all ages.

The BiblioLife Network

This project was made possible in part by the BiblioLife Network (BLN), a project aimed at addressing some of the huge challenges facing book preservationists around the world. The BLN includes libraries, library networks, archives, subject matter experts, online communities and library service providers. We believe every book ever published should be available as a high-quality print reproduction; printed on-demand anywhere in the world. This insures the ongoing accessibility of the content and helps generate sustainable revenue for the libraries and organizations that work to preserve these important materials.

The following book is in the "public domain" and represents an authentic reproduction of the text as printed by the original publisher. While we have attempted to accurately maintain the integrity of the original work, there are sometimes problems with the original work or the micro-film from which the books were digitized. This can result in minor errors in reproduction. Possible imperfections include missing and blurred pages, poor pictures, markings and other reproduction issues beyond our control. Because this work is culturally important, we have made it available as part of our commitment to protecting, preserving, and promoting the world's literature.

GUIDE TO FOLD-OUTS MAPS and OVERSIZED IMAGES

The book you are reading was digitized from microfilm captured over the past thirty to forty years. Years after the creation of the original microfilm, the book was converted to digital files and made available in an online database.

In an online database, page images do not need to conform to the size restrictions found in a printed book. When converting these images back into a printed bound book, the page sizes are standardized in ways that maintain the detail of the original. For large images, such as fold-out maps, the original page image is split into two or more pages

Guidelines used to determine how to split the page image follows:

- Some images are split vertically; large images require vertical and horizontal splits.
- For horizontal splits, the content is split left to right.
- For vertical splits, the content is split from top to bottom.
- For both vertical and horizontal splits, the image is processed from top left to bottom right.

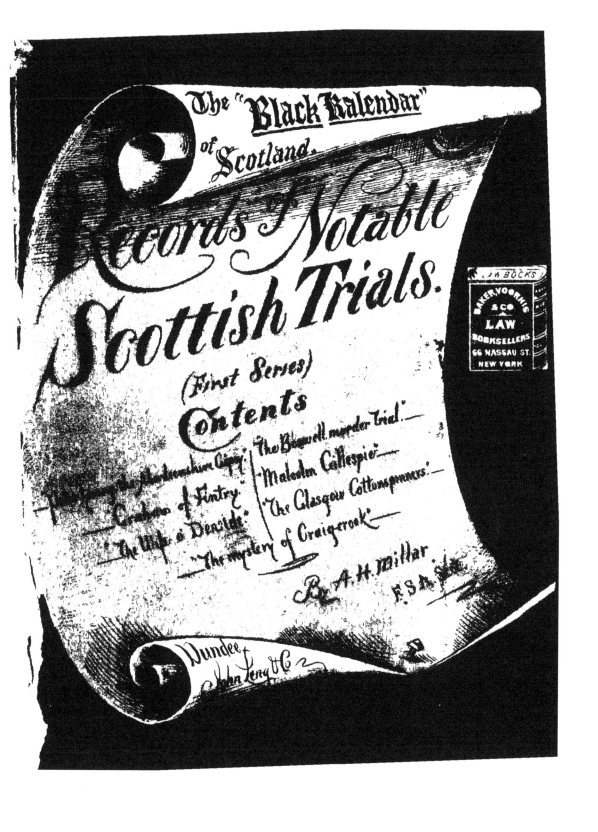

The Black Kalendar of Scotland:

RECORDS OF

NOTABLE SCOTTISH TRIALS

BY

A. H. MILLAR, F.S.A. Scot.

AUTHOR OF THE HISTORY OF ROB ROY, THE STORY OF QUEEN MARY, &c.

With Illustrations by MARTIN ANDERSON

FIRST SERIES

Laws are handed down
Like an hereditary sore disease
From race to race and slowly glide along
From one spot to another. Reason turns
To foolishness, beneficence becomes
A heavy ill.
—*Goeth*

DUNDEE AND LONDON	JOHN LENG & CO.
EDINBURGH	JOHN MENZIES & CO.
CUPAR FIFE,	WESTWOOD & SON
ABERDEEN,	W. & W. LINDSAY

1884

121(8)

Nu 611

John Leng & Co
Printers and Lithograph
Bell Street, Dundee

PREFACE

———

THESE Trials have been selected more for the historical information which they contain than for any sensationalism connected with them. Accuracy and completeness have been sought after rather than elegance of literary style; and the letters describing the deathbed of Sir ALEXANDER BOSWELL, which have not hitherto been published, should render this account of his famous duel specially interesting. The illustrations have been reproduced from sketches made at the different places by Mr MARTIN ANDERSON. The Author's grateful acknowledgments are due to Mrs BOSWELL, Balmuto House; Chief Constable M'CALL, Glasgow; A. C. LAMB, Esq., F.S.A. Scot., Dundee; ALEX. MACLAUCHLAN, Esq., Perth; JAMES RETTIE, Esq., Aberdeen (the publisher of Seaton's picture of the Old Tolbooth); DAVID SMALL, Esq., Artist, Glasgow; &c.

DUNDEE, *January* 1884.

INDEX.

———

OLD PRISON AND TOWN HOUSE, PERTH
From a Painting made in 1834 by Mr Alex Maclauchlan

INTRODUCTORY.

Historians are at length beginning to under stand that the history of a nation's progress cannot be adequately written from the records of courtly pageants or of aggressive wars, and historical research of late years has been directed rather towards the condition of the people than to the opulence of the king The wars which absorbed the attention of the time are now only considered with reference to their interruption of Commerce, and the condition of the lower orders at stated periods, has lately been taken as affording a more definite gauge of advancement than could be given either by the dubious success of arms or by the triumphs of diplomacy. The upper classes may find it convenient to conform to the strict morals of severer nations, but the state of a country can only be ascertained by a consideration of those seething masses of humanity by whose labours the upper classes exist, and from whom we receive alike our greatest patriots and our most atrocious criminals No history of Scotland which ignores them can be complete, and it is our intention, in the series of articles here initiated, to give some idea of the under current of life in Scotland during the wide period which they shall embrace. We shall not indulge in imaginary flights, convinced as we are that

"Truth is strange
Stranger than fiction.

but we shall endeavour to arrange our subjects in such a fashion that, whilst they may interest the most casual reader, they may be of incalculable service to the student of Scottish history. No fact shall be stated without authority, no evidence led which a court of law would reject.

During the course of these papers we shall reproduce sketches of some of the most famous Tolbooths of olden times in Scotland, as well as many of those Criminal Courts which have been the scenes of forensic triumphs and of notable vindications of law and order. At the head of this article we place a sketch of the ancient Tolbooth of Perth, taken from a painting by A. Maclauchlan, Esq, executed in 1834, and regarding which he writes thus :—

The building in centre of picture is the Old Town House and the building with the tower, to the left, is the old prison, formerly part of the Chapel of the Virgin. The Chapel of the Virgin at one time occupied the whole site and was erected at a very early period, for it is described as having been in a ruinous condition in 1210, one of the periodical floods of the Tay having nearly destroyed it.

It was repaired, and continued to occupy the site at foot of High Street extending right across the street and shutting out the view of the river, until 1621.

This site was exactly at the west end of the old bridge, access to which was had through an arch way, and to the river by a stair called "Our Lady's Steps." In 1621 the bridge, which had recently been rebuilt, was entirely swept away by a flood in the Tay, which also destroyed the portion of the Chapel of the Virgin next the river.

The Chapel having been secularised at the Reformation, no attempt was made to restore it, and in 1696 the Town House—including Council Room, offices, weigh house, &c—was built, and remained as seen in the picture until 1839, when it was removed and the High Street opened up to the river. The portion of the Chapel which escaped the flood—that at the left of the picture, with the tower and small spire—was used from the Reformation till the early years of the present century as the prison for the county and city, and continued to be used as the Police Office and police cells till four or five years ago. The ancient crypt of the chapel was divided by massive stone walls into cells, and these were excessively gloomy—the heavy arched stone work overhead—without windows or opening of any kind except the door.

A consistent, but doubtful, Perth tradition says this portion of the Chapel was restored about the middle of the fifteenth century, and the tower erected by Cochran, architect to and favourite of James III and ancestor of the Earls of Dundonald. This last remaining portion, the cells of which had long been severely condemned by successive Government inspectors, was removed in 1876 and the present handsome Town House erected by Mr A Heiton, architect.

The Circuit Court was held in a hall above the cells, which had probably been used as the Chapel proper, and executions took place on a platform which ran from the front of this room to the door of the weigh house seen in the picture.

This Court, on the demolition of the Town House in 1859 was fitted up as a Council Chamber, and was used as such till the erection of the present new buildings.

The Circuit Court was conducted in a way that would rather astonish the present generation. The public were admitted to a small gallery at the east end of the Court on payment of 3d each, and thirsty auditors were provided with Edinburgh ale by the jailer at 6d per bottle.

PETER YOUNG, THE ABERDEENSHIRE GIPSY

PART I

'Steek the aumrie, lock the kist
Else some gear may weel be mist
Donald Caird finds orra things
Where Allan Gregor fand the tings,
Dunts o kebluck taits o woo,
Whyles a hen and whyles a soo
Webs or duds frae hedge or yaird—
'Ware the wuddie Donald Caird'—*Scott*

The Gipsies, or "Egyptians, as they are called in old records, appear in Scottish history at a very early date. No race amongst the varieties of the human species has given rise to more speculation than the Gipsies and the most erudite investigators have been baffled in all attempts to discover their origin. Some antiquaries have looked upon them as one of the lost tribes of Israel, whilst others as confidently ascribe to them a pre-historic date, and remove the place of their origin to the remotest shores of India. Their language is said to be a corrupt form of the Sanscrit dialect still in use in the Mooltan, on the Indus, and it is asserted that they were expelled from India by the cruelties of Timour Leng in 1400 A D. After wandering over the southern portions of Europe, they settled principally in Spain, finding protection under the Moors, and that country has been their chief seat ever since. From this spot they spread themselves throughout France and Britain, adhering with marvellous tenacity to their ancient customs, and keeping themselves as a distinct race, a peculiar people.

Their first appearance in Scottish history is made during the reign of James IV, and several of them appeared as dancers before his successor at Holyrood House in 1530, and are styled indifferently "Egyptians" or "Moors." But though thus introduced under Royal patronage, they soon forfeited the favour with which they had been received. Their thieving propensities erelong rendered them obnoxious to the law abiding Scots, and though there are letters in existence, both from James IV and James V, extending protection to two several "Earls of Little Egypt,' there are more ominous appearances made by the Gipsies in the statute book of the realm. Thus in 1636 the Privy Council passed an Act against them so drastic in its nature that it seems to imply that the Gipsies were considered incorrigible. We may quote this Act as a curiosity of Criminal Law, and as indicating unmistakably the feelings with which the race was regarded —

"Apud Edr, 10 Novembris 1636.

Forsameikle as Sir Arthur Douglas of Quitting hame haveing litel e tane and apprehendit some of the vagabond and counterfut theives and limmars callit Egyptianis he presentit and delyverit thame to the Sheriff principall of the Sherefdome of Edinburghe, within the constabularie of Hadington, quhair they have remained this month, or thairby, and quhairas the keeping of thame longer within the said Tolbooth is troublesome and burdenable to the town of Hadington, and fosters the said theives in ane opinion of impunitie, to the in couriageing of the rest of that infamous byke of lawles limmars to continow in their theivish trade, Thairfore the Lords of Secret Counsell ordanis the Shireff of Hadinton or his depute to pronounce doome and sentence of death agains so manie counteriout Theives as ar men, and againis so manie of the weomen as wants children, ordaining the men to be hangit and the weoman to be drowned, and that suche of the weomin as hes children to be scourgit throw the burgh of Hadinton and Brunt in the cheeke, and ordanis and commandis the Provost and Baillies of Hadinton to caus this doome be execute vpon the saidis persons accordinglie'

From this time forward the Gipsies never succeeded in regaining the favour which they had lost, and they became the pariahs of Scottish society, trusted by no one, suspected by all. They had ever been famous as artificers, but their trades seemed merely assumed as a cloak to hide their lawless and nefarious purposes, and they lived by poaching and horse stealing even during the period when these were capital crimes.

The chief seat of the Scottish Gipsies was at Yetholm, and here the King or Queen kept court until very recent times, but numerous families of them "settled'—if that term may be used—in various parts of the country, and led a thoroughly Bohemian life. The district of Lochgelly, in Fifeshire, was long a favourite residence with them, and a considerable number still infested that locality in the early years of this century. Aberdeenshire was also one of their chosen spots, and it was in this quarter where Peter Young, whose story we are now to relate, first saw the light of day.

He was born in the year 1765, and though his life was a short one he experienced within its brief space as many strange adventures as fall to the lot of much older men. His parents were connected with a troop of "curds," or travelling tinkers, who wandered throughout Aberdeenshire, and his earliest years were spent beneath the canvas of their tent, and in the full enjoyment of unrestrained freedom. The training thus received was not calculated to make him a useful member of society, and neither the precept nor example of his parents and associates was likely to improve him. The character of those with whom his lot was cast may be judged from the fact that "persons of the name of Young are to be found in every gang or cairds of whose apprehension there are any notices about this time." Under these circumstances little could be expected from him, and the superiority which he latterly obtained amongst them was due to his hardihood and address in eluding justice or escaping from its grasp. Though only twenty three years of age when he was "justified"—as the old term goes—at Edinburgh, he had the reputation of having broken out of every prison in Scotland, and his name was famous as a hero of romance whilst he was yet in his teens.

We have not been able to discover upon what foundation, other than tradition, his fame rests; for the only public records of his crimes and 'hairbreadth 'scapes which we can find merely cover the last two years of his life. In 1786 he was confined in the jail at Perth for some petty theft, and whilst there he succeeded in making good his escape, liberating at the same time two women who were his fellow prisoners. One of these was Agnes Brown, a notorious Gipsy criminal who had originally belonged to the tribe at Lochgelly, and had been associated throughout her long life with crime in all its most repulsive phases. She had been sentenced to banishment in 1753 for theft committed at the Michael Fair of Kinkell, but the sentence had not been fully carried out, and she had remained in prison for the dreary period of thirty three years, until this gallant youth came to set her free. She made no good use of her liberty, however, for in the following year (1787) she was apprehended for picking pockets in the crowd gathered to witness an execution, and was whipped through the streets of Aberdeen, and transported for seven years.

Nor did Peter Young himself over value the freedom which he had won at so great a risk, as in a few months afterwards he was busily engaged at his former occupation. Though barely twenty one years of age, he had burdened himself with a wife, whom he associated with him in his most daring exploits. If there be any truth in heredity, Jean Wilson was well fitted to aid him, as she could trace back a pedigree of crime. Her mother, Margaret Brown, had been tried at Perth in 1776, and sentenced to seven years transportation, but she succeeded in effecting her escape from jail after she had endured two years confinement. She fell under the power of the law again however, in 1788, and was incarcerated in Aberdeen Jail at the time when both her daughter and son in law were confined there under sentence of death.

In concert with his wife, Young had planned and executed a daring robbery by housebreaking in Portsoy, but luck had deserted him, and they were captured and brought to Aberdeen for trial. After a lengthened investigation they were both found guilty, and sentenced to death. The execution of Peter Young and his wife was appointed to take place on 16th November 1787, but, as the old Scottish proverb truly declares, "there's mony a slip atween the crag and the wuddy."

Old Tolbooth of Aberdeen in 1806 (*from Seaton's Picture of Castle Street*)

PART II

On Donald Caird the doom was stern,
Craig to tether legs to airn
But Donald Caird wi mickle study
Caught the gift to cheat the wuddie,
Rings of airn and bolts of steel
Fell like ice frae hand and heel!
Watch the sheep in fauld and g en,
Donald Caird s come again!"
                                    —*Scott*

The sentence of death which had been pro

nounced against Peter Young at the Aberdeen Autumn Circuit Court was to be carried into execution upon the 16th of November 1787 The same doom awaited his wife, but as she was declared to be in a state of pregnancy her term of life was extended by the sentence of the Court till August in the following year Young s career was thus likely to reach an abrupt termination, and his youthful partner was involved in his ruin.

The Scottish prisons of the time seem to have been guarded with inexcusable laxity. Though strongly built so far as masonry was concerned, and furnished with "yrne yetts" calculated to resist all efforts to gain access from the outside, they did not invariably restrain their occupants; and Peter Young had already discovered that

> ' Stone walls do not a prison make
> Nor iron bars a cage '

Modern improvements have swept away the greater portion of the Tolbooth of Aberdeen, but the adventurous visitor may yet discover the vaulted cell beneath the ancient steeple in which Peter Young was probably confined. The roof rises to a height of about ten feet from the stone floor at its greatest altitude, and the bracketting from which the vaults spring is barely six feet high. Along the wall furthest removed from the window an iron rod of 1½ inch diameter is fixed, and upon it the sliding shackles may still be seen by which the most atrocious malefactors were confined. The window space is enclosed by transverse bars, but is otherwise quite open to the weather; and the hapless wretches who may have been chained to the opposite wall must have bided the pelting of many a pitiless storm.

Young had escaped from many of the Scottish prisons before this time, when he was merely imprisoned upon lesser charges, and it was not likely that he would tamely remain within the Tolbooth of Aberdeen now that his life was in danger. He determined thus far to make a bold effort for life and liberty.

Circumstances were greatly in his favour as Andrew Gray, the jailer, was extremely lax in the exercise of his duty. From the record of proceedings afterwards taken against the latter, we find that he made the Tolbooth a mere change house, where liquors might be freely purchased either by the prisoners or their visitors. The keys were entrusted to the keeping of a servant, who refused entrance to no one that could offer a few pence for the privilege; and Young found no difficulty in procuring from his friends such tools as were necessary to effect his release. He was delicately formed, and his wrists and ankles were so small that he could extricate himself without much trouble from the shackles and handcuffs which were imposed to restrain him; and when once free to move about his prison, he soon found means to utilise the saw knives with which his friends had supplied him. His first task was to release his fellow prisoners from their bonds, and they set to work upon the iron window bars and speedily cleared the aperture of all obstruction. During this operation they

narrowly escaped detection, for two of their saw knives accidentally fell into the street and were picked up by some passers by and handed to the jailer; but Gray, "good, easy man," was not in the least troubled by this discovery, and did not feel called upon to interfere. Young made his escape therefore with comparative ease, and liberated the whole of his fellow prisoners at the same time. The Tolbooth of Aberdeen was left literally tenantless.

[*Note*—A strange tale is told of this escape which differs somewhat from the above. It is related that when the jailer came to inquire if he wanted anything for the night, he sprang upon him, took his keys from him, and ordered him to lie on his back upon the floor, threatening to take his life if he dared to move. Young then went through the building and released all his fellow prisoners, and unlocked the front gate so as to let them all escape. To his dismay he found that there was a bolt on the *outside* of the door, but his great physical strength enabled him to overcome this difficulty. The armed sentinel, expecting no attack from the *inside* of the jail, was taken by surprise, and Young, seizing his firelock, stood sentry over him till all the captives had escaped. He then politely returned the firelock to the soldier, and followed his companions to Deeside. Though this story is more romantic than the one we have adopted, the latter we believe to be the true version, as it appears in the legal proceedings against Young and Gray, the jailer.]

It is hardly credible that such a daring exploit as this could have been accomplished in the very midst of a populous town without attracting the notice of the inhabitants; yet it is a veritable fact that all the prisoners made good their escape, and might have preserved their liberty but for their foolhardiness. A party of six of them, consisting of Young and his wife, an old soldier called Bartlett, a youth named Paul, who had been condemned to death for sheep stealing, and John Munro and Patrick Anderson, two well known malefactors, set out by Deeside, intending probably to shape their course either for Montrose or Dundee, and soon placed many miles betwixt themselves and Aberdeen. It may be imagined, however, that such a strange company could not pass through Kincardineshire without attracting some attention; and the officers who had been despatched in pursuit of them soon came upon their traces. Young's knowledge of the country, gained during his wandering life, had enabled him to plan a bold attempt at housebreaking in the locality of Mill of Kincardine; but whilst in the very act of committing this new crime the runaways were overtaken by their pursuers. Four of them were secured, but Young and Anderson managed to elude their vigilance and get clear away. The other prisoners were led back to Aberdeen, and placed under stricter surveillance than formerly.

The magistrates of the city immediately issued a proclamation offering a reward of twenty guineas for the apprehension of Young, and describing his appearance in these terms— ' A stout young man, pock pitted, aged about twenty two, with a remarkably sharp eye, about five feet ten inches high, thin made, has an arch sneering look, is a native of Deeside, in the county of Aberdeen, the language of which county he speaks. He is further described as wearing ' a tartan short jacket of large squares or lozens, trousers of the same stuff, and a bonnet, so that he is rather a remarkable figure." Yet, despite his "kenspeckle" appearance, Young put the authorities to defiance, and showed himself openly in the streets of Perth, where his former exploits had already made him notorious. At length word was sent to Aberdeen two months after his escape that he was in custody at Arbroath, but ere the officer from the former place could arrive to identify him he had again broken from prison. The news of this fresh adventure soon spread through the district, and bands of volunteer detectives set out from Arbroath to scour the country in search of him. They were at length successful in apprehending him near Montrose, and he was borne back in triumph to Arbroath Jail. Unwilling to risk another escape, the officers from Aberdeen conveyed him to that city in a post chaise, closely guarded by a company of soldiers, having first placed his feet in irons and his wrists in manacles. In this fashion he was conducted back to his old quarters in the Tolbooth of Aberdeen, and lodged there securely upon New Year's Day, 1788.

The magistrates as custodiers of his person now found themselves in a strange predicament. It was true that Peter Young had been regularly tried, convicted, and sentenced in the previous autumn, but it was not the less certain that the prisoner, upon whom the doom of death had been pronounced, had made his escape from their custody, and the question arose as to whether *this* man was really the convict. It is needless to say that he denied his identity steadfastly, and the authorities scarcely felt justified in running the risk of executing the wrong man. To relieve themselves of this responsibility the whole matter was reported to the High Court of Justiciary in Edinburgh, and a warrant was granted to bring him from Aberdeen to be examined before the Lords. On the 19th of January he was again despatched under a strong guard for the south.

The journey was a tedious one, and the party rested for the night at Perth, lodging their prisoner within the cell which he had formerly occupied in Perth Jail. It is probable that he had concealed some of his implements in this apartment, as he succeeded during the night in severing the iron fetters which bound him, and but for a sudden interruption would have again escaped. Ultimately, however, he was safely delivered to the authorities in Edinburgh, and securely confined in the Tolbooth there. His efforts for liberty were not yet over, for it is related that " within an hour after he had been committed the inner turnkey, having come into his cell to see what he was about, found him busily employed in cutting one of his leg irons with the blade of a shoemaker's knife which he had converted into a saw. On his being minutely searched, two of these instruments were found concealed between the inner and outer soles of one of his shoes."

He was brought before the High Court of Justiciary on 3d March, and when asked what he had to say against the sentence of death being carried into effect he boldly asserted that he was not the man. The Lords were thus placed in a serious difficulty. They could not try him again for a capital offence without assuming that he was *not* Peter Young, since the long established usage of Scots Law forbids that a man be tried twice for the same crime. Yet if their prisoner was not Peter Young they had really no crime to lay to his charge. The advocates who had taken up his case—the famous Henry Erskine and Charles Hope, afterwards Lord President—claimed that he should be tried by a jury as the question of his identity was one of *fact* not of *law*, and the life of an innocent man might thus be forfeited without his having had the usual right of a regular trial. The case was argued at great length and with much ability on both sides, and it was not until the 15th of March that a decision was finally given. There were six of the Lords of Justiciary on the bench at that time, and after a protracted debate it was found that four of them believed that no jury was required in this case, and that they had simply to satisfy themselves of the identity of Peter Young with the prisoner, and then order the former sentence to be executed against him. Amongst these, Lord Hailes, the eminent antiquary, took the lead as senior judge, and quoted many historical precedents in support of this view. Lords Henderland and Stonefield and the Lord Justice Clerk agreed with him, but Lords Eskgrove and Swinton dissented strongly from his conclusions, but, of course, without effect. Two witnesses only were called to swear to the identity of the prisoner with the convicted Peter Young, and no theory whatever was advanced in his defence He was sentenced to be executed at Edinburgh on the 2d of April

Considerable discussion was occasioned by this decision It seemed as though the Court of Justiciary was assuming the power to dispense with jury trial when it suited its convenience, and quite a commotion was caused throughout the country by this idea The public, jealous of an infringement upon their rights, and moved also by the tales of Young's audacity, kindness to his fellow prisoners, and faithfulness to his wife, made powerful efforts to have his sentence cancelled Their representations were effectual with the King thus far that a respite was granted, and the date of the execution altered to the 2d of July

Meanwhile, warned by their past experience his jailers had taken special means to keep him securely within their grasp They had a strongly railed iron cage prepared for him, in which this unfortunate man spent the few remaining days of his life, never for a moment left unattended, and guarded as though he were a dangerous animal No reprieve followed upon his respite, and he suffered the extreme penalty of the law upon the day appointed His wife's sentence was commuted to transportation for seven years, but she was kept in the Tolbooth of Aberdeen till June 1791 —five years after her trial—and then shipped to New South Wales, never more to be heard of

The excitement caused by this peculiar case was not readily allayed Many a fierce debate has been held over it, and even yet we may encounter legal gentlemen who have grave doubts as to the accuracy of the Lords' procedure, even though they admit that, according to the notions of the time, there were few criminals who more richly merited his doom than Peter Young, the Aberdeenshire Gipsy

MAINS CASTLE, FROM THE COURT YARD

GRAHAM OF FINTRY, A STORY OF MAINS CASTLE

PART I

' *Angelo*—We must not make a scare-crow of the law,
    Setting it up to fear the birds of prey,
    And let it keep one shape, till custom make it
    Their perch, and not their terror

               —*Measure for Measure*

There is a marked difference betwixt the history of the Feudal System in England and in Scotland The check which the English Barons gave to King John at Runnymede was practically a limitation of the power of the Crown in the interests of the people , and Magna Charta finally secured the freedom of the subject by curtailing the absolute despotism of the monarch But in Scotland the case was far different The frequent changes in her rulers from the time of Malcolm Ceanmohr onwards had made it necessary for the kings who hoped to keep the throne to cultivate the affection and support of her meanest subjects , and they soon discovered that the love and esteem of the lower orders formed a strong bulwark and sure retreat in times of danger

When James I of Scotland returned to his kingdom after his long captivity he found the realm in a state of dire confusion During his protracted absence the Barons had run riot in the land, and every man did what seemed right in his own eyes, regardless either of justice or humanity With profound foresight the King saw that the only method at his disposal for checking this usurpation of power was for him to make the people his allies against the petty despots who tyrannised over them His plan succeeded marvellously The power of law, administered with that justice which eminently distinguished him, soon made itself felt throughout the distracted kingdom , and though he fell a victim to the infuriate rage of the Barons, he was regarded by the people as a martyr in the cause of order Thenceforth there was a Holy Alliance between the King and the Peasant for the overthrow of the hateful Feudal System

The struggle, however, was a long and dreary one, and for centuries it might well be questioned whether the foes within the kingdom were not worse than the enemies without It was not, indeed, until the reign of James VI that the Crown felt itself strong enough to attempt the suppression of the power of the nobles and even then it might have failed but for the dissensions which arose amongst the nobility themselves The vast revenues of the Church had become the prey of the nobles and they quarrelled like angry wolves over their spoil, each turning his hand against his brother Out of this Chaos came that Kosmos of law and order under whose beneficent rule existence is made possible to us That the reader may have some idea of the terrors of the Old System, and witness in imagination the growth of the New, we purpose relating a true tale of this transition period

> Of many changes aptly joined
> Is bodied forth the second whole
> Heard gradual on less the soul
> Of Discord race the rising wind ,
>
> ' A wind to puff your idol fires,
> And heap their ashes on the head
> To shame the boast so often made
> That we are wiser than our sires '

Sir David Graham of Fintry, though possessing no higher dignity than that of a Knight, could claim kinship with the noblest in the land, and even boast of a Royal descent The founder of his family was the son of a Princess of Scotland, and he is connected by birth and marriage with the Earls of Angus and Montrose He had an extensive patrimony in Carrondale, Stirlingshire, but having acquired the lands of Strathdichty he erected a baronial residence on the banks of Gellie Burn, near Dundee, and transferred his household to the shire of Angus To perpetuate the memory of the spot whence he had sprung, he named his new house after the old one, calling it the Castle of Fintry Strangely enough, both the castle and the estate have changed their names within the last century The one is now known as Mains Castle, the other as Linlithen He probably began to build the Castle in 1562, as that date may still be traced over one of the gateways, and had doubtless found it habitable in 1567, the period when our story begins

No one of the fierce Barons of that time had been more strenuous in defence of his feudal rights than Sir David Graham He had claimed an absolute right over his vassals, had upheld his power by "furk and fosse, by pit and gallows ," and had ruled his subjects with an iron hand The disturbed state of the country during the troubled reign of Mary Queen of Scots seemed to give him license, and he took full advantage of it Even the servants of his neighbours who offended him suffered at his hands , and he made common cause with the wildest young bloods of the nobility Whilst the country was divided between the retainers of Moray and Mary, the Laird of Fintry took occasion to gratify his private revenge

There was a certain man named John Pegot, who lived at this time in Balnaboth, on the estate of Clova His superior was one of the Ogilvys of Airlie, but he had chosen to support the side espoused by Ogilvy of Inverquharity Lord Ogilvy of Airlie was a boon companion of Sir David Graham of Fintry, and these two valiant Knights agreed—over a bottle, probably—that they would teach Pegot to behave otherwise Airlie did not wish to appear in the matter, and Graham undertook the execution of their plan without his aid Summoning a few of his vassals, he rode from Mains Castle to Balnaboth, beyond Kirriemuir, and entering the house of Pegot, "quhair he was than in quyat and sober maner, beleveand ne harme nor injurie to have been done to him be ony personis, bot to have levit vnder Goddis peax and our souerane lordis, ' Sir David and his accomplices, "violenthe, maisterfullie, and perforce, tuke the said vmqle Johnne furth of his awin duelling hous to Erlis Stradichtie [Mains Castle], quhair the said David and remanent personnes foirsaidis of his speciall cawsing, hounding, sending, devysing, arte, partctaking, assistance and ratihibitioune, as said is, detenit, and held him in captiuitie thairintill, be the space of viij dayis or thairby thaireftir , committand thairthrow, manefest oppressioune vpoun him, hie being our souerane lordis frie liege , and vsurpand of his hienes auctoritie vpoune thame, in hie and manefest contemptioun thairof "

A most thorough search into the records of the time has failed to disclose the crime of John Pegot, and we are almost forced to believe that the Laird of Fintry had no special ill will towards this unfortunate individual, but merely wished to testify by his sufferings his great contempt for the Ogilvys who had not joined with him

John Pegot was lodged for more than a week in the newly built dungeons of Mains Castle, and was, most likely, the first occupant of this dreary abode By some means—not now discoverable—he managed to escape the toils of his captor, and threw himself upon the protection of Sir John Ogilvy of Inverquharity, who was then at enmity with Sir David Graham of Fintry Inverquharity's complaint commanded attention, and Sir David and his two brothers, Walter and James Graham, were "callit to vnderlye the law, befoir the Justice or his Depuitis, in the Tolbuyth of Edinburghe, the tent day of Februare, in the zeir of God Im Vc lxvij zeiris"

Few Scotsmen will fail to recall the terrible tidings which this date disclosed It was the day succeeding that fearful night when Darnley fell a victim to the lust and cruelty of Bothwell Sir David Graham made his appearance in Court, defying his accusers, but the alarming tidings of Darnley's murder postponed all business He had besides found a protector willing to screen him from the vengeance of the law in the person of his relative the Earl of Angus and that nobleman took advantage of an ancient legal privilege that he might shield his protégé

From a very early period in the history of Scotland the country had been divided into tracts of territory which were placed in the custody of prominent noblemen, that the laws might be administered as though in the presence of the King This jurisdiction could only be conferred by the monarch, and the lands over which it extended were given to its holder *in liberam regalitatem*, and thence termed a Regality The Lord of the Regality had absolute power over all the inhabitants, and no appeal could be made against him save to the King himself Indeed, so far reaching was his sway that he could demand the custody of any of his subjects from any other Lord of Regality, no matter what offences he might be charged with, provided he gave security that ' justice would be lawfully administered " It will thus be seen that this form of procedure was the reverse of that at present in practice, for criminals are now tried near the spot where the crime was committed, not at the place of their birth nor among their own friends The accused when thus demanded by the Lord of his Regality was said to be 'repledged (*repleza* is the old Scots law term), and this method in those lawless times became "a fruitful source of injustice and oppression, and was often employed to frustrate the ends of law "

The interposition of the Earl of Angus at this period procured the release of Sir David Graham of Fintry and his two brothers—Walter and James Graham—upon the pledge that they would appear to answer their accusers ' in the toune of Kirrimuir, place wont and used for haulding of Courtis thairintill, the xviij day of May next thaireftir, in the zeir of God Im Vc lxviij zeiris" (1568) Sir David and his brethren returned to Strathdichty to complete the building of Mains Castle and to devise means of evading the punishment which threatened them

STAIRCASE IN LOWER MAINS CASTLE

THF REGALITY COURT OF KIRRIEMUIR

PART II

" Beneath these battlements, within those walls
    Power dwelt amidst her passions in proud state
    Each robber chief upheld his arméd halls,
    Doing his evil will nor less elate
    Than mightier heroes of a longer date.
                        —*Byron.*

The misfortunes of Scotland proved of great advantage to Sir David Graham and his associates When the day came round for their trial at the Court of Regality in Kirriemuir, the country was really plunged into greater distress than ever The hapless Queen Mary had been imprisoned in Lochleven Castle by her ruthless persecutors, and had made a romantic escape from their toils, and was again at liberty And upon this very 8th day of May 1568 she raised her standard at Hamilton, and prepared for a final conflict with her enemies Intelligence of this movement had reached Kirriemuir, and as Sir David Graham was known to be a sympathiser with the Queen, it was deemed advisable to postpone the diet until the decisive conflict between Mary and her subjects had taken place The Knight of Fintry, knowing the state of trepidation into which the Regent's party had been thrown by the Queen's escape, appeared boldly within the Court-house and dared his "unfriends" to proceed against him The Justiciary Record declares that "albeit the said David and his collegis foirsaid comperit, zit in respect of the trubles quhilk oc curit within the realme for the tyme, justice thane culd nocht be ministret in the said matei, but wes continewit to the last day of Junii nixto cum thaireftir." This postponement was a distinc

triumph for Sir David, as in those troublous times no one could tell accurately which party would finally be uppermost The Queen had still her battle to fight, but it was not impossible that she might ultimately regain the throne from which she had been violently deposed,

The imprisonment of John Pegot in Mains Castle had now assumed quite a political aspect His case was no longer a question betwixt a baron and a vassal, it was practically a debate between the Queen's supporters and the Regent Moray's party The district of Angus and the Mearns looked on anxiously whilst the plea continued, knowing that its import was greater than appeared on the surface

Ere the Court of Regality met again the fatal battle of Langside had been lost and won, and Mary was a fugitive upon alien soil Yet so insecure were the members of the Court as to the final outcome of the civil war then raging that they deemed it advisable to postpone once more the hearing of this important case Many of the Queen's ad herents were still in arms The Earl of Huntly was ranging through Aberdeenshire at the head of a considerable army, and several of the leading noblemen on the east coast of Scotland were ready to rise in defence of the Queen Her mis fortunes had increased rather than diminished their ardour, and they only waited the advent of a competent leader to renew their efforts in her cause The Bailies of the Court of Regality deemed it prudent, therefore, to leave this de batable case over for another month, and took surety that the accused persons would appear to answer the charge against them on "the xxvij day of July next thaireftir following"

A curious combination of circumstances arose at this time. The Bailies of Regality, upon whom the trial of this case fell, were Sir John Ogilvy of Inverqubarity and James Scrymgeour of Glaswall. The former of these was open to the charge of partial counsel, since John Pegot had adhered to him in preference to his own superior of Clova, and only a well balanced mind could be expected to judge fairly in such a dispute. We fear that there is some foundation for the supposition that the case had been postponed so as to admit of its coming before Sir John for trial, that he might thereby deal a blow to the Marian party in Forfarshire. If that was the intention of the Regent Moray's supporters, it was thoroughly defeated by Sir David Graham and his associates.

The civil war had set father against son and brother against kinsman, and the feeling of animosity came largely into this peculiar case. Sir David's staunchest friend was Lord Ogilvy of Airlie, yet his judge was to be Ogilvy of Inverquharity, his companion's brother in law. Besides, the crime of John Pegot had been an adherence to the party which this judge had espoused, and his capture would thus seem more heinous to Sir John Ogilvy than to one less interested in the matter. All these considerations were, doubtless, carefully estimated by Sir David Graham, and, seeing little chance of his receiving impartial justice at the hands of his judge, he determined to execute a most daring move.

The supporters of Mary's claim to the throne were being gradually thinned away by the ill-success of their endeavours, yet a few of the east country nobles held together for her defence, and pledged her ambiguously in their dining chambers. Amongst these chivalric but deluded men the most prominent were the Earl of Huntly, the Earl of Crawford, Lord Ogilvy of Airlie, and Sir David Graham of Fintry. These nobles bound themselves together to aid each other against their common enemies, and though Queen Mary's case seemed for the time quite hopeless, they still looked for a turn of Fortune's wheel. The situation of Sir David called forth their sympathy, and they decided to aid him in a tangible and effectual manner. They drew together all the armed retainers whom they could muster in the neighbourhood of Kirriemuir, so that they might intimidate the Court of Regality by a display of physical strength. This method of conducting a lawsuit had already been objected to, and it was now looked upon as a confession of weakness if the accused had many armed friends amongst the audience in Court.

But Graham and his associates were determined to take Justice by the forelock, regardless of laws which could not be adequately administered during this unsettled time. The four confederates brought together about a thousand men, fully armed, and prepared for any emergency. Their course of conduct is quaintly recorded in the phraseology of the time within the Records of Justiciary, and from these we may transcribe this strange story of masterful resistance to the law. The ancient document runs thus:—

"Vpoune the quhilk twentie sevin day of July foirsaid, compeirit Johnne Ogilvye of Inuerquharratie, knycht, and James Scrymegeour of Glaswall, baillers of said Regalitie in that pairt within the said toune of Keremuir, and than, at the said place, vsit and wont for haulding of Courtis thair intill, fencit and held Court in dew tyme of day, think and to have proceidit to the administratioune of justice in the said mater; In the meyntyme, the said Dauid Grahame of Fintrie, knycht, getand knawlege thairof, and vnderstanding him giltie of the said cryme, and naw was willing to compeir and vndirly the law thairfoir, joynit him with vmqle George, Erle of Huntlie; Dauid, Erle of Crawfurd; James, Lord Ogilbye; quhilkis threw his persuisione and counsale, parte taking, denysing assistance and ratihabitioune, to geddir with the said Dauidis self and his complicis, in proper persoun, with conuocatioune of the Kingis liegis, to the nowmer of ane thowsand men or thairby; boddin in fer of weir with swordis, jakkis, steil bonnetis, speris, culveringis, and vtheris wappinis, inuasiue, incontrair the tenour of the Actis of Parliament; come to the said toune of Keremuir, the said xxvij day of July, the zeir of God Im. Vc lxvij zeiris, and stoppit the haulding of the said Court, and all administratioune of Justice thairin; causing the saidis bailzeis, thair clerk, and vtheris memberis of Court, for fer of thair lyvis, to ryse and depairt thairfra, the samin Court being dewlie fencit of befoir, as said is; And nocht onlie stoppit the haulding of the said Court, but thai intendit purpoislie of verrie malice, to have bereft the saidis Judgeis, and vtheris convenit and assisting thame in setting forward of justice the said day of their lyvis. Lyke as, indeid, the said Dauid, accumpaneit as said is, than inuadit, followit, and persewit thame for their bodelie harme and slauchter; leveand nathing that micht have brocht his wickit and vngodlie interpryse to effect, and had nocht faillit to have performit the same gif God had nocht provydit remeid."

There is something very ludicrous in this story of an accused person coming to his trial at the head of an armed force, and chasing away the Court and the officers from the hall where justice was to be administered. Yet it was not without its parallel in those unsettled times. Thus, when the Earl of Lennox accused Bothwell of the murder of Darnley, he refused to appear in Court to support his charge unless he would be allowed to bring three thousand armed men along with him to Edinburgh, whom he had raised for this purpose. And Sir David Graham's demonstration had the effect of staying all proceedings against him for a long time. He resumed his position amongst the Forfar nobles, as though no crime had been laid to his charge, and everyone agreed to forget John Pegot and his wrongs.

Justice in those days was tardy and uncertain, and was most frequently used for purposes of oppression and revenge. The charge against Sir David Graham was allowed to sleep for *ten years*, and when at length he was brought to trial upon 29th June 1577, it was more a farce than a reality. His defenders were "The File of Montrose, The Lard of Balfour, The Master of Gray, The Dene of Glasgw," and two advocates, and the names of the members of Assize were as follows :—

Gilbert Ogilbye of that Ilk	Robert Durhame of the
Thomas Fotheringhame of	Grange
Powrie.	Henry Guthere of Colestoune
Alex. Guthrie of that Ilk	George Somer of Balzordie
George Halliburtoune of Pet	Paul Fossie of that Ilk
cure	David Lindesay of Edzell
Robert Erskyn feare of Dun	Dd Guthrie, feare of Kincal
George Gray of Schellhill	drum
George Drummond of the	The Laird of Auchinlek
Blair	Alex. Lauder of Winmoquhe

It is interesting to notice how many of these names still survive in the territories mentioned.

When the case was opened one of the advocates for the defence "producit ane wryting subscryuit be vmqle Johnne Pegot in Bannabeith, declaring the defendaris to be innocent of all cryme committit to the said Johne, and that he was onlie moueit be malice of vtheris personis to persew the same."

The pursuers protested against this paper being read, but the presiding Justice allowed it, and the assize "fand and de lyuerit, for the maist part [i.e., by a majority] the saidis haill personnes accusit on pannell, to be clenzit and acquite" of all the crimes charged against them. Surely this was a most "lame and impotent conclusion" to a case which had been so long delayed, and yet it stands so recorded in the Justiciary Annals of the time.

Many puzzling questions will present themselves to the reader of this strange story. Had John Pegot been bribed by the Regent's party to trump up a false accusation against one of Queen Mary's defenders? Or, on the other hand, had Sir David induced him to abandon his charge, and profess that it was untrue? These are points which can never be decided, but this story is full of instruction to him who considers it attentively. It shows the King disputing with the Baron over a relic of feudal power, and declares unmistakably that the meanest subject had the right to demand protection by the ægis of law from the oppression of his superiors.

———

Note.—We have had considerable difficulty in determining the dates given in the above story, for this reason. Up till 1600 the year in Scotland began not on the 1st of January, but on the 25th of March. Thus February 1567 was really later than December 1567, though in our present chronology the case would be reversed. We are inclined to think, however, that the version which we have given above is the correct one.

INTERIOR OF CELL

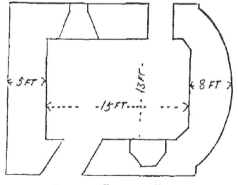

GROUND PLAN OF CELL.

THE FARM HOUSE OF WEST DENSIDE

THE WIFE O' DENSIDE

PART I

"'Tis pleasant through the loop holes of retreat
To peep at such a world to see the stir
Of the great Babel and not feel the crowd
To hear the roar she sends through all her gates
At a safe distance where the dying sound
Falls a soft murmur on the uninjured ear
— *Cowper*

The farm of West Denside occupies a most picturesque situation amongst the elevated uplands which rise to the north of Broughty Ferry Its topographical position takes the visitor by surprise The winding road by which it is reached strikes northwards from Broughty Ferry to Forfar, and passes through some of the finest scenery in the shire of Angus When once the traveller has got rid of the modern villas of Broughty Ferry which have now crept up to the very summit of the hill that overlooks that antique burgh, he finds himself transported at once by "the backward flowing tide of Time" to a period more than three centuries ago The ancient castle of Claypots, part of which was built in 1569, stands close by the wayside, and still shows some traces of its former strength and beauty And though the romantic story of its having been built by Cardinal Beaton, of infamous memory, is **quite incredible, it is not less interesting as a proof**

that the Protestant Baron, Gilbert Strathauchtyne of Carmyllie, who erected it, had as refined taste in architecture as the accomplished Roman Prelate himself The whole country through which this road runs is rich in historical associations, and within a circuit of a few miles the remains of the ancient seats of some of the earliest recorded Forfarshire families may still be found On the banks of the Fithie Water, which joins the Dichty by the side of this road, stands the grey ruin of Ballumbie Castle, the feudal keep of the Anglo Norman family of Lovell, who made their appearance in this quarter probably in the time of Edward I, but have long since disappeared from the land The reader of Scottish history cannot look without emotion upon these mouldering stones when he remembers that they formed the home of the intrepid Catherine Douglas, whose vain attempt to save King James I from assassination, by sacrificing her right arm to the fury of his assailants, has been the frequent theme of poets and of painters

Not far from this spot the moss covered remains of the baronial castle of Gilchrist, first Earl of Angus, may be discovered To him Malcolm Ceanmohr committed the charge of this important shire seven hundred years ago, and from him are descended the Ogilvies of Airley, of Inverquaarity, and of Clova, with their numerous branches These ruins stand upon the estate of Wedderburn, formerly called Easter Powrie, and in this proprietary the old families of Wedderburn of Kingennie and Scrymgeour of Dudhope have been united

The tortuous road leads to the quaint hamlet of Murroes—a corruption of Muirhouse—whose kirk and graveyard stand at some distance from the highway The place and its surroundings might easily presuade the traveller that his short walk of three miles from Broughty Ferry had carried him back through two centuries of time, and introduced him to an obsolete state of existence The rising ground shuts out all appearance of the Tay's broad estuary, and the ridge of the Fifeshire hills and the peaks of the Lomonds seem but continuations of the ground on which he stands No trace of city life is visible, and the spires and smoke stalks of Dundee have disappeared as by magic He is in the midst of a rural country, and all around him are sloping meads and fertile fields, whose verdant undulations plainly testify to man's conquest over Nature The barren muir, whence its name was originally derived, can no longer be discovered, for ages of industry have reclaimed the land, and caused the wilderness to blossom like the rose The swelling mounds which rise and fall in infinite variety may speak to the geologist of the turbulent volcanic upheavals by which they were formed, and the valleys and ravines may tell of the irresistible glaciers and foaming torrents which have scooped out vale and river bed from their barren surface But to the unscientific eye the scene presents a not less poetical though superficial aspect, and the beholder cannot fail to notice the brilliant success which has crowned man's contest with the elements throughout countless generations in this spot, and rewarded his persevering toil with the fruits of the earth in abundance.

> How fair a prospect rises to the eye,
> Where beauty vies in all her vernal forms,
> For ever pleasant and for ever new !
> Swells the exulting thought, expands the soul
> Drowning each ruder care a blooming train
> Of bright ideas rushes on the mind
> Imagination rouses at the scene
> And backward through the gloom of ages past
> Beholds Arcadia, like a rural queen
> Encircled with her swains and rosy nymphs,
> The mazy dance conducting on the green

The road beyond Murroes Kirk attains a still greater elevation, and rises with many a bend and sweeping curve to a very considerable altitude

About three miles from the Kirk on the eastern side of the road, and at some distance from the hedgerow, a white house may be noticed standing on an eminence in the midst of a field, and facing southwards By traversing the path leading to it an entirely new aspect of the country becomes visible The height upon which it is situated overlooks the country through which the traveller has passed, and instead of a limited scene, shut in by grassy hills and embosomed in woods, he beholds a wide horizon enclosing a vast stretch of flood and field, and *presenting every variety of pasture and sylvan scenery* Southwards the Tay majestically spreads forth its waters ere it loses itself in the North Sea, and the white line of breakers at Buddon Ness indicates the position of the " Roaring Lions " and the Bar of Tay Over the narrow isthmus which terminates Fifeshire the treacherous waters of St Andrews Bay are visible, and the hoary Tower of St Regulus and the quaint spires of the ancient Cathedral City may be distinctly discerned The dim white speck which glitters in mid-ocean far to the south east is the Bell Rock Lighthouse, the column which crowns the Hill of Downie is the Panmure Testimonial, and along the coast faint indications may be detected of the numerous hamlets and villages which stretch from Broughty to Arbroath Westward the spectator may,

> With eye enamour d mark the many wreaths
> Of pillar d smoke, high curling to the clouds,

which point out the site of Dundee, and he will immediately recognise the peak of the Law elevated from the midst of this sulphurous vapour The hills of Fifeshire and Perthshire rise in tumultuous confusion on the far western horizon, whilst from this position the bold outline of the Sidlaws may be traced until lost in the hazy distance To the north the view is bounded by the rising ground immediately behind, which reaches a height of seven hundred feet above the sea level, and directly in front of the house the ground slopes rapidly downward from the terrace on which it stands, presenting to the eye a restless sea of verdure The cool breeze from the sea tempers the fiercest day of July, and invigorates without enervating even in the depth of winter

Such is the position, such the appearance of the house of West Denside, and one might well imagine that the inhabitants of such a spot should be secure from the sins and the sorrows which attend upon city life —

> Thrice happy he ! who on the sunless side
> Of a romantic mountain forest-crown d.
> Beneath the whole collected shade reclin s,
> Or in the gelid caverns woodbine-wrought,
> And fresh bedewed with ever-spouting streams,

Sits coolly calm   while all the world without,
Unsatisfied and sick tosses in noon
Emblem instructive of the virtuous man
Who keeps his temper d mind serene and pure,
And every passion aptly harmonised
Amid a jarring world with vice inflamed

Yet all experience teaches that the fairest scene will not moderate the evil promptings of ambition nor mitigate the pangs of remorse , will not secure from temptation, nor avert the Nemesis of retribution Even a very limited knowledge of human nature will convince the optimist that it is merely in the poet's dreamy vision that

' Man superior walks
Amid the glad creation musing praise
And looking lively gratitude

For it was in this very place of Denside, which we have been thus describing, and which seems so far removed from the reach of passion or the taint of sin, that one of the most moving tragedies of modern times was enacted The name of "the wife o' Denside" has long been familiar throughout the east coast of Scotland , and it is now our purpose to relate the true story of that incident with which her name is associated in a coherent fashion It is needless to say that many absurd traditions have already grown around the tale, and fanciful additions to the facts and unwarranted deductions from them have long been current in Forfarshire Having made a careful examination of all the evidence bearing upon this case which is now procurable, and a personal inspection of all the localities referred to, we think we shall be able to relate the episode in a fashion not hitherto attempted

The farms of East Denside, Dodd, and West Denside are all upon the estate of Douglas, and are the property of the Earl of Home About the year 1825 all these farms were occupied and wrought by a farmer named Smith and his family, and he had selected the house of West Denside as his residence The sketch which we supply shows the place as it is at present, but at the period to which we allude the whole building did not exceed one storey in height, and the roof was covered with grey slate The ground floor, with which we are mostly concerned, is nearly in its former state The space in front, occupied as garden ground, is surrounded by a high boxwood hedge, which must have taken many years to attain its present stature , and this plot is reached by a flight of steps which lead down from the terrace on which the house is erected These particulars may serve to render our story more intelligible to the reader

The Smith family consisted of the father, his wife Mary Elder or Smith, two sons, Alexander and George, and two daughters There were three female servants connected with the farm, Barbara Small, Jean Norrie, and Margaret Warden, the latter two of whom slept together within the house The farmer himself was considerably older than his wife, and was a man greatly respected by all who encountered him Mrs Smith was also looked upon as a hard working and thrifty housewife, though perhaps somewhat uplifted by the prosperity which had rewarded her husband's industry One of her daughters was married to James Miller, who acted as foreman, and the two sons were employed on the farm These were the principal *dramatis personæ* who took part in the tragedy of Denside

C

INTERIOR OF KITCHEN AT WEST DENSIDE

PART II

'Oh wae s me for the hour Willie
  Wh(n we thegi h(r met
Oh wac s me for the ti ie Willie,
  That our first try,t was s(t !
Oh wae s me for the loamn ,reen
  Where we were wont to gae
And wae s me for the de,tiny
  That ,art me love thee sae '

                    — *Motherwell*

Margaret Warden, one of the servants at Den
side, was the daughter of a widow who lived not
far from the neighbourhood   Her father had died
when she was fifteen years of age, and
during the ten years which elapsed between
that time and the period of our story
she had been engaged as a servant on some
of the farms in the vicinity   The widow had been
left with one son and two daughters, and the
destitution which she endured had excited the
sympathy of several of her neighbours   Amongst
them was a sister of Mrs Smith of Denside called
Mrs Machan, who had taken considerable interest
in the Warden family, and assisted the unfor
tunate widow in her helplessness   Through her
influence the daughter Margaret obtained a situa
tion as a servant at Denside, and the other
members of the family were indebted to her for
many kindnesses   Unfortunately her goodwill
towards Margaret Warden was the cause ultimately
of that unhappy creature's destruction

The world flowed smoothly with Margaret
Warden for some years after she had entered the
service of the Smiths at Denside, and being of a

light hearted and amiable temperament, she soon
became a favourite with her fellow servants   But
when she was about twenty one years of age a
heavy cloud of misfortune overshadowed her   She
had trusted in man's faithfulness, and been deceived,
betrayed, ruined, and was forced to drain the
bitter cup of sorrow which she had prepared for
herself

> O agony keen agony '
>   For trusting heart to find
> That vows believed were vows conceived
>   As light as summer wind
>
> O agony deep agony !
>   For heart that s proud and high,
> To learn of Fate how desolate
>   It may be ere it die "

She retired to her mother's cot to conceal her
shame, and under the protection of the maternal
roof she brought forth the child of her sin and
sorrow

This event seemed likely to cause a rupture be
tween the Smiths and Margaret Warden, but the
good offices of Mrs Machan brought about a recon
ciliation, and she returned to resume her former
occupation at Denside   Time will mitigate the
severest pangs of remorse, and the rolling years
which bring sorrow with them bear away the sad
memories of past misery   Though not naturally of
a frivolous character, Margaret was not deeply re
flective, and the kindness of her employers and
fellow servants soon taught her to forget the dis
grace which she had suffered   The fault had been

apparently overlooked and forgiven, and she strove to regain her reputation by unwearied assiduity Nor were her efforts unrewarded Mrs Smith entrusted her with the control of those depart ments which had formerly been in her charge, and all around her seemed to have forgotten the saddest incident in her career

But even in this peaceful scene unknown dangers surrounded her and threatened her peace Her gentle demeanour had attracted the notice of George Smith, the younger son of the family, and he had paid her particular attentions upon several notable occasions A thousand contending emotions would arise within her breast at these times—her vanity would be flattered that the master's son should take notice of her ; ambition might whisper that his love opened out a new career for her ; and the tenderer feeling of affec tion for one who could overlook her faults and par don her weaknesses naturally supervened The difference in their social position was great, and experience might have taught her to beware of falsehood ; yet theirs was but a repetition of " the old, old story"—

> "Oh ! Love will venture in
> Whaur he daurna weel be seen ;
> Oh ! Love will venture in
> Whaur Wisdom ance has been "

The young laird had declared his love, and been accepted for some time before his parents were aware of it There had been many stolen inter views between George Smith and Margaret War den ere the news of his amour reached his mother , and they had plighted their troth repeatedly,

> " Under the hawthorn in the dale,"

long before she knew it Mrs Smith's own pride prevented her from seeing the drama which was being enacted before her eyes, and, like many others in her circumstances, she received her first intimation of the affair from some good natured outsider The very hint of such a thing appalled her She had been striving by thrift and economy to lay the foundations of a great fortune at Denside, and she had looked forward to the marriage of her sons as alone necessary for the completion of the edifice Were they to unite with some of the ancient families in the neighbour hood she should feel that her mission was accom plished, and that her life of hard work and money saving had been really well spent But now the dream of her existence seemed about to be over thrown If that were true which her friends had repeated, George Smith had wilfully thwarted her plans, and involved her ideas of future greatness in total ruin. She would watch for every indica tion of so great a catastrophe.

Her diligence in this respect was soon rewarded The lovers anticipating her objections, had planned their interviews discreetly

> ' They couldna meet in the green forest,
> Nor yet in the ba nor bower, '

but they exchanged their vows beneath the shade of the barn beside the house, in a spot so near their home as to be unsuspected The vigilance of the wife of Denside, however, ultimately dis covered their meeting place, and all her fears were confirmed She found the son, upon whose mar riage her hopes of greatness were built, breathing his tale of love into the ear of one whose social position was far beneath his, and whose moral character was not without a flaw There is little wonder that one of her stamp, however mild and gentle in ordinary circumstances, broke forth furi ously upon the delinquents when she saw them in this situation The reprimand which she bestowed upon her son was mild and maternal, but the abuse which she heaped upon the devoted Margaret's head was unmeasured and intemperate Knowing the former error of her un happy servant, Mrs Smith would easily persuade herself that her son was the dupe of a designing woman ; and she used language towards her which would only have been justified by the vilest conduct on Warden's part The un fortunate girl, stung by her reproaches and irri tated by her accusations, refused to remain under her roof, and took the way sorrowfully from Den side towards the meaner abode of her mother

That was a sad night in the home of the Wardens The aged mother returned from her labours in the fields to find her prodigal daughter seated tearfully by the fireside, enduring meekly the upbraidings of her brother, and unable to revile again To her questionings little reply was vouchsafed, and the old woman retired to rest dreading the revelations which the following morning would make She was not long kept in suspense Mrs Smith had been in the habit of driving her dairy produce to Dundee when Margaret Warden could not be spared from the farm ; and on this occasion she called at Warden's house to inquire after the absentee She found Margaret alone in the house, but what passed between mistress and maid can never be known When Mrs Warden entered she found Mrs Smith urging Margaret to go with her to a doctor in Dundee, but the girl resolutely refused to accompany her At this time (July—August 1826) typhus fever and cholera morbus were rag ing in the vicinity, and Mrs Warden imagined for the moment that her daughter had been sent home through dread of her being affected by these scourges of humanity. She hastened, therefore, to assure Mrs Smith that her daughter had been bled quite recently, and this was then considered the safest febrifuge and precaution against contagion. Finding all her efforts to induce Margaret to accompany her quite unavailing, the wife of Denside set out on her journey to Dundee alone, being convoyed merely to her machine by the mother of her servant. The distance which these two women had to traverse was not great, yet the conversation which passed between them on the way is of great importance to our narrative. The only account of it which can be procured is derived from the evidence, given under oath, of Mrs Warden.

"What do you think is wrong with your daughter?" asked Mrs Smith, when they had got beyond the house.

Mrs Warden replied that "she didna ken."

"I wish she binna wi burn," said her companion, ventilating the fear which possessed her own bosom.

"That," said the mother, discreetly, "is best kent to hersel."

And then Mrs Smith, annoyed by her cautious reticence, launched forth into a violent attack upon poor Margaret. She reminded her mother of her past ill conduct, pointed out how she had forgiven her previous mistake, expecting her to reform; and plainly accused her of having again forgotten her self respect and forfeited the regard of her employers. It was useless for Mrs Warden to reply to these accusations, for her own fears had already suggested them; but she was hardly prepared for the remark which followed upon them.

"If Margaret is in that condition," said Mrs Smith, "it will bring disgrace both upon you and me."

Only one conclusion could be drawn from this speech—that some one of the Smith family was involved in Margaret's sin, if sin there was in the case. After this remark, Mrs Smith's final leave-taking of Mrs Warden was fearfully ominous. She said that "she was going to the doctor in Dundee to get something for herself, and she would see and get something for Margaret also."

Margaret was anxiously awaiting her mother's return, and questioned her closely as to her conversation with Mrs Smith. Especially was she desirous to know if the name of her lover, George Smith, had transpired; but her anxiety was of no avail. Her mother could tell her nothing which she did not already know, and she decided to return that night to Denside and brave the anger of her mistress.

Some confusion arises here in the evidence. It is asserted, on the one hand, that Mrs Smith sought to induce her to return, and to say nothing as to the cause of her absence lest the master of Denside should hear of it. To some extent Mrs Smith seems to have stood in awe of her husband, and she saw that she could not blame Margaret Warden without incriminating her own son; but whether this was the consideration which weighed with her in prompting her to invite the fated girl back to her house is beyond human knowledge. On the other hand, it is maintained that Margaret returned to Denside of her own free will, and brought upon herself the terrible fate which overtook her by her precipitate action. The reader must himself decide as to which of these courses was the likelier for her to pursue. We are only concerned at present to state that that night she returned to Denside—never to leave it again.

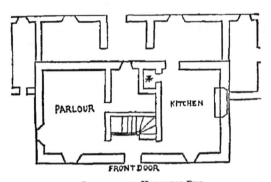

POSITION OF KITCHEN BED
GROUND PLAN OF THE HOUSE OF WEST DENSIDE.

PART III

" When bees are sair'd wi sippin sweets
  The flourish hasna lang to blaw,
When frae the tree we pu the fruit
  How sune the leaves begin to fa !
When harvest yields great rowth of grain
  The winter means to linger lang,
And still the keenest at the kirn
  Is first to sing the waesome sang

—*W S Fisher*

The harvest of 1826 was an early one, and much of the grain was already cut ere Margaret Warden returned to Denside There was one field of oats, however, immediately in front of the house which had been later than the rest of ripening, and shortly after her return to her old quarters she was sent, along with two sisters who wrought on the farm—Ann and Agnes Gruar—to assist in shearing the crop at this place She had confessed her condition to Mrs Smith and that lady had prescribed fasting and hard work, in conjunction with what she would give her, as the likeliest means of obviating the consequences of her guilt But Margaret was unfitted mentally and bodily either for a severe regimen of diet or for extreme labour, and her spirits sank under the infliction She was worse in health than usual on the special day to which we refer, and after many vain endeavours to accomplish the task apportioned to her, she sat down despairingly beside the ungathered sheaves, and poured forth her misery into the ears of her companions She told them the state into which she had been brought by her trustfulness, and spoke of her fears lest her lover should prove untrue She related what had taken place between herself and the mistress, and explained that she felt it impossible for her to endure

longer either the physical or mental torture to which she was subjected

' Oh ' threesome rigs are hard to shear
  For her whase heart nae hand may claim

And when she remembered what she had suffered at the hands of her relatives on a former occasion, she protested that she would rather take her own life than submit to similar treatment To Ann Gruar especially she opened her mind, telling her that " she was not able for her work, that she must leave Denside, and did not know where to go, as she could not go to her mothers,' and saying repeatedly "that she would put an ill end to herself She uttered this threat so seriously that Ann Gruar half believed that she was sincere in her avowed intention, and sought to dissuade her from it But she persisted so firmly that she would make away with herself that her hearer grew terrified by her earnestness, and "went away saying, 'God keep me! and told the circumstances to one of her companions in the field

Tradition records that at this moment, whilst Margaret Warden was sitting helpless and despairing in the field, and mourning over her fate with bitter tears, the Wife o' Denside approached her from the house, and, seeing her pitiable condition, offered her a flagon of tea to comfort and refresh her The kindly action touched the poor sinner's heart, and regretting the injustice which she had done her by accusing her of harshness, she gladly partook of the proffered refreshment, and strove to resume her occupation The cheering draught revived her for a time, and she managed to complete her task for the day

This occurrence took place upon a Monday On

Tuesday Margaret Warden was at work in the fields as usual, apparently as light hearted as she ever had been before the eventful day when she spoke of suicide The kindness of her mistress, possibly, had led her to renew her hopes that she would yet be forgiven by Mrs Smith, and received as a daughter in law She was willing, therefore, to follow her directions implicitly, and to resign herself to her charge without question That night when she returned from her labours out of doors she sat down by the fire to rest herself, and fell asleep in her chair, whilst her companion and bed fellow, Jean Norrie, was working about the kitchen When their usual bed time had arrived, and while they were sitting by the ingle, Mrs Smith entered the apartment from the parlour, with a glass in her hand, containing some liquid which she kept stirring with a spoon What was her purpose in thus breaking in upon their privacy ? Jean Norrie's description of the interview and its results runs thus —

" Mrs Smith came into the kitchen, and said she would let us both taste what was in the glass, and that ' she had taen her sairin' o t before she cam' but the house ' It was a pretty large dram glass, and was about full She dipped the teaspoon into the glass, and put it to my mouth, and gave the rest to Margaret Warden, who drank it off She had one piece of sugar with her, which she also gave to Margaret Warden. The stuff in the glass was *white like* I have tasted castor oil, but the stuff in the glass did not taste like any castor oil that I ever tasted Mrs Smith gave me castor oil once before, and the stuff in the glass did not taste like it I have seen cream of-tartar, and it was as like it as anything I ever saw Our usual bed time was ten o'clock, and it was just about that time There was none of the family in the kitchen at the time Warden and I went to bed immediately afterwards, and in the morning Warden was taken ill When I wakened she was striking a light, and turned sick I led her to bed, and she lay down I cannot say positively that she vomited at that time

" I went out to my work and returned at dinner time, and found Warden still in bed and complaining When I came back in the evening I found her yet in bed, and asked her how she did ?

" She said, taking hold of my hands, ' *Oh, what I ha'e bidden this day !*'

" I asked her if the Smiths had been *owning* her ?

" She said, ' *Rather too weel* '

" I signified to her that I thought she was dying, and she said, ' *Some fowk wad be glad o' that* '

" Warden complained very much all the time of her distress of a sair side and inside I slept with her on Wednesday night, and when I wakened I found her awake also She was very ill on Thursday—worse than the day before She vomited very much, and was much affected by purging She complained greatly of thirst, and I repeatedly gave her water, which she immediately threw up again. I was about the house all that day, and Warden frequently called for her mother Her mother lives at some distance from Denside on the road to Dundee She asked for her mother in presence of Mrs Smith, who said, ' *Wheesht till your physic operate* ' I understood that Mrs Smith had given her physic that day The mistress said it was castor oil She asked me what I thought would be good for Warden ? Would whisky do her good ? I said, ' She had got enough of that, or something else, for such purging and vomiting I never saw ' Mrs Smith then turned about and went ben Warden said to me, ' Say nothing to her about it ' She said that her mistress had burned her inside with whisky I advised her to take no more of these drinks, but she said that Mrs Smith said they were good for a *wheezle* in her breath I said, Dinna tell me it's for your breath, I ken better,' and she answered, ' I ken ither things too ' She had aye a wheezle in her breath sin' ever I kent her, sometimes better and sometimes waur She was sensible on Thursday, but on Friday she drowsed and was *queer like* Her mother came to her on Friday On that day she called me to her bedside and said, ' You ken, Jean, wha has been the occasion o' me lyin' here ?' I said, ' No She replied, ' Dinna say naething ' I said, ' Dinna *you* say naething, for I dinna ken ' Warden said, ' They'll get their rewards ' I answered, ' If it's onybody you're blamin' you'll surely forgi'e them ,' and she said she would. Ann Gruar and Warden's mother were present. I said, ' I've told you before no to tak' ony mair o' thae drinks the mistress gi'ed ye.' Warden said, ' Ay, ha'e ye ' "

As Norrie's evidence indicates, the mother had by this time arrived, and had overheard much of the conversation between the fellow servants Her own evidence corroborated the main points alluded to by Jean Norrie, and supplied some valuable information besides, bearing directly upon this case Before reciting it a word of explanation is due

During the course of this story we have done our utmost to explicate the true facts of this important affair We have now to lay before the reader the evidence upon which the jury in a criminal trial decided To arrive at the truth in this matter, we have kept constantly before us *three distinct accounts* of the trial, which took place shortly afterwards, as they are reported in the file of the *Dundee Advertiser*, in a reprint from the *Dun-*

dee *Courier*, and in a "specially reported" account of the trial published at Montrose in 1827 The version which we have formed is collated from these three accounts We have striven to weave the story into a connected form, but have not tampered with the facts in any way We take up the story where Jean Norrie left it, and now record the incidents which happened in her absence, as related by Mrs Warden

"When Norrie went away, I asked Margaret 'if onybody had gien her onything, or onybody had hurt her?' She said, 'Jean Norrie can tell you a' aboot it' I said, 'You can tell yoursel Margaret then said, 'My mistress gae me it I could ask her nae mair, I was so sorry There was naething mair said on the subject

A new and important witness now appears on the scene The illness of Margaret Warden was so serious that it was thought advisable to call in the aid of a medical practitioner Dr Taylor, of Broughty Ferry, was the nearest and most trusted mediciner in the locality, and he was summoned by Mrs Smith to the bedside of Margaret Warden A glance at the ground plan of Denside—prepared on the spot—will make his testimony thoroughly intelligible His verbatim evidence runs thus —

"I was sent for on Friday to visit Margaret Warden I arrived at mid day I met Mrs Smith at the door knitting her stocking *She took me into the parlour* I asked, 'What was the matter with the servant?' She said she had been ill with vomiting and pain in her bowels ever since Tuesday I asked 'why she had been so long in sending for medical assistance?' She said, 'She was not aware her complaint was so dangerous, and she was a light headed cutty, and they had not paid that attention to her they might have done' I asked 'if anything had been given to her?' and she said, '*Nothing but castor oil*' I understood this to have been in the course of the illness Mrs Smith then said that it was reported that the girl was with child, and asked if I would know it if I saw her? I said it was very probable that I might She asked whether it was

not likely the vomiting and purging would carry off the child, if there was one, adding, 'it would be a stain on the family?' I said it might or it might not have that effect I then said that I had come for the purpose of seeing the patient, and did not choose to indulge in such conversation I was taken to Margaret Warden's bedside, and found her coming out of a fit of vomiting She was very ghastly, and fell over almost insensible I could feel no pulsation at the wrist or the temples The pulsation of the heart was very indistinct, and beat about 150 or 160 a minute The extremities were perfectly cold and a cold perspiration was over the whole body I attempted to rouse her, and asked her when she was taken ill? After repeating the question two or three times, she said she had been taken ill on Tuesday night with purging She was so exhausted that I did not consider myself justified in putting more questions on that subject I understood her to be with child for about three months

She did not say whether she thought herself dying She said nothing from which I could infer that she had done herself ill The moment she answered a question she fell over quite exhausted When I left the kitchen, Mrs Smith asked me to go back to the parlour, and inquired what I thought of Warden? I said I thought she would die in a few hours, and explained that I had not prescribed any medicine for her, as I made it a rule not to prescribe for a dying person Mrs Smith said 'she had sent for a medical man to take the responsibility off her shoulders, and asked if I thought she was with child?' I said I had every reason to believe she was Mrs Smith then asked 'if the vomiting and purging would carry it off?' I answered, 'It might or it might not' She remarked 'that she would take care, though, that it did, as the gudeman would tear down the house about her'"

And Dr Taylor and Mrs Smith retired, and left Margaret Warden upon her deathbed—to die by her own suicidal hand, or by the ruthless poison of a murderess

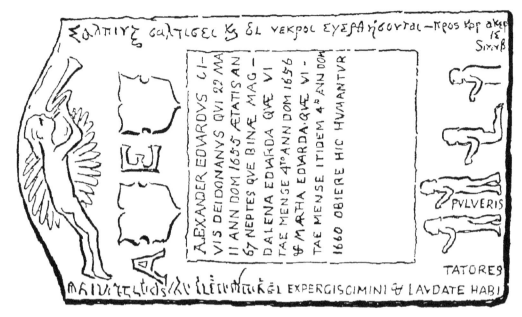

ΣΑΛΠΙΓΞ ϹΑΛΤΙϹΕΙ ϗ ΟΙ ΝΕΚΡΟΙ ΕΥΕΡΑ ήϲονται—προς κορ ακερ

ΑLEXANDER EDOARDVS CI-
VIS DEIDONANVS QVI 22 MA
II ANN DOM 1655 ÆTATIS AN
67 NEPTES QVE BINÆ MAG -
DALENA EDOARDA QVÆ VI
TAE MENSE 4° ANN DOM 1656
& MARTHA EDOARDA QVÆ VI -
TAE MENSE ITIDEM 4° ANN DOM
1660 OBIERE HIC HVMANTVR

Siκηβ

PVLVERIS

TATORES

ΜΑΙΥΛΤϹΛΛ⸱Ι⸱... ΕΧPERGISCIMINI & LAVDATE HABI

TOMBSTONE, MURROES CHURCHYARD

PART IV.

"In tears I came into this world of woe ,
In tears I sink into the shades below ,
In tears I pass d through life s contracted span—
Such is the hapless state of feeble man
Crawling on earth his wret hed lot he mourns,
And, thankful to his native dust returns
　　　　　—From the Greek of Palladas

After three days of severe suffering, Margaret Warden succumbed to the power of the poison which she had taken, or which had been administered to her, and breathed her last at nine o'clock on the evening of Friday At the moment of her death she was surrounded by her own personal friends—her mother, Jean Norrie, and Ann Gruar were all present—yet she uttered no word, either of crimination or confession, other than what we have already recorded The appearance of the corpse immediately after death was so unnatural as to attract attention Jean Norrie described it as "of a blackish colour," and Mrs Warden deponed that she "assisted to dress the body—it was of a dark colour Even Dr Taylor had noticed that the patient's arms "had a dark appearance," but the idea of poisoning had not occurred to him, probably because Mrs Smith's suggestions had supplied another explanation The testimony of these witnesses, though founded merely upon the external aspect of the deceased, seems to imply that her death had taken place under such suspicious circumstances as to require investigation But no such investigation was made, and the body of Margaret Warden—whether suicide or victim—was to be hurriedly interred in what should have been her final resting place

Word was sent to her brother on Saturday—the day after her death—of the sad occurrence, and he was requested to come to Denside to assist at her funeral on Sunday Mrs Smith's sister in-law—the wife of her husband's brother had heard of the death, and visited Denside on Saturday Her story as to the situation of affairs bears so immediately upon this portion of our narrative that it may be reproduced verbatim at this stage —

"I was at Denside the day after Margaret Warden's death I asked if it was the fever she had died of, and *Mrs Smith said it was* I asked if she had given her any medicine, and she said she had given her nothing but some castor oil on the Tuesday night I also asked if the girl had been in the family way ' She said she had heard so, *but did not believe it* I remember that the body was of a blue colour, and Mrs Smith said the doctor had told her that all who died of the fever were of that colour; that the colour was not so bad the day before; and that the doctor had told her that if the colour was bad to-day, it would be worse to morrow"

It is worthy of notice that fever as the cause of Warden's death was never suggested at any other time or to any other person. Dr Taylor supposed, from a cursory examination, that the disease was *cholera morbus*, and Mrs Smith afterwards declared that she understood from him that it was water in the chest, *though he denied under oath that he had ever said so to her.* The notion of either suicide or murder was not mooted at this juncture, but a coffin was speedily prepared, and the unfortunate woman was buried in a "shame hasted" manner, with all the tokens of her sinfulness, in the kirkyard of Murroes, on the *second day* after her demise. The mother "saw the body chested and the lid screwed down." The brother, Robert Warden, "saw the coffin taken from the bed at Denside, did not observe the coffin particularly till it was lowered into the grave, there were the letters 'M W, aged 25,' upon the lid of it."

Here should have ended the story of Margaret Warden. The brief tragedy of her life had been consummated, and after her mournful experience of man's perfidy and woman's trustfulness she had apparently found shelter from "the slings and arrows of outrageous fortune" literally within

> "The darkness of a nameless tomb."

No stone was raised to mark the spot where she had been laid to rest, and there was nothing whereby her body might be identified save the brief inscription upon her coffin lid—now buried far beneath the sod—which told how few and evil had been the days of her years. Even yet it is not possible to discover the precise place where her grave was made in the quiet old kirkyard of Murroes, nor has a thorough search in the locality disclosed the position of the turf which covers her *final* abode in that ancient God's acre,

> "Where little flowers are gleaming
> And the long green grass is streaming
> O er the gone, forever gone."

We say *final* abode, for even the sleep of death in which she lay was not to remain undisturbed.

At the time of Margaret Warden's death only two persons had any grounds for supposing, from her own statements, that she had been the victim of foul play, and these were her mother and her fellow servant, Jean Norrie. On Saturday, the day after the death, "when they were coming to the coffining," Mrs Warden repeated the conversation she had had with Margaret to her other daughter, but enjoined secrecy upon her regarding it. She did not tell her son

nor any one else at that time, "because it could not bring back her daughter from the grave, and would bring such disgrace upon the family." Gratitude towards Mrs Smith's sister also weighed with her in deciding that she should suppress any charge against the household at Denside, and, so far as she was concerned, she intended leaving the death of her daughter a profound mystery which the earth had covered and which should not be revealed until the great day of account had arrived.

There are some crimes which will not hide, and murder is popularly supposed to be amongst them. One might have thought that the death of this obscure servant girl in an out of the way farmhouse, in circumstances not necessarily implying murder, would have been suffered to sink into oblivion with rapidity. The lack of a proper official inquiry into cases of sudden death in Scotland affords peculiar facilities for the perpetration of the highest of all crimes, and the body of Margaret Warden—whether suicide or victim—might have rested in the grave till the resurrection so far as the legal authorities in Scotland were concerned. And it says little for the activity of our law reformers that the remarks of the *Dundee Advertiser* of October 5th, 1826—nearly sixty years ago—upon this case are quite as applicable to our own day. They bring before the reader the course of our story as it appeared to the contemporaries of the unfortunate woman, and narrate briefly the events which took place immediately after her death, to which we shall have to refer at greater length —

"We envy our southern fellow subjects in nothing so intensely as their possession of the admirable institution of a coroner's inquest, and the melancholy case we are about to state affords one of the every day proofs of the necessity of introducing that institution into Scotland without delay—that the characters of individuals innocently implicated in the death of a fellow mortal may be protected by the prompt proceedings of a coroner's inquest, or the laws of our country, when outraged, vindicated more speedily and with greater certainty than in the absence of such an institution they can be. Margaret Warden, a young woman in the service of David Smith, farmer at Denside, in the parish of Monikie, was, on Wednesday, 6th ult, seized with a violent illness, which continued till Friday, the 8th. Dr Taylor, of Broughty Ferry, was sent for on Friday, and arrived at Denside about two o'clock in the afternoon. He found the woman in the act of vomiting, her extremities cold, and her whole appearance exhibiting every symptom of approaching dissolution, occasioned, as he thought, by *cholera morbus*, a prevailing distemper. He was satisfied that his patient was beyond the power of medical aid, and left the house without prescribing for her. She died in a few hours afterwards. On Sunday the body was interred in the Parish Churchyard of Murroes. Upwards of a week afterwards a rumour arose, and was circulated far and wide, that a young woman who had been pregnant by a farmer's son had been poisoned by his mother, and various were the names of individuals, and as various their places of abode and the circumstances connected with the supposed atrocity, that floated on the breath of the public. At last information was communicated to the Sheriff of Forfarshire that a young woman had died under suspicious circumstances at Denside, in the parish of Monikie. But the body by this time had been interred about twenty days, and it was therefore thought a hopeless task to discover the cause of the woman's death. After a consultation with a medical gentleman, however, it was resolved that the body should be raised, and on Saturday last [30th September] this was done in presence of Drs Ramsay, Johnston, and Taylor. The body was laid on a gravestone, and dissected in the open air by Dr Johnston, and after testing the contents of the stomach a report was drawn up, which decidedly attributes the woman's death to the poison of arsenic. It is also reported that the woman had been three or four months pregnant. Portions of the contents of the stomach have been sent to the Crown Agent at Edinburgh with the view of their being tested by the learned in that city. Corruption had so quickly done its work that her face, when the body was taken from the grave, could not be recognised by her friends. Mrs Mary Elder or Smith, the farmer's wife, has been examined before Christopher Kerr, Esq, Sheriff Substitute, and committed to the gaol of Dundee for further examination."

From the above contemporary account it will be seen that a *post mortem* examination of a body took place in the churchyard of Murroes. Was that the body of Margaret Warden? Absolute accuracy in this matter is necessary, as we shall find when the case comes before the Court. Let us look for a moment at the evidence whereby the body was identified.

Dr Taylor saw Margaret Warden on her death bed. He believed that she was affected with *cholera morbus*. He was present at the exhumation of a body in Murroes Kirkyard. It was a woman's body, showed signs of pregnancy, but had no trace of *cholera morbus*. From the result of an analysis made by him and others he believed this woman—whoever she might have been—had died from the administration of arsenic.

Robert Warden, the deceased's brother, was the only party present at the exhumation who had also witnessed the burial. He testifies that "he came from Denside with the funeral. The coffin was lying in the kitchen bed—the only one in the kitchen. Knows Dr Ramsay, Dr Johnston, and Dr Taylor. Saw a body taken out of the grave where his sister was buried, about three weeks after the interment, saw the same coffin taken out that he saw put in, there was no alteration in the grave."

As doubts were *hinted* at the trial which afterwards took place as to the identity of the body, it may be judicious to settle this matter at once. We have seen that there was a plate on the coffin which would serve to identify it. That plate was seen by Robert Warden when the body was lowered into the grave at first, and noticed by him when it was exhumed. The features were not recognisable, but the evidence of her brother should be conclusive. It is not likely that he could have forgotten the spot where the remains of his sister were laid three weeks before, and, even if he had, the lettering on the plate would be sufficient for him. And if we reject the sworn evidence of this solitary witness as to the identity of the body, we are forced to adopt the monstrous supposition that some other person in the neighbourhood was in the same state as Margaret Warden, that she had died about the same time as she did, and that she was buried surreptitiously, not only in the same grave, but actually *in the same coffin* which had conveyed Margaret's body from Denside to Murroes! The very statement of the case is its own refutation. No fact was ever more clearly established in a Court of law than this, that Margaret Warden died through the deadly action of arsenic. Had she, when plunged in the depths of despair by the dread of an exposure of her sin and frailty, laid violent hands upon herself and taken away her own life in defiance of the commandments of God and the laws of man? This was the difficult problem which the authorities of Forfarshire had now to solve.

The flat stone in the graveyard of Murroes upon which the body was laid for examination is still pointed out to the inquisitive stranger, but it has other and older claims to the regard of the visitor and the antiquary. It covers the mortal part of Alexander Edward, father of the Rev. Robert Edward, Episcopal minister of Murroes in the time of Charles II, and author of a Latin account of Angus. This peculiar work of monumental art has been carefully deciphered by the Rev. Mr Nicoll, present pastor of Murroes parish (1883), to whom we are indebted for a copy of the unique inscriptions which it bears As our illustration shows, the subject of the carved work is the resurrection An angel is represented in the upper portion blowing the last trump, whilst at the base four figures are shown in the act of rising from their graves The central inscription is in Latin, and may be thus translated —" Alexander Edward, citizen of Dundee who died 22d May, A D 1655, in the 67th year of his age, [and] two grand daughters—Magdalen Edward, in the 4th month of her life, A D 1650, and Martha Edward, also in the 4th month of her life, A D 1660, are [all] buried here "

Around the edge of the stone there are three inscriptions in as many different languages, a Hebrew quotation from Isaiah xxvi 19, having its Latin translation appended—" Awake and sing, ye that dwell in dust ," and on the opposite side the phrase from I Corinthians, xv 52—" For the trumpet shall sound and the dead shall arise," lettered in Greek characters

There is something strangely, weirdly suggestive in the fact that this resurrection stone—erected nearly two hundred years before the death of Margaret Warden—should be utilised as her temporary resting place after she had become a veritable ' dweller in the dust '" Had the dead really arisen to vindicate the inscrutable purposes of Providence,

'And justify the ways of God to Man ?'

THE FOUR MILE HOUSE

PART V.

" Oh ! wae betide my cruel mither,
　An ill death may she dee,
She turned fair Annie frae the door,
　Wha died for love o' me !
　　　—*Annie o Lochryan*

When once the law had been put in motion with reference to this case, no delay was suffered to interfere with its initiatory action The exhumation took place on Saturday, a portion of the intestines was taken away in a sealed box for further examination, and tests were applied on Sunday so as to make it evident that poison had been the cause of death On Monday the Sheriff Substitute arranged to have a precognition of the family at Denside taken, but it was suddenly found that Mrs Smith was too ill to be brought to Dundee for that purpose Popular rumour had already accused her of being intimately concerned in the matter, and the Procurator Fiscal—the late Dr John Boyd Baxter—instructed Dr Johnston to ascertain her condition To avoid the danger of bringing her to Dundee, it was arranged that the Sheriff Substitute and the Fiscal should meet her at an inn called the Four Mile House, about midway between Denside and Dundee, provided Dr Johnston found her well enough to accompany him thither

As an attempt was afterwards made to discredit

the statements which she emitted at this time, upon the ground that she was in a hysterical state and unfit for judicial examination, it may be as well to give Dr Johnston's version of the story at this stage. His deposition, under oath, is thus recorded —

" I was asked by the Procurator Fiscal to go to Denside to visit Mrs Smith, to ascertain whether she was in a fit state to go to Four Mile House to be examined before the Sheriff Substitute, and went accordingly. I found her, not in excellent health, but in a state that she might go to that place to be examined. At first she was unwilling to go, but after I explained to her husband that I could not certify that she was not able to go, she was induced to go. It was then arranged that she, her husband, and one of her sons should travel to Four Mile House in the chaise with me. On the road I spoke to Mr Smith regarding his friend Mr S——, of P——, in order to divert their attention from the subject of the examination. Mr Smith, however, remarked that 'none of his friends could have anticipated such a report as had gone abroad against his wife,' and added that 'there must be something more in the matter than he was aware of, otherwise gentlemen would not be travelling about the country in carriages.' 'He had heard,' he said, 'that poison had been found in the stomach of the deceased.' I replied, certainly there had, but I hoped that none of his family had given it. Mrs Smith said that 'Margaret Warden had vomited so much before her death that she did not think anything could have remained on her stomach.' Mr Smith mentioned that 'there was more than one of the farm servants who had heard the deceased say that she would put away with herself.' In the lobby of Four-Mile House I asked Mrs Smith whether she found herself any worse? and she replied she was not. I gave it as my opinion that she was in a fit state for examination. If I had had any doubt on the subject, I would have mentioned it."

Dr Johnston was not present at the examination, but the evidence of those who were there corroborates his statement as to the condition of Mrs Smith. Sheriff Substitute Kerr says—"Mrs Smith was in her sound senses at the time—quite calm and collected, *until the last question was put to her.* She at first answered the question correctly, but when it was put a second time she became much agitated. She fell back on her chair very suddenly, but as suddenly recovered." Procurator Fiscal Baxter deponed —"Mr Smith was present during the whole time of the examination, and made no objections. Mrs Smith was calm and

collected till near the conclusion. *At the last question she became agitated.* She was a good deal agitated when signing her declaration." James Yeaman, jun, of Affleck, J P, was also present at this examination, and declares that "she was perfectly collected at the commencement. Her husband was in the room, and made no objection to her being examined. She became very much agitated when a certain question was put to her by Mr Kerr." Other witnesses gave corroborative evidence, making it very clear that Mrs Smith was in full possession of her senses, and perfectly calm when she emitted her first declaration.

By a strange oversight none of the published accounts of the case contain other than vague references to this important declaration, but as it is our purpose to state the circumstances fairly and truthfully, so as to dispel many of the unfounded rumours which have long circulated in the locality regarding it, we have put ourselves to considerable trouble to obtain an authentic copy of the document. Its value as evidence can hardly be over estimated. It was the first reply of Mrs Smith to her accusers, the earliest explanation of the death of Margaret Warden vouchsafed by her. The reader will notice that the declarant contradicts many of the witnesses from whose evidence we have already quoted, and he must determine for himself as to which party is most worthy of credence.

"First Declaration

" At the Four Mile House, in the parish of Monifieth, the 2d day of October 1826 —In presence of Christopher Kerr, Esq, one of the Sheriff Substitutes for the Dundee district of Forfarshire,—

"Appeared Mary Elder, wife of David Smith, farmer of Denside, in the parish of Monikie, who, being examined, declares that she is about forty two years of age, That she had a servant named Margaret Warden, who died at Denside on the evening of Friday, the 8th day of September last, about half an hour after nine o'clock in the evening, That Margaret Warden became unwell about midnight, as she thinks, in the night between Tuesday, the 5th, and Wednesday, the 6th of September, That at daylight, on Friday morning, the declarant sent notice of the girl's illness to Dr Taylor at Broughty Ferry, That both on Wednesday and Thursday, and until about one o'clock on Friday, the girl vomited and purged much, That the declarant and Jean Norrie, the fellow-servant, sat up with the girl on the night between Thursday and Friday, That the girl did not appear to be sensible during Thursday, for she did not appear to know the declarant or her daughters but occasionally she knew those who were about her; That on Friday she knew her mother, named her sometimes, and asked her to look if the doctor was coming; That the deceased had a shortness of breath during all the time she was in the declarant's service, and was sometimes away from her service as unwell; That the declarant did not know anything particular in the deceased's state of health previous to her becoming unwell, as before declared to—except that she generally had more difficulty in breathing towards bed time, and the declarant thought she had more difficulty in breathing during the preceding week; That the deceased was employed at her usual work on Friday before she became unwell about midnight, as before declared to; That the declarant was in the house when Dr Taylor came to visit the girl on the day on which she died; That the declarant took Dr Taylor into the parlour when he came into the house before he saw the girl, and asked him whether he knew the girl; and told him of her state; That the declarant asked him to endeavour to ascertain if she was with child, for the girl was rather of loose character; That she did not say to Dr Taylor that she thought the girl dying; That she did not say anything to Dr Taylor as to the likelihood of the vomiting and purging to which the girl was then subject carrying off the child, if there was one, nor did she put any question to him regarding the possibility of such a result; That the declarant did not suspect or believe that the girl was with child, nor had she ever heard any rumour that she was so before the girl's death; That the girl was away from her service about the beginning of harvest, in her mother's house, unwell, and the declarant called at the house to see her, and she then inquired at her mother what could be the matter with her, and whether she thought that she was with child? That about a fortnight before the girl became unwell the declarant gave to her a doze of castor oil before going to bed; That she gave her another doze of castor oil either on the evening of Monday, the 4th of September, or on the evening of Tuesday, the 5th, she is not sure which, but she thinks it was Monday night; That it was administered among some 'lozenger wine' in a dram glass or tumbler; That the declarant bought the castor oil on the Friday immediately preceding the girl's death; That she bought it out of the shop of Mrs Jolly, druggist, in Dundee, and was supplied with it by Mrs Jolly herself, or at least in her presence; That the declarant bought at that same time some 'arnetta' for dyeing, and some mustard, but nothing else; That Jean Norrie was present when the castor oil was administered, but no other person was present;

That the declarant never had any poisonous articles about her house to her knowledge,—except that persons have been employed to put away rats, but declarant had no knowledge of the means they used, and if any poisonous article was used by them they furnished it themselves, and the declarant and her family had nothing to do with it; That the last time any person was employed at Denside putting away rats was about two years ago; That the declarant has been in the practice of getting druggists' goods from Mr Alexander, surgeon, Dundee, but she has no recollection of getting any such article from any other person but Mr Alexander and Mrs Jolly; That the declarant *got no drug or other such article from any other person than Mrs Jolly, on the Friday preceding the death of the girl* * All which she declares to be truth

(Signed)   "MARY ELDER
"CHRIS KERR"

The importance of this last question is very great, since nearly the whole case turns upon it, for it is very evident that if Mrs Smith only administered castor oil which she had purchased from Mrs Jolly, and yet arsenic was the cause of Margaret Warden's death, it would be impossible to connect the Wife of Denside with the mysterious demise of her erring servant. But this was the only question in her examination at which she stumbled, and her hesitancy was so evident that it did not escape the notice of any of the witnesses present. Mr Kerr felt it to be his duty to commit her to the gaol in Dundee for further examination, and she was conveyed thither from the Four-Mile House that night.

On the following morning, application was made to the Sheriff Substitute by her friends requesting him to attend her that she might emit a second declaration. He states himself that he would not have re-examined her so soon except for this application; but he arranged to meet the Fiscal in her place of confinement, as suggested, and there to hear her new explanation. This declaration, like the former one, is not republished in any accounts of her trial, and we need make no further apology for its appearance here than we have already done. It is sufficient for our purpose to state that both Sheriff and Fiscal bore testimony that she was in her sober senses on the second as on the first day, and that her later declaration was emitted voluntarily

" *Second Declaration*
At Dundee, the 3d day of October 1826
In presence of Christopher Kerr, Esq, one of the

This is the passage particularised in the evidence of Messrs Kerr, Baxter, and Yeaman

Sheriff Substitutes for the Dundee district of Forfarshire

"Appeared Mary Elder or Smith, present prisoner in the Tolbooth of Dundee, and the declaration emitted by her on the 2d day of October current, in presence of the said Sheriff Substitute, having been read to her, she adheres thereto, with this explanation —That she now recollects that she got from Mr William Dick, surgeon in Dundee, on the Friday immediately preceding Margaret Warden's death, something to put away rats, that about a fortnight before that time Mr Dick's daughters, three in number, were at Denside, and the declarant asked them to say to their father that she wished he would give her something to put away the rats from Denside, and when she was in Dundee she got something from him upon the said Friday immediately preceding Margaret Warden's death for that purpose Declares that with this explanation she adheres to her said declaration, and she has no other addition to make thereto, or alteration to make thereon Declares that she had no recollection of this circumstance at the time when she emitted her said declaration, but she recollected it after she was brought to prison last night, and she then told her son that she had something further to communicate, And being interrogated, declares that she did not mention either to Mr Dick or to his daughters any particular thing that she wanted, but only asked for something that would put away the rats, Declares that she is not sure whether it was Mr Dick himself, or his wife, who gave her the article to put away the rats, but she is sure she was not told by either of them what the article was—at least she does not think she was told, That she was not told it was poison so far as she remembers, and she cannot say whether 'poison' was written upon it or not, That there was some writing on it, but she does not know what it was Interrogated specially whether the declarant asked Dr Dick to give her arsenic on the Friday before declared to ?

Declares that she did not Interrogated— What she did with the article she got from Dr Dick ? Declares—That Mrs Dick recommended her to put it into the holes and craps of the walls ; and she put it, on Monday, into the holes and craps in a loft above the bothie, That Margaret Warden was present in the kitchen when the declarant got a plate to mix it with meal, but nobody else was present when the declarant was employed in disposing of the article, That the declarant did not tell Jean Norrie of having got the article or what she had done with it, nor, so far as she knows, did any other of the servants know of it, That Denside is very much infested with rats, That, in going into the byre, a drove, like a drove of cattle, may be seen, That the servants complain that they are disturbed by them in their beds, All which she declares to be the truth

(Signed) "MARY ELDER
"CHRIS KERR "

It is far from our intention to prejudice the reader either in favour of or against Mrs Smith, and we have thought it best, therefore, to lay the authentic evidence before him and allow him to form his own conclusion The secrecy with which the initiatory steps are taken in Scotland when a charge of murder is to be preferred makes it impossible for us now to discover what precise action took place after the two declarations had been emitted by Mrs Smith, but we find that she "was fully committed for trial" on the afternoon of 12th October, and on Thursday, 12th December, she "was served with an indictment to take her trial before the High Court of Justiciary at Edinburgh on Thursday, the 28th December current The *Dundee Advertiser* of that date records that "on Tuesday morning (26th December) Mrs Smith was sent off to Edinburgh to stand her trial before the High Court of Justiciary this day " Elaborate preparations had been made for her defence, and Francis Jeffrey and Henry Cockburn, then the leaders of the Scottish Bar, were retained as her advocates

INTERIOR OF JUSTICIARY COURT, EDINBURGH

PART VI

"The world is still deceived with ornament
In law, what plea so tainted and corrupt
But being seasoned with a gracious voice
Obscures the show of evil?   — *Shakespeare*

The interest in the Denside case up to this point has been somewhat sensational, but it was now to present those exceptional *legal* features which have caused it to be frequently referred to as a phenomenon in law. The question as to the legality of the proceedings to which it gave rise has been frequently debated, and, as much has apprehension exists regarding it, a simple statement of the difficulty may serve to make the matter clear.

The greatest grievance formerly endured by suspected persons in Scotland was the long delay which frequently took place in bringing their cases to trial. The power which the Barons had of imprisoning their vassals upon suspicion, and keeping them in durance for an indeterminate period, had been assumed by the Lords of Justiciary, to whom their prerogatives had been committed; and Scotland laboured under this infliction long after the famous Habeas Corpus Act had been granted to England. At length William III,

finding it desirable to court the favour of the Scottish people, gave his assent to the celebrated "Act for Preventing Wrongous Imprisonments, and against Undue Delays in Tryals" (Sess. IX., Parl. I. Will. III., Act. 6), which is usually referred to as "the Habeas Corpus of Scotland." By this important Act it is provided that any prisoner may present an application for immediate trial to any competent Judge, and the latter must, within twenty four hours after receipt of this application, enjoin upon the Lord Advocate or other prosecutor to fix a dyet for tryal within sixty days thereafter, or otherwise the prisoner would be set at liberty, and freed from any further trial for the same offence. The proceedings in Court were also limited to a period within forty days; and thus, by this invaluable Act, no Scottish prisoner need be detained in durance, without a judgment, beyond the extreme limit of a hundred days.

Mrs. Smith's agents had taken advantage of this provision in the Act of 1701 by the peculiar process called "running criminal letters," and had thus brought on her trial at a very early stage. This necessity caused the Crown Prosecutor to hurry on his evidence, lest the accused should escape entirely The Lord Advocate of the time, upon whom the task of prosecution fell, was Sir William Rae of St Catherines, son of the famous Lord Justice Clerk Eskgrove, and M P at this time for the Anstruther Easter (now St Andrews) Burghs It had been his lot to cross swords in forensic combat with some of the foremost members of the Scottish Bar, and his frequent defeats when opposed to Jeffrey and Cockburn, as on this occasion, made him doubtful of the result of the action

Up to the last moment no clue had been afforded him of the line of defence to be adopted by his opponents The two declarations by Mrs Smith seemed to make his task easy, the latter especially connecting her with the purchase of arsenic, the poison whereby death had been caused, and no other adequate theory had been started at this time to account for the violent end of Margaret Warden He must have therefore supposed that it was a simple case of murder, requiring no special care on his part to secure the conviction of the accused But in this supposition he was grievously mistaken He learned on the day immediately preceding the trial that it was intended to advance a theory of suicide as the main defence, and that a large number of witnesses were to be summoned to establish this plea He felt it to be his duty to examine those witnesses, as it was impossible for him to tell what credit a jury might give to the statements of the parties A postponement of the trial was therefore necessary that the ends of justice might not be defeated

Accordingly when the Court met on the morning of the 28th of December, he rose at once to explain his position He stated ' that it was incumbent upon him, in the discharge of his public duty, to move the continuance of the diet in this case It was not necessary in doing this to state his reasons, but as he wished all the motives which guided him in his public duty to be known, he would mention that it was only yesterday that he had been informed of the nature of a defence which was to be made for the prisoner—which was that the person who had died had poisoned herself He understood that forty one witnesses were to be adduced for the defence, which was so contradictory of the evidence which had been laid before him in the case, that, although he regretted to put the jury and the witnesses to the trouble of returning, yet he would not do his duty if he did not first proceed to investigate the grounds on which that defence was to be supported before he proceeded with the prosecution In these circumstances he had not thought it necessary to bring

the accused into Court, and he now moved their Lordships to continue the diet against her till Friday, the 12th of January "

The Judges on the bench were the Lord-Justice Clerk (Boyle), Lord Meadowbank, and Lord Alloway, and they concurred in pronouncing an interlocutor postponing the trial as desired From the statement which we have quoted, it will be apparent to every candid reader that no other course was open to Sir Wm Rae than that which he had adopted, yet his action in the matter gave rise to much angry comment One Dundee newspaper of the time records that "the reasons assigned by the Lord Advocate for putting off this trial, and subjecting the unfortunate husband of the prisoner to the very heavy expense of preparing a second time for the defence, are not deemed quite satisfactory It was notorious in this quarter that one of the pleas for establishing Mrs Smith's innocence was founded on expressions said to have been used by the girl, implying a determination to destroy herself " These animadversions upon Sir Wm Rae's conduct were really unmerited, for we are in a position to show that the postponement of the trial must have been acquiesced in by Mrs Smith's counsel, since they had not secured at this time, nor long after, the witnesses upon whom they depended to establish the theory of suicide

Mr Smyth, advocate, was sent by Crown counsel to precognosce the forty one witnesses, but he had not completed his examination of them when the date of the adjourned trial arrived A fresh postponement was necessary—as much in the interests of the defence as of the prosecution—and the 5th of February was finally appointed as the day for the disposal of this protracted case Even up till this period the evidence for the defence had not been completed Mrs Smith had alluded in her first declaration to some one who had been "employed to put away rats" at Denside, and it was very necessary that this party should be discovered. It was also currently reported that Margaret Warden had declared her intention to commit suicide to occasional visitors to the kitchen, as well as to her fellow-servants, and if it could be shown that she intended to take her own life, and that the rat catcher had left the means within her power, a strong presumption of suicide would be afforded But the latter important witness could not be discovered, although strenuous efforts were made to obtain intelligence of his whereabouts As a proof that the second postponement had been also assented to by the defender's counsel, we may mention that an advertisement asking information concerning him was inserted in the *Dundee Advertiser* of 25th January, a fortnight after the proposed date of the second trial This advertisement is only obscurely referred to in the published accounts of the trial, but as the witnesses for whom inquiry was made were evidently looked upon as important for the defence, we have thought it advisable to reprint this strange document

"To the Benevolent

"Andrew Murray, Rat catcher, is particularly requested to call at Mr Smith's, Farmer at Denside, in the parish of Monikie, on or before Wednesday the 31st current, and those who may know where he is are respectfully solicited to inform him of the present notice All his expenses will be paid

"It is also earnestly requested that any person who can give information that might lead to finding out a woman of the description under mentioned, will communicate the same, without delay to Mr Smith, or to his agents, Macewan & Miller writers in Dundee The woman alluded to is middle aged, and was lately travelling in Fife selling matches, she was accompanied by a boy of about ten years of age, who had a white mouse carrying in a box She is said to have some time resided in the Hilltown or Wellgate of Dundee

This advertisement was effectual in producing both of the witnesses inquired after, but whether their evidence was worth all this trouble the reader must decide when it is laid before him

The trial of Mrs Smith was doomed to be an exceptional one for many reasons When the case was brought before the Court for the *third* time an incident occurred to retard its progress, which is almost unparalleled in the annals of Scottish Judicature The graphic account of this episode contained in the *Dundee Advertiser* of 8th February 1827 fully relates this peculiar incident in these terms —

"*The trial of Mrs Smith* —This trial, which, as we formerly noticed, had been postponed in an unusual manner by a stretch of the almost regal powers possessed by the Lord Advocate, was commenced at Edinburgh on Monday, at nine o'clock in the morning before a bench consisting of all the Lords of Justiciary After an objection to the relevancy of the indictment had been stated and repelled, the examination of the witnesses for the Crown proceeded About five o'clock the tenth of these witnesses (Dr Christison) was in the course of being examined, when an unearthly groan was heard in Court, and all eyes were turned to the jury box—from whence it had proceeded It was found that one of the jurymen (Mr Thom-

son, blockmaker, Leith) had fallen into an epileptic fit Dr Christison sprung from the witnesses' box, and, along with several other medical gentlemen then in Court, went to his assistance He was conveyed into an adjoining room, where means were used to recover him, whilst the Court sat waiting the result At six o'clock he had not returned, and two medical gentlemen [Professor Christison and Dr Macintosh] were then examined as to the probability of his being able to resume his duties as a juryman that evening They concurred in saying that although he was considerably recovered, a relapse might be apprehended that it was unlikely he could continue to act during the greater part of the night as a juryman After the Court had expressed its opinion that it would be improper to put him again into the jury box the Lord Advocate submitted that in accordance with what had taken place in a former case—the only one of the same nature on record—the jury should be discharged, and a future day fixed for proceeding with the trial to which day the Court should adjourn The counsel for the panel thought that mode of proceeding incompetent in this case The Court found that the trial could not proceed, and continued the case till Monday next at ten o'clock, when the question of competence will be discussed The Court on the motion of Mr Jeffrey cautioned persons connected with the newspapers or other publications against giving publicity to any part of the evidence as they would have to answer for the consequences '

The exceptional incident which had occurred took this case out of the range of ordinary trials, and it soon became evident that Mrs Smith's agents intended to avail themselves of this fact The jurymen and witnesses were discharged but instructed by the Court to reappear upon Monday, 12th February, to proceed with this important case Counsel on both sides were to be prepared with arguments as to the legality of carrying on the trial or dismissing the panel from the bar The new turn which the case had taken intensified the excitement in the country regarding it and it was confidently anticipated that the decision of the Court in this peculiar circumstances would regulate all future proceedings Seldom had the Court of Justiciary been so fully attended by all classes as on the day appointed for the settlement of this matter The bench was occupied by all the Lords of Justiciary, and the leaders of the legal profession had assembled in great numbers to hear a decision which should affect their practice in all time coming

D

Part VII

'Law is law—law is law an as in such and so forth, and hereby, and aforesaid provided always nevertheless notwithstanding the law is as once as a new laid egg and not to be understood by a idle headed people'—*Scrivas*

When the case of Mrs Smith was called the Lord Advocate rose and stated briefly "that, in consequence of what took place on Monday last, he held all the proceedings of that day null and void from the time the interlocutor of relevancy was pronounced, but that the case might be opened for discussion, he should now move the Court to proceed to ballot for a new jury." Mr Cockburn opposed this motion, contending that this action was quite incompetent. His speech occupied nearly two hours in delivery, and was marked with all that thoroughness of research, accuracy, and eloquence which were his chief characteristics. Briefly stated, his arguments took this form —

A new jury could not be balloted from the forty five jurymen originally summoned, because it was necessary that forty five names should be in the ballot box, but it was evident that only forty four could now be there. Besides, the thirty members who had been discharged when the first jury was elected had mingled with the community—a circumstance utterly repugnant to Scottish legal tradition. Further, he contended that as the case for the prosecution had been nearly completed when the unfortunate interruption took place, the prisoner had really "tholed an assize," and could not be tried again for the same offence upon the same criminal letters. No case precisely similar had ever occurred, and it was dangerous to establish a precedent which seemed so plainly to contradict the fundamental principles of Scottish criminal law. He maintained that the jury had been discharged by an interlocutor of the Court, and could not be reassembled to try this case anew upon the former libel. The Prosecutor seemed to consider that the case was merely adjourned and was still going on, but this was evidently a misapprehension, since there was now no complete jury, nor could there be unless a new trial were ordered, and a new leet of forty five jurors summoned. He maintained that "from the moment the jury is sworn it is not in the power of the Prosecutor to abandon his case, there can be no desertion of the diet,—no adjournment, and if any accident supervene, the instance must necessarily fall." He asserted that the Court had no power to call witnesses to repeat evidence which they had already given, since the citation upon which they had been called was thoroughly exhausted, and he warned the Court that they were assuming a power for which they had no warrant in thus attempting to try a prisoner twice for the same offence, upon the same libel, and with only a fraction of the original jury. There was no doubt but that the jury had been discharged, and though in some cases the Court could liberate jurymen from attendance, they had no right to liberate fifteen of them, especially as they had already sat upon the case. If this principle were correct, the Court might liberate twenty, twenty five, or even the whole, and try the prisoner without a jury at all. But, on the contrary, if the forty five are present, the Court has no right to liberate even one of them. The argument on the relevancy must take place before the whole forty five, and the panel is entitled to have it discussed before she is called on to plead. The only plea upon which the action of the Court could be defended was that of expediency—a most dangerous excuse for such an arbitrary proceeding.

In reply, Mr Dundas maintained that the order of the Court adjourning the diet practically left the matter in the same state in which it was before the proof began, and he contended that the prisoner could not be said to have "tholed an assize" until a verdict had been returned. He examined the authorities and cases referred to by Mr Cockburn, and explained their precise bearing upon the case. He stated that the prisoner was bound to have the trial completed, even in her own defence, since all the evidence that had been led was against her, and if she were dismissed she would have no opportunity of disproving it. The Solicitor General did not think it necessary to add anything to Mr Dundas's speech, and concurred with him in his arguments.

Mr Jeffrey then addressed the Court for the prisoner in a speech which has been often referred to as a model of forensic eloquence. His chief argument was that the accident which had destroyed the perfect corporate existence of the jury should really have quashed the proceedings, and the Court had no power to appoint a new diet for trial until a new indictment had been served. When the jury is charged with the libel, it is charged irrecoverably, till an interposition of Providence put a stop to the trial. Whatever, therefore, destroys them being as a jury necessarily terminates the libel with which they are identified, and, of course, the instance on which that libel proceeds. Besides, the clear intention of the Act of 1701, under which this trial had been begun, was, by fixing peremptory dicts, to enable the prisoner, in certain cases, to escape without a trial, for the humanity of the law is even above its justice.

When he had concluded, the Court pronounced a distinct opinion sustaining the motion of the Lord Advocate, and directing that the trial should proceed upon the former libel, that a jury should be balloted from the original list of forty-five assizers, and that the same witnesses should again attend to repeat their evidence. In fact, the former proceedings were to be obliterated from the time when the libel was found relevant, and the whole case tried a second time. The importance of this case as regulating future practice was thoroughly understood, and, to put the matter beyond doubt, each of the six Lords on the bench delivered separate opinions, though they were unanimous in recommending the course adopted. Lord Pitmilly remarked "that it would be a disgrace to our Criminal Code if means did not exist of preventing the escape of criminals in circumstances like the present," and Lord Gillies admitted "that the remedy adopted in the present instance is sanctioned neither by statute, by precedent, nor by practice." The Denside case thus marks an epoch in Scottish criminal procedure, and is taken out of the range of ordinary murder trials by the exceptional incident which had occurred. As the arguments upon this point had occupied the Court from ten o'clock in the morning till five o'clock in the afternoon, the case was again adjourned till Monday, 19th February.

Never in the whole course of the history of Scottish jurisprudence had a similar scene been enacted to that which was witnessed in the Court of Justiciary on the morning of that day. All the Lords of Justiciary were present, and it was only when the case was called that its difference from all previous trials became apparent. The proceedings now began from the point when the relevancy of the libel had been proved, and as all the former actions of the preceding dict before this point were held as forming a portion of the present process, the strange phenomenon was presented of a prisoner put upon her trial for life without the libel being read, or herself asked to plead. The Court had clearly assumed arbitrary powers, which revived recollections of the lawless times of three centuries ago.

When the jury was about to be elected by ballot, the prisoner's counsel objected to allowing the former list of forty-five to be taken, as fifteen of them had already been discharged, and the others had not been summoned for that day. The objection was repelled without discussion, as it was

thought the decision of the Court had provided for it. Curiously enough, we cannot find two of the lists of jurors finally chosen to agree together as to their names and designations. The first witness called was Christopher Kerr, Sheriff-Substitute for Dundee district of Forfarshire. Before he was sworn Mr Cockburn objected to him and to all other witnesses who might be examined on this trial as ultroneous—that is, voluntary witnesses—since they had not been cited to attend this dict, but this objection was also over-ruled by the Court without discussion. Mr Kerr then gave evidence as to the state of the prisoner when her two declarations were made, and he was corroborated by J. Boyd Baxter, the Procurator Fiscal. The Lord Advocate then moved that the two declarations be read, but Mr Jeffrey objected to them, upon the ground that 'the panel was subject to a hysterical affection—a wandering and sickness of mind—and that she was particularly in that state the night before, and for some days previous to, the first declaration being taken. That position he offered to prove at this stage by medical evidence, but it was agreed to defer the reading of the documents until further on in the trial. The examination of witnesses was then proceeded with.

Jean Norrie related the whole of the circumstances of Margaret Warden's illness and death in the same terms as we have done in our narrative. Her evidence was given in a clear and intelligible manner, and even the close cross-examination of Mr Jeffrey did not shake her testimony. Only two matters really require our attention at this point—the intention of Warden to commit suicide, and what opportunity she could have. Jean Norrie "remembered of Warden saying in the field one day when she was holing a pickle potatoes, that she didna ken what to do, 'she wad surely do some ill to hersel.' Witness did not think that she intended to do so, though she said it, for she was a rash creature of her words." In reply to Lord Gillies Norrie said 'she never heard that Warden bought any drugs or medicines. She said she had some pills which she had got from the mistress, and they were the only drugs she ever saw her have. She further stated that 'she never saw any rats about the byre, never saw any rats there till after Warden's death, when she saw one in the barn. Before Warden's death she never heard of poison being used to kill rats; never saw any poison in the loft above the bothy. Before Warden's death she does not recollect of hearing the panel or any of the men speak about rats. After Warden was dead and buried she heard some talk about rats.

Barbara Small, lived at Denside, in the house of

James Millar, the foreman of the farm [...] in la[...] Mrs Smith, saw Warden several times dur[...]g her [...] [...]s of her life. Neverthe[...]t he at any [...] th[...] [...] put himself [...]d[...]. "Are Warden [...]d in, par]" I said to witness, that she had died of water in tr [...]chest, and she said Dr Taylor told her so. She was often in the byre, and never saw any rats there. She took charge of Mrs Millar's children. Panel never told witness that there was poison laid about the house. She never forbade witness to take the children into the loft above th[...] co by.

Mary Gibson, niece of Mrs Smith, saw Warden several times during her illness, but did not give any additional particulars.

Mrs Warden['s] evidence has already been largely [...] in our description of the detailed scene. She betrayed some anxiety to screen the Densi[...]e family from any evil result through her testimony. Her son Robert Warden, gave evidence as to the funeral, and Ann Gruar related the moment which we have already described, when Warden dec[...]red her intention to take her life.

Usually the most puzzling portion of a trial for poisoning is that which deals with the medical evidence, yet it is rarely that witnesses engaged in *post mortem* investigations agree so decidedly as in this case. Dr Taylor, Broughty Ferry, was the only one who had seen the deceased upon her death bed, and he had then taken her symptoms to indicate *cholera morbus*, but his examination of the body, together with Drs Johnston and Ramsay, altered this opinion, and he declared that "he had now no doubt that Warden

died of poison, and that the poison was arsenic." The only hitch in his evidence arose from his unwillingness to identify the body as that of Margaret Warden. "He could not say it was the body of a person he had seen, but it was certainly taken from the same grave in which the body of Margaret Warden was buried." Dr Johnston, Dundee, described the tests which he had applied for the detection of arsenic at great length, and conclusively proved, by cumulative as well as special evidence, that death had resulted from the administration of this poison. Dr Ramsay concurred in the report and had come to the same conclusion as his colleagues in the matter. Professor Christison had been employed to test portions of the intestines by the Crown agent, and his methods of investigation were unknown to and different from those employed by the Dundee doctors, yet they conclusively proved that arsenic in large doses had been administered, and had certainly caused death. This witness endured a most severe cross-examination from both Mr Jeffrey and the Lord Advocate, but he never for a moment wavered in his assertion as to the nature of the poison and the results which had ensued.

Thus far the evidence distinctly showed that Margaret Warden's death had been caused by arsenic, but there was as yet nothing to prove that the prisoner had any such poison in her possession at any time near the date of the decease. It was now the duty of the Lord Advocate to lead the evidence at his command upon this most important point.

PART VIII

"*Œdipus*—By what methods may be found
The faint marked footsteps of this long past guilt?"
    —*Sophocles*

William Dick, surgeon in Dundee, was well acquainted with the Smith family, having been the medical attendant at Denside for a long time, though not for some five or six years before the trial. He kept drugs for his private practice. Two of his daughters had been on a visit to Denside in the August preceding Warden's death, and Mrs Smith had told one of them to ask her father to make up some poison for rats, saying she would call for it her self on the following Friday. This request was made on Monday 21st August, but Miss Dick forgot to deliver the message, and Mrs Smith omitted to call until Friday the 1st of September. Dr Dick was out when she called, and when he returned

he found her in the kitchen, and she said to him, "You've forgot the poison for the rats." He asked her, "What poison?" She said "Some poison I sent for to kill rats." He asked if she had any cats, and she replied that she had, but that she was no better for them. He told her that he had nothing of the kind, but if it would oblige her he would get it from an apothecary's shop. She desired him to do so, and as he wanted some articles for himself, he went to the shop of Mr Russell, apothecary, and ordered his shopman to put up some arsenic for a friend. The quantity supplied was to be an ounce or an ounce and a half, it was put into paper, and marked "arsenic" on one side and "poison" on the other, this was enclosed in another paper, which was also tied up marked in the same manner. It was about twelve o'clock when Mrs Smith first called, and she was back at his house before one, and received the arsenic out of his own hands. He told her to mix it up with a little oatmeal and cautioned her either to make it up with her own hands or to see it done, for fear of accident. *He told her it was arsenic.* She also got a small dose of laxative medicine—not castor oil—it was 20 grains jalap and 5 grains calomel.

Dr Dick was examined by the Sheriff on the forenoon of the day upon which Mrs Smith was apprehended. He did not conceal the circumstance of having procured arsenic for her, and this was probably the reason why Mr Kerr had put the crucial question which had discovered Mrs Smith and evoked a second declaration. Mr Cockburn cross-examined this witness, and elicited the information that he had known Mrs Smith for forty years, and had always considered her a humane person—liberal to her poor neighbours. She had been subject to hysterics, but he had not seen her in that state for a dozen years.

Andrew Russell, shopman to David Russell, apothecary, recollected having sold an ounce of oxide of arsenic to Dr Dick at the time specified. He marked "arsenic" and "poison" on the package.

Mrs Jolly, druggist, Dundee, knew Mrs Smith. Not long before her apprehension she called on witness, and having asked a word with her, stated her case and she recommended castor oil. Mrs Smith said she had taken castor oil without effect, and asked if there was nothing else that would answer the same purpose. Witness gave her an ounce of castor oil, and there might be some white mustard along with it.

Mrs Margaret Kerr or Smith, wife of the prisoner's husband's brother, was at Denside the day after Warden's death, asked if it was fever she had died of, and prisoner said it was. She understood that it was typhus fever to which she alluded, as it was then going about. She had seen her on the Sunday before she was apprehended, having been sent for as she had taken ill. Mrs Smith was in hysterics, and unable to tell her complaint. Witness remained with her till nine o'clock next day (2d October), when she had recovered a little, but was not out of bed. She had known her to be affected in that way before, and had taken her out of church in that state. The fit made her insensible, and she forgot she had been in church, and could not speak correctly, even the second day, after a similar attack.

Thomas Brown did not know his exact age, but it was about twelve years; he was employed as herd at Denside from two months before Whitsunday till Martinmas last. He slept in the bothy, was

never disturbed with rats there, never heard rats in the loft above the bothy, and did not recollect seeing any in the byre, he saw a dead rat in the barn one morning, but never observed any others about the place. He knew Margaret Warden, who is now dead, had no conversation about getting poison to kill rats, and never was sent for any arsenic. He was the only boy about the town [farm steading]. He had been often about the loft but never saw anything like oatmeal lying about it.

John Smith, farm servant at Denside, is no relation of Mrs Smith. Saw Margaret Warden on the day before she was taken ill. She was then in good health and spirits, and was making comment in the field. He did not recollect having seen any rats in the course of last summer, though he slept in the bothy. He recollected in the loft no quantity last summer, and suspected it was rats, but never heard of arsenic being laid there before Warden's death. Never saw any dead rats about Denside. In cross-examination he deponed that he saw rats the winter before last, they were in great numbers about the stable and byres, and the hose harness was much destroyed by them about Whitsunday last. There was poultry about the farm. He had heard Mrs Smith say that many of them had died and that she thought the rats had killed them.

As the witnesses for the prosecution had now been all examined, the Lord Advocate proposed that the declarations should be read. Mr Jeffrey, on the part of the panel, objected to the last declaration being read because at the time it was emitted it was shown to a man of nervous attack of hysteria, and therefore was not in a state to be examined. When he had challenged the first reading of these declarations he had offered medical proofs to her state of health, and he now adduced evidence to show that these documents were not to be relied on.

Mr Lyon Alexander, surgeon in Dundee, knew Mrs Smith, was called to go to Denside in a great hurry on the Monday [2d October] on which she was apprehended, and arrived there betwixt twelve and one o'clock in the morning. Mrs Smith was then in a state of stupor and insensibility, and appeared, when he entered the house, to be labouring under a violent nervous attack. She was far from being recovered when he left her at five o'clock in the morning. At that time she was talking of persons as present who were not. He did not think that she was at that time in a state

The author of this account [of the trial] is in error in transcribing the whist in this instance. Mr Mackenzie and Mr Menzies are mentioned. We find one Mackenzie as in S.S.C. in one, Menzies as advocate, but think that Jeffrey would conduct this case personally

to be examined on suspicion of having committed
a crime. The recovery from these attacks is gene
rally tedious. A person may be past that stage
when he states illusions for reality, and yet be far
from being recovered. Dr Alexander saw Mrs
Smith in gaol next evening. She had then a very
indistinct idea of what had passed the night before.
Loss and imperfection of memory is a frequent
concomitant of the disease. Her friends said that
she had received a severe shock that day by having
a grandchild nearly drowned. It was not his
opinion that she was in a fit state to be examined
in the forenoon between the times he saw her.

As the cross examination of this witness is im
portant, we transcribe it as it is found in the
Dundee Advertiser of 22d February 1827, and in no
other account of this trial :—

Dr Lyon Alexander, witness—

By the Lord Advocate—Witness thinks, accord
ing to his experience, that in her case it was im
possible for her to be examined that day.

By Lord Meadowbank—The pulse was nearly
natural.

By the Lord Advocate—Witness was called by a
man servant, who said that they were afraid she
[Mrs Smith] would be gone before he got out. He
had attended the Denside family for five or six
years.

The evidence transcribed above refers mainly to
the state of the accused before incarceration. The
succeeding testimony shows the state into which
she had fallen after her imprisonment, and though
adduced for her assistance it seems to be decidedly
against her.

Mr John Crichton, surgeon, Dundee, visited
Mrs Smith in the gaol there on an evening in
December. The people in the gaol were applying
hot flannels. It he could give the complaint a
name he would call it violent hysteria, approaching
to epilepsy. She was not *then* in a state to speak
coherently.

On this evidence it may be remarked that it is
puzzling to see how the state of Mrs Smith's health
in December, at least two months after her incar
ceration, could affect the credibility of the declara
tions emitted on 2d and 3d October. And though
this witness strongly asserted his belief that the
illness of Mrs Smith in prison was not feigned, the
symptoms he describes are precisely those which
would appear in a nervous patient actually under
an accusation involving a capital punishment.

Mrs Margaret Machan, sister of Mrs Smith, saw
her on the morning of her apprehension. She was
then confined to bed. Witness assisted to dress
her that she might go to Four Mile House, and
she fainted three times while she was doing so.
Witness admitted to the Lord Advocate that she

did not continue long in the faint. Dr Johnston
was in the house at the time, but she did not call
him, because she had seen her many times as bad
as that.

James Yeaman, jr., of Affleck, saw Mrs Smith
at Four Mile House, and heard her declaration.
She was perfectly collected until the last question
was put to her. Patrick Mackay, messenger, was
also present at this examination. Mrs Smith was
collected at the commencement, but towards the
close, when a certain question was put, she became
very much agitated, fell back in her chair, but
soon recovered. No objection was made to her
examination at the time on the ground of her
alleged illness.

Having heard the evidence adduced for the
rejection or reception of the declarations,
the Court repelled the objection without an
answer from the Public Prosecutor, stating that
the effect of the declaration must be left for the
jury to decide upon. These documents were
accordingly read, and this closed the case for the
prosecution.

The exculpatory evidence was founded entirely
upon the notion that Mrs Smith had procured
poison for rats; that Margaret Warden had seen
her mixing it, and that the unfortunate deceased,
goaded to extremity by her condition, had com
mitted suicide to conceal her shame. Strenuous
efforts were made to establish this theory, although
the "forty one witnesses" with whom the prose
cutors were threatened did not come forward.

Annie Dick, daughter of Dr Dick, detailed the
cause of her visit to Denside, and mentioned that
Mrs Smith had asked her to request her father to
procure some poison for the rats there. She had
forgot to deliver her message, but when Mrs Smith
called, she believes she got the required mixture.
When Mrs Smith spoke to her about the poison,
both Margaret Warden and Jean Norrie were
present.

Grace Dick corroborated her sister's evidence in
every particular.

The testimony of Andrew Murray, the rat
catcher, who had been advertised for, suggested
another theory as to the means whereby Margaret
Warden committed suicide. He stated that he
had been at Denside "in the way of business" for
the first time about three and a half years before,
and had left some medicine (poison) to destroy
rats, consisting of oatmeal, arsenic, and some anise.
Was there about two years afterwards to
destroy vermin in the Mill of Affleck, then in the
possession of Mr Smith, and had left some medicine
with Mrs Smith at that time. Was at Denside on
Sunday week, being called in by the advertisement,
and found vermin there—"the small Scots rat,

and mice siclike " He only left medicine where persons were of that character who could be trusted with it He did not actually see any rats when last at Denside, but only traces of them

James Miller, foreman of the farm of Denside, and son in law of Mrs Smith, had seen rats about the farm at Whitsunday, but not after In cross examination he stated that he was in the bothie some days after Margaret Warden's death He was taken up by one of Mr Smith's sons to see some stuff in the ' crips" of the walls, said to be poison for rats This was a day or two after Mrs Smith's apprehension

William Sturrock, wright, had some conversa tion with Mrs Smith in June last year as to rats at Denside, and she said that she must have the rat catcher back, or some medicine to destroy them

Agnes Gruar corroborated the evidence of her sister Ann as to Warden's threat to destroy her self, and Ann Lees also asserted that she had once heard the deceased use similar language

Mrs Hamilton or M'Hattle, the woman who was advertised for, gave what she considered important evidence as to Warden's suicidal intention She was a kind of hawker, and had been in the habit of visiting Denside generally at night, as she frequently got free lodgings in the barn She was there two or three weeks before Warden died When Warden showed her to bed, she asked if witness would come and speak She burst into tears, and said, what would she do, for she was not able for her work, and she had got rough usage from her mother and brother on a former occasion Wit ness said, a mother's heart was aye kindly, and

she would be the first to pity her Warden said before she would be tossed and handled in the way she was before she would put an end to her self Witness took her by the hand, and implored her not to speak in that manner Warden then grasped her by both hands and bade her speak low, for there was some one in the close She begged her not to reveal what she had said, for if she thought that she would put an end to herself before morning Witness promised not to tell, and kept the secret until after Warden's death

This woman M'Hattle had a boy along with her, and it was now the purpose of the defender's counsel to suggest that he had been sent by Warden to purchase poison Robert Lasson, merchant, Broughty Ferry, recollected of a boy coming into the shop, who asked for twopence worth of arsenic He did not get the arsenic, never having sold any but his wife said, "Was it not cream of tartar?" The boy said, "No, no, it was poison he wanted " Mrs Lasson said he would get it at the doctor's This happened on the Monday or Tuesday of the week on which Warden died

Dr Andrew Fyffe objected to some of the tests applied to discover the arsenic, and Dr Macintosh was of opinion that all the symptons of Warden decease indicated rather a death from chole than from poison He admitted, however, that the presence of arsenic in the stomach proved that death had been caused by poisoning

This concluded the evidence for the defence, and the Lord Advocate began his address to the jury at 11 o'clock at night

---

PART IX

Parolles—Nay, 'tis strange 'tis very strange that is the brief and the tedious of it and he is a most facinorous spirit that will not acknowledge it to be the——
Lafeu—Very hand of heaven
Par—Ay, so I say
                                   —*All's Well that Ends Well*

The speech of Sir William Rae, the Lord Advocate, was clear and precise, and as he had to go over so much evidence, it occupied fully two hours in delivery He pointed out that poison had been found in the stomach of the deceased, so as unquestionably to have caused her death Dr Fyffe, in his evidence for the defence had attempted to show that the arsenic found in her body was *sulphuret*, whilst that sold by Mr Russell was *oxide*, but Dr Christison had explained that a chemical change in the stomach would convert the oxide

into a sulphuret, and as a matter of fact *both* form of arsenic were traced by the tests applied It had been proved that Mrs Smith had poison in her possession, and that she had given a false reason for this, as no rats had been seen by the servants on the farm The evi dence of the rat catcher, who had only visited the place at long intervals, and who confessed that he had not seen rats, but only traces of them, could not overthrow the testimony of those who were constant residents in the place He maintained that the assertion as to Mrs Smith's illness before her examination had not been established, and he alluded to the strange remark which she made when on her way to Four Mile House, that she thought the violent vomiting would have cleansed the stomach of everything. He pointed out the discrepancy between the first and second declarations, and compared her denial that she knew it was arsenic with the decided evidence of Dr Dick, contending that these contradictions carried convincing proof of guilt. Still more striking was the fact that she had given so many different versions of the cause of Margaret Warden's illness to various people, each incompatible with the other. Her interview with Dr Taylor, and the conversation which took place between them, must have considerable weight with the jury. He ridiculed the idea that the girl had poisoned herself. No sufficient motive had been suggested for such an act. It was incredible that she, who had already a child four years of age, should be so delicate in her feelings and so overcome with shame at her condition as to take away her own life with suicidal hand. There had been no concealment in the former case, and her rank in life precluded the notion that she had felt her shame to be worse than death. No clear evidence had been led to show that she was really serious in her threats of self destruction, and all the testimony given on this point was rendered doubtful by her dying declaration. That the panel could have administered medicines for the purpose of procuring abortion was also incredible, for she had not used the articles calculated for that purpose, but had chosen instead a drug of the deadliest kind. The case was one which rested entirely upon circumstantial evidence; but the jury must not take the circumstances one by one. They must view them all together, and then say if they could come to any other conclusion than that the panel did administer poison to the woman and that she had come to her death thereby. On the whole view of the case, he considered himself justified in claiming from them a verdict of guilty.

Mr Jeffrey followed on behalf of the prisoner. "His speech," says one authority, "was for the most part delivered in a slow, solemn and impressive style, not common to this orator. Towards the conclusion, whilst presenting a view of the general bearing of the whole evidence and enforcing the necessity of having the most clear and convincing proof to warrant the taking away of life, his elocution became exceedingly rapid and animated—exhibiting a fine specimen of the masterly and correct combination of fact, argument and declamation for which he is distinguished. His speech occupied about two hours and a half."

In this case he said, the jury had no alternative but to set at liberty the prisoner as a person unjustly accused, or to condemn her to death as a murderess. When they considered the total absence of any motive for such an atrocious act, and the calm and cheerful manner in which the panel had ministered to the deceased, day after day, during her illness, they would ask their consciences could she be guilty of so detestable a crime. If so, it was a crime of such barbarity, a guilt so abominable that no language could adequately characterise it. He cautioned them against being misled by the feelings of indignation so natural in such cases; to consider the character of benevolence the prisoner had so long borne, the motive for the crime charged so feeble, and that there was no proof that she had ever regarded the object of her supposed vengeance with any feeling of hostility. But, he would ask, was there any evidence that the deceased had died by poison at all? And here the learned gentleman, while he expressed his admiration of the science of medicine and of many of its professors, stated that he could place little reliance on the tests to discover poison. Those tests which were considered almost infallible a few years ago were now entirely disused as fallacious, and other tests employed which, perhaps, in the course of time, might be equally thrown aside for the same reason. He objected to the dates quoted in the indictment—Tuesday and Friday—as those on which it was averred that poison had been administered. No evidence had been offered as to Friday, and yet the whole of the medical witnesses concurred in stating that if the dose given on Tuesday were arsenic, the deceased could not have survived so long. He contended that it was not competent for the prosecutor to argue that poison *might* have been given on Wednesday or Thursday. His proof must be limited to the days specifically mentioned in the charge, yet even his own witnesses asserted that it was highly improbable, almost impossible, that the girl could have lived till Friday. It was perhaps possible, but would the jury be asked for a verdict on a mere *possibility* of guilt? They were bound to consider rather if there was a possibility of *innocence*, and if there was so, they were bound to acquit.

It was true that the panel bought poison, and that poison was arsenic; but the reason of this was clear from the evidence. A professional rat catcher had been repeatedly employed at Denside. He had been there four years before, and had returned fifteen months before the girl's death, and had killed rats by poison. Besides, Mrs Smith went publicly to buy arsenic. It was sought before Dr Dick's whole family, which was not likely had any unlawful use of it been intended. As to the dying words of the deceased, there were two editions; but he contended that it was totally inconsistent with these words, the idea that they inferred the prisoner's guilt. It was much more probable that they were applied to her own relations, or to the young man who had deceived her. But assuming that arsenic was found in the stomach, and that the deceased had died thereby, he contended that there was a much greater probability that she had taken it herself than that it had been administered by her mistress. That she had threatened self destruction repeatedly was sworn to by six different witnesses. It was in unimpeachable evidence that she had declared her intention in a serious, solemn, and sorrowful manner, and in a tone which struck awe and horror into the minds of the hearers and produced those calm and serious remonstrances which the witnesses had repeated. Assuming, therefore, that she had died by poison, he would ask whether it was possible to believe, in the face of all the evidence of her kindness and partiality for the deceased, that Mrs Smith had harboured in her breast a vengeance so brutal? Was it not much more probable that Margaret Warden, actuated by a sullen and irritable temper, in the circumstances of destitution which appeared before her, and having the temptation within her reach, died by her own act?

"If, gentlemen of the jury,' he said in conclusion, 'you have any doubt upon this point, you are bound to acquit the prisoner. You will look at the case in every point of view, and say whether you can find a clear verdict of guilty. I think that is impossible. I do not expect a triumphant vindication. I ask merely a verdict of acquittal, and I am entitled to expect it if there remain any mere doubt of guilt. I leave it to your consciences to say if you can convict any person on such evidence as is laid before you. With some confidence I ask a verdict of not guilty, but I *demand* a verdict of not proven."

The summing up of the Lord Justice Clerk began at three o'clock on Tuesday morning, and continued till half past five. As usual the jury rose when his speech began, but, contrary to custom, they were not asked to resume their seats, and were forced to stand during the whole time of its delivery, though their endurance had already been severely taxed. In describing this speech one writer says:—"His Lordship went over the evidence at great length, dwelling with much emphasis on those parts of it which made against the prisoner. His Lordship's impression, evidently, was that the prisoner was guilty." He began by cautioning the jury to guard specially against any prejudice which they might have taken through what they had heard out of doors in the very peculiar circumstances which had occurred. He over ruled Mr Jeffrey's objection as to the precise day when the

poison was administered by showing from the criminal letters that the prosecutor had taken a latitude of days in the words 'or one or other of the days &c. As to counsel's objection to the admissibility of the first declaration—it had already been accepted by the Court, and must have its effect upon the jury. In his opinion both declarations carried on their face proof of the soundness and sanity of the prisoner when they were emitted. The first question for the jury was—Did Margaret Warden die of poison, and was that poison arsenic? If these two points were not established, all the other evidence fell to the ground. The symptoms of her illness did not necessarily infer poison, but when poison was found in the stomach all the medical witnesses agreed that the symptoms were caused by its presence. It is absurd to assert that we must reject all medical evidence as Mr Jeffrey suggests, because it is possible that more exact tests for poison may be discovered at some future time. His Lordship thought the jury must be satisfied that she died through the administration of arsenic. The next question was—What evidence had they that it was administered by the panel? They found Mrs Smith in the possession of arsenic at the supposed time of administration. Burning pain was one of the symptoms of this poison, and they found that the deceased complained of burning pain after receiving whisky or something else from her mistress. Panel had herself admitted that she gave her castor oil on Thursday. The declarations were not only self contradictory, but could not be made to agree with the evidence. Speaking of Mrs Warden's testimony, he said, 'If you are to believe her, Margaret Warden had distinctly accused her mistress of giving her something which had caused her distress. This was at a time when she thought herself dying; and if she had taken the poison herself, and not told her mother, she must have been the greatest hypocrite on earth to go out of the world with a lie in her mouth, indicating that she had got from another what had brought her to that state, while conscious that she had taken it herself.'

In considering the exculpatory evidence, his Lordship examined at great length the theory of suicide sought to be thereby established. After an elaborate analysis of the testimony, he proceeded:

"In the last place, you will consider whether you are satisfied that there is evidence sufficient to prove that, though she died by poison, Margaret Warden was her own murderer. At this conclusion I cannot myself arrive unless I am to believe the whole of the evidence for the prisoner, and disregard that of the other witnesses. From all that I have heard, I cannot believe that she took the poison herself There is no vestige of evidence, not one witness among the cloud of witnesses which has been brought before us, that testifies to any other person having bought arsenic but the prisoner The case is undoubtedly one of great importance, and you must consider it carefully If you have no doubts you will express your conviction by a verdict of guilty If otherwise, the rule of law is that where the scales of justice hang even, the person accused is entitled to the benefit of the most favourable construction "

When his Lordship had concluded his charge, the jury expressed a wish to retire, and they were instructed to prepare and seal their verdict, and deliver it at two o'clock in the afternoon Accordingly at that time the Court reassembled, and the jury having taken their seats, their Chancellor delivered a written verdict, all in one voice finding the libel *Not Proven* The Lord Justice Clerk then addressed them in this peculiar fashion — "Gentlemen, I now discharge you from your duty The Court have reason to be satisfied with the patience and attention you have bestowed upon this extraordinary and very painful case The verdict you have just returned, gentlemen, is *your verdict*, and I now discharge you from any other duty in the case "

Turning to Mrs Smith, he said—" Mary Elder or Smith, the jury appointed to try the criminal charge against you have returned a verdict, in one voice, finding that charge Not Proven They have not concurred in a verdict finding you not guilty, and, in now dismissing you from that bar, I leave it to your own conscience, before God, to apply their verdict in such a way as may be most conducive to your welfare in this world, and to your eternal welfare hereafter " The prisoner was then dismissed *simpliciter* from the bar

Thus was terminated one of the most exceptional trials of modern times We have been tempted to detail the case with some prolixity, principally because of the strange local features it presents, but also partly to counteract the absurd traditions regarding it which have long circulated in the neighbourhood of the scene of this tragedy The popular voice condemned Mrs Smith from the first, even before her defence was known , and scandal such as this grows more difficult to contradict as the years go by But we have now laid before the reader an impartial statement of this story, and he must judge for himself how far the many scurrilous ballads of the time were wrong when they boldly asserted the guilt of " The Wife o' Denside "

During our researches in connection with this

trial we came across the details of a curious incident connected with it which may be worth relating On the 18th of January 1827 a young man called at Denside, and introduced himself to Mr Smith as one of Mr Francis Jeffrey s clerks He had been sent to Dundee, he said, for the purpose of precognoscing some of the witnesses, but had run short of funds , and, as he was likely to be at considerable expense still, he had his master's authority to ask for £10, which would be deducted from his bill at the final settlement He mentioned that he had visited Mrs Smith in prison before he left Edinburgh It so happened that Mr Smith had not so much cash by him at the time as to comply with this demand, but he arranged to meet the young man on the following day at Crichton s tavern in the Murraygate, and advance him the money required Before going to the tavern on Friday, Mr Smith took the precaution to call on his Dundee agent, who told him at once that the fellow must be a swindler The officers of police were made acquainted with the affair, and it was planned that Mr Smith should still keep his appointment, pay the money, and take a receipt for it, so as to convict the "clerk" of fraud Mr Smith, accompanied by his son, his agent, and Sergeant Dow of the police, went accordingly to the tavern, and, after the two latter gentlemen had been secreted in the room with them, the young man was admitted to an interview The instant the receipt was granted, and two £5 notes handed to the impostor, the agent stepped forward, examined the document, and told the man he must go to the Police Office. He refused , but Sergeant Dow then came on the scene, and took him into custody, despite his protestations that he had committed no crime, since he had not lifted the money from the table He was afterwards identified as a deserter from the 25th Regiment, named Peter Smith or Gow, who had been concerned in the theft of some rings from a house in Dundee, and he was committed to prison for fifteen days Charges of theft were also laid against him from Aberdeen and from Forfar On the 3d of February he was taken to the jail of Forfar, and detained there some time whilst the case against him from that quarter was preparing , but he was ultimately sent back to Dundee in the early part of May At a Sheriff Court held in Dundee by Sheriff Substitute Robertson on 12th May, he was accused of falsehood, fraud, and wilful imposition practised upon Mr Smith of Denside, and at once pleaded guilty to the charge He was asked how long he had been imprisoned, and replied, "Four months , ' but the Procurator Fiscal explained that he had only been in custody with reference to this charge for two months. The Sheriff Substitute considered the crime to which he had pled guilty a serious one, a more deliberate piece of villainy could not, in his opinion, have been practised He had called upon Mr Smith when his mind must have been in great distress, and had sought to use his misfortunes to perpetrate a heartless fraud He would not consider a sentence short of three months' imprisonment adequate to the offence, and the prisoner was sentenced accordingly

---

THE BOSWELL-MURDER TRIAL—A FIFESHIRE DUEL

PART I

> ' *Face* — Sir, for the *Duels*
> The *Doctor* I assure you shall inform you
> To the least shadow of a hair and show you
> An instrument he has of his own making
> Wherewith no sooner shall you make report
> Of any quarrel, but he will take the height on't
> Most instantly and tell in what degree
> Of safety it lies in or Mortality
> And how it may be borne
>   — *The Alchemist* (*Ben Jonson*)

So vast has been the influence which public opinion has exerted of late years in changing our manners and customs from those prevalent amongst our forefathers, that it is difficult for us to credit their existence so near our own time It is no exaggeration to say that during the last half century our social habits have been quite revolutionised, our political ideas radically altered, and the whole course of existence in these British Isles greatly changed from its former channel Free Trade, the growth of steam driven industry and commerce, Parliamentary reform, the abolition of the taxes upon knowledge, and the freedom of the press have all combined to render us as different in our style of living from our immediate predecessors as they differed from the Cavaliers and Roundheads of the Protectorate Especially is this noticeable in that growth of a regard for law which is eminently a product of these latter days The citizen no longer fears to trust the protection of his life, his honour, and his goods to the care of the servants of his Sovereign, being well assured that the Press will preserve him from injustice or shield him from unmerited disgrace, should the officials of the law neglect or overstep their duty And yet the time is not long gone since each man found it necessary to take arms in his own defence, and to vindicate his outraged honour at the point of the sword Duelling survived as a relic of mediæval barbarism even within the memory of our senescent contemporaries, and it is our purpose to relate one of the most notable of the cases of this insane system of manslaughter which have occurred during this century Before detailing the circumstances, it may be instructive to trace the progress of this strange custom from early times.

Authorities are divided as to the origin of duelling—one class of writers maintaining, that it has existed in one form or other from the very earliest times, whilst another asserts that it is "a practice altogether peculiar to the modern world, since no traces of it are to be found among any of the nations of antiquity Strictly speaking, the latter theory is correct, for although there are several instances upon record of single combats fought by warriors in front of hostile armies, these have nothing in common with the duel as we understand it. Upon this subject an acute writer has remarked —"That one man should endanger or lose his own life, or take away that of another, for an offence in ninety nine cases out of a hundred confessedly undeserving the punishment menaced or inflicted, that this should be every where done in defiance of law and religion, that the perpetrating the act should be esteemed meritorious—resistance to it dishonourable, and that this anomalous violation of humanity, law, and religion should be the claimed and exclusive privilege of the most refined and best educated portion of society, are facts, for the history and exemplification of which, strange to say, we must limit our inquiries to the civilised communities of Christendom '

Both Tacitus and Cæsar assert that "the elder Germans determined disputed claims to property and even to office by the sword," and there is no reason to doubt this assertion So early as A D 501 a law of Gundebald, King of the Burgundians, enjoined this custom, and Frothius, the Dane, made a decree declaring, in dubious Latin, that " it was sublime for those who disputed over words to try a fall ' Gradually the dangers of an appeal to the sword dawned upon the beclouded Gothic mind, but the custom had become so general that it was difficult to repress it In A D 701 we find Luitprand confessing that "we are not convinced of the justice of what is called the judgment of God, since we have found that many innocent persons have perished in defending a good cause, but this custom is of such antiquity amongst the Lombards that we cannot abolish it, notwithstanding its impiety ' So gross had this evil become in the reign of Charlemagne, and so widely was it spread, that not only the parties in a common suit of law, but the witnesses, and even the judges, were constantly summoned to do mortal battle in support of the justice of their cause, the truth of their testimony, or the uprightness of their decision Many attempts were made to limit its ravages by those enlightened rulers who saw the endless havoc thus made amongst their subjects, and the Church sought to divert the people from an appeal to the sword by instituting those elaborate ordeals—of fire, of water, and of the dead hand—which they asserted to be infallible guides to the truth in any disputed matter But the practice of the duel was never abandoned, and the warlike monarchs of France looked upon it as an unchallengeable proof of personal prowess The tournaments, where Knights fought together *à outrance*, for love, and slew or were slain for amusement, doubtless fostered this lax way of viewing an antiquated custom, and served to preserve it even into civilised times

John Locke, in his "Essay on Civil Government,' puts the question in a very clear light "It is,' he says, "out of a man's power so to submit himself to another as to give him a liberty to destroy him, God and nature never allowing a man so to abandon himself as to neglect his own preservation, and since he cannot take away his own life, neither can he give power to another to take it" This reflection is so very obvious that we wonder it did not occur to some ardent churchman of the Middle Ages, when the crime of duelling was rampant It is true that Louis le Débonnaire sought to limit the duel to the decision of criminal or of grave civil causes only, but he was forced to abandon his purpose and suffer the obnoxious system to resume its sway

In Scotland this Gothic custom had maintained its power and immolated its victims for a long and dreary period before any attempt was made to repress it The first trace of legislation against duelling in Scotland which we can find is in Act passed by James VI in 1600, and which is couched in these decided terms —

"Anent Singular Combats

"Oure Soueran Lord and Estaittis of this p'nt parliament Considering the great *Libertie* that sindrie persones takis In provoking vtheris to singular combattis vpoun suddan and frivoll querrellis, q lk heavngenderit great Inconveniences within this Realme THAIRFOIR statutis and ordinis that na persone in tyme cuming without his hienes licence fecht ony singular combatt Vnder the pane of dead, and his moveable geir escheat to

his hienes vse And the provocar to be punischit with ane mair Ignominious dead nor the defendar at the plea sure of his M tie '

This Act clearly brought amateur duelling under the denomination of murder, though it reserved to the King the right to appoint a trial by combat should he see fit to resume that almost obsolete custom But this law though sufficiently rigorous in its penalties must have been loosely administered, since it utterly failed to put a stop to the practice of duelling The stormy reign of Charles I doubtless gave rise to many private political quarrels, which could only be settled by an appeal to the sword, and in the year after his execution, whilst Scotland was nominally under the dominion of Charles II, an Act was passed (4th July 1650) "discharging all dewells or combatts under the certificatioun conteanit in the paper approvin in pliament and ordaned to be published at the mercatt croce of Edr' Still severer measures were found necessary under the Protectorate of Oliver Cromwell, and on the 29th of June 1654 his famous " Ordinance against Challenges, Duels, and all Provocations thereunto' was issued This document declares that " Whereas the fighting of Duels upon private Quarrels is a thing in itself displeasing to God unbecoming Christians, and contrary to all good order and government, and forasmuch as the same is a growing evil in this Nation, for preventing whereof there is a present necessity of some more severe law then hitherto hath been made in that behalf, Be it therefore Ordained by His Highness the Lord Protector of the Commonwealth, &c" The provisions of this Ordinance are as follows —The challenger, the acceptor of a challenge or the bearer of the same, shall be committed to prison, without bail, for six months, and shall not be set free until he has entered in recognisance, with two or more sureties, " to be of the good Behaviour during the space of one whole year then next ensuing ' Any one challenged who does not disclose the fact to a Justice of the Peace within twenty four hours after the receipt of such challenge shall be held to have accepted it, and be punished accordingly Any duel or combat on which death ensues shall be judged to be murder and if a duel be actually fought, though death do not ensue both principals and seconds shall be banished for life from the Commonwealth, and if afterwards found therein they shall suffer death The using of provoking words or gestures shall make any one who so strives to cause a duel subject to a fine to be bound over to keep the peace and to make such reparation to the party wronged as the Judge shall deem fit All persons who know of any intent to fight a duel shall forthwith apprehend, or cause to be apprehended, the parties concerned and if they fail to do so they shall be liable to a forfeit of ten pounds of lawful English money for the use of the poor of the parish where the offence was committed Challenges given or accepted in any part of the Commonwealth, though fought elsewhere, shall be held as offences committed within its bounds, and punished accordingly

Even these stringent measures were quite ineffectual to repress the evil custom, and the restoration of Charles II was accompanied by a perfect craze for duelling In 1679 that monarch issued a proclamation declaring ' that duels are most frequent, and that the utmost rigour of the law would be exercised against them ," but it is very certain that his own favourites at the Court were the greatest sinners in this respect ' The mania says one writer on the subject, "spread to all ranks Doctors met in consultation with drawn swords Mead and Woodward fought under the gate of Gresham College Woodward's foot slipped, and he fell ' Take your life ' exclaimed Mead ' Anything but your physic,' replied Woodward ' Amongst the nobility it was considered as a proof of good breeding to have been engaged in this special form of murder, and the arm of the law was paralysed and impotent to restrain the murderer or avenge his victim Affronts were systematised according to a code of honour, whereby one might learn how far he might be insulted without feeling it necessary to demand his opponent's life, and the passion for duelling became as prevalent and absorbing as the craze for commercial speculation, or the mania for gambling

During the reign of William III another attempt was made to restrict this fatal propensity by a measure passed in 1696, entitled "Act against Duells, which runs thus —

"Our Sovereign Lord, with advice and consent of the Estates of Parliament, Statutes and Enacts That whosoever, principall or second or other interposed person, gives a challenge to fight a Duell or single Combat or whosoever accepts the same, or whosoever either principall or second on either side engages therein albeit no fighting insue shall be punished by the pain of banishment and escheat of moveables without prejudice to the Act already made against the fighting of Duells, which His Majestie, with consent forsaid, hereby Ratifies and Confirms

This Act seems to have been quite as inoperative as its predecessors, and society, thoroughly demoralised upon this subject, disregarded the harmless fulminations of the law Some feeling was awakened throughout the country by the melancholy murder of the fourth Duke of Hamilton in Hyde Park by the veteran duellist, Lord Mohun, on Sunday, 15th November 1712, but it now became apparent that indignation was aroused rather because of some suspicions of foul play than from any moral objections to the duel A Bill against duelling was brought into Parliament, but thrown out on the second reading In the following year (1713) the subject was introduced in the Queen's Speech, and she declared that "the practice of duelling requires some speedy and effectual remedy '

But the Bill which followed upon this statement was again thrown out and this fatal custom was still left rampant It was evident that no new laws were necessary but simply the proper administration of those in existence yet that was rarely tried at all, and even then with limited success It was not until a moral reformation had been initiated during the reign of George III through the agency of the Dissenters, that any abatement of this evil became evident Duels became rarer when the voice of Religion was heard, and when

Fashion declared against the wearing of swords, and yet in the sixty years of George III's reign, not less than 170 duels are known to have been fought, involving the murder of nearly seventy persons But as this long term of sovereignty drew towards a close, it was felt that public opinion had become so altered upon this subject that the old Acts against duelling might safely be rescinded, especially as they had been so long ignored and inefficiently administered On the 3d of July 1819 the Act 59th Geo III , c 70, became law, whereby it was provided that the two Acts of James VI and William III ,

which we have quoted entirely, *should be repealed* Duelling was thus placed in the position which it had occupied two hundred and twenty years before, and could no longer be looked upon as a special crime

The member who carried this important Act through Parliament was Sir Alexander Boswell of Auchinleck He was only a short time in the House this was "his solitary piece of legislation ," and ne was one of the first to fall a victim to the barbarism which he had thus reintroduced The story of that fatal incident we have now to relate

AUCHINLECK HOUSE, ERECTED IN 1780 BY LORD AUCHINLECK

PART II

Benedick—"I ll tell thee what, Prince a college of wit-crackers cannot flout me out of my humour Dost thou think I care for a satire, or an epigram ? No if a man will be beaten with brains, he shall wear nothing hand some about him "
           —*Much Ado about Nothing*

The family of the Boswells of Auchinleck, to which race Sir Alexander Boswell belonged, had been famous in the annals of Scottish Jurisprudence for generations before his time It is supposed that they had originally settled in Scotland whilst David I occupied the throne (1124 1153), and they became located in Fifeshire early in the fifteenth century—Sir John Boswell having obtained possession of the barony of Balmuto through his marriage with Mariota, daughter of Sir John Glen His grandson, David Boswell, married twice, and whilst the children of the first marriage carried on the family of Boswell of Balmuto, his son Thomas, by the

second marriage, obtained the barony of Auchinleck in Ayrshire from James IV , and became the first of that branch of the race It was his misfortune to share the fate of his master at Flodden Field, but the family became connected with some of the foremost of the nobility in Scotland through the marriage of his only son and successor, David Boswell of Auchinleck, with Lady Janet Hamilton, daughter of the first Earl of Arran, and great granddaughter of James II

The first lawyer of note in the family was James Boswell of Auchinleck, who married the Lady Elizabeth Bruce, the daughter of the Earl of Kincardine, in 1704 His son Alexander rose to eminence in legal circles, and long occupied a prominent place amongst the Lords of Session, under the title of Lord Auchinleck But it was reserved for his grandson James, the biographer of Dr Johnson, to elevate the name of Boswell to a unique position in literature, and to attain by the simplest means an honourable place amongst the British Classics Yet it is curious that, though he is constantly referred to as "the prince of biographers," and lauded as inapproachable in this special department, no adequate sketch of his own life has ever been written. This is not the place for such a work, but as we imagine that nothing could give a better idea of the mental constitution of his son, Sir Alexander Boswell, whose melancholy story we have to relate, than a glimpse into the home circle wherein that unfortunate man was reared, we may be pardoned for digressing so as to bring before the reader some of the traits of the biographer's character not hitherto made public

James Boswell, the father of the duellist, was born at Edinburgh, 29th October 1740 He studied Civil Law at the Universities of Edinburgh and Glasgow, and was called at an early age to the Scottish Bar He removed to England for the purpose of studying to become an English barrister, but he seems to have been carried away for some time by the seductive influence of London life The position of his father, Lord Auchinleck, had put him on terms of intimacy with the literary leaders of the day, and he seems to have been especially friendly with Sir David Dalrymple, afterwards the celebrated Lord Hailes In the library at New Hailes, there is still preserved a series of letters from Boswell to Lord Hailes, which epistles throw much light upon his character in his early days They are all dated in 1763 —the very year when he became acquainted with Dr Johnson In the first of them he asks Lord Hailes "to interpose with his father, who has threatened to disinherit him on account of his roving and unsettled ways" "Tell him," he writes, "to have patience with me for a year or two, and I may be what he pleases" The next letter is dated in June, and is full of penitence for the past and hope for the future "My great object," he says, "is to attain a proper conduct in life How sad will it be if I turn no better than I am? I have much vivacity, which leads me to dissipation and folly This, I think, I can restrain But I will be moderate, and not aim at a stiff sageness and buckram correctness I must, however, own to you that I have at bottom a melancholy cast, which dissipation relieves by making me thoughtless, and, therefore an easier though a more contemptible animal I dread a return of this malady I am always apprehensive of it."

Surely that was a strange attraction of opposites which led such a character as Boswell confesses himself to be into close and life long relationship with Dr Johnson The critics have been puzzled by it ever since, and have even imputed motives of vanity upon both sides in default of other explanation But as it was precisely at this time— May 1763—when these two met, it will be seen that Boswell was then in that wavering state of mind when the least incident will determine a man's career, and the kind notice of Johnson, and his wise advice to the unsettled youth, raised an inextinguishable feeling of gratitude in Boswell's bosom The letters to Lord Hailes describe many of their interviews, and in one of them this remarkable passage occurs—

"I thank God that I have got acquainted with Mr Johnson He has done me infinite service. He has assisted me to obtain peace of mind, he has assisted me to become a rational Christian I hope I shall ever remain so"

The strange friendship thus formed lasted without interruption until Dr Johnson's death in 1784 Six years afterwards, Boswell, who had attempted no literary work save an elaborate treatise upon the Douglas Peerage Case, and a pamphlet against a proposed reform in the Court of Session—which latter *brochure* is described as "exceeding all his other compositions in extravagance and absurdity" —suddenly astonished the world of letters by his "Tour in the Hebrides" and his "Life of Dr Johnson" We think it may safely be said that no book has ever given rise to so much contradictory criticism as the latter, nor endured so much objurgation without its vitality being impaired Boswell's contemporaries made merry over it, and ransacked the vocabulary of Billingsgate to find terms sufficiently rude in which they might denounce or deride him Many of these bitter jeers against him have been collected in a manuscript volume written by Lord Hailes, and their general tone may be understood from the following example —

Loud and fierce blew the wind while Johnson slept sound,
And dreamt he was treading on classical ground
But Boswell, amazed at the tempest's wild roar
Cryed Gentlemen sailors pray set me on shoar
Shall stinking salt water thus choak up my breath?—
O, no let me die a good natural death
Avast! quoth the master since such death you chuse,
Here take this rope's end and we'll fasten the noose
And then shall the truth of that old saw be found—
If you're born to be hanged you can never be drowned "

Still more violent were the strains in which Dr Wolcot (Peter Pindar) addressed him, though Time has brought about the strange result that what the poet intended as bombastic, ludicrous prophecy has now become serious reality As the works of this forgotten satirist are no longer read, we may venture to quote a few lines as a novelty —

" O Boswell Bozzy, Bruce, whate'er thy name,
Thou mighty shark for anecdote and fame,

Thou Jackall leading Lion Johnson forth
To eat Macpherson in est his native North
To fr ghten gray Professors with his roar
And shake the Hebrides from shore to shore
Al bu
Triumphant th m through T me s vast gulf shalt sail,
The poet of our terary Whale
Close to the classic Rambler shalt thou cling
Close as a supple courtier to a king
Fate shall not shake thee off with all its power
Stuck like a rat to some old ivied tower

Yes ' whilst the Rambler shall a comet blaze,
And gild a world of darkness with his rays
Thee too, that world with wonderment shall hail
A lively, bouncing cracker at his tail

It has taken a long time for this comic predic
tion to reach realisation, and it would form a
curious study to note how criticism has drawn
round from active scorn and opposition to Boswell
and his great work until it has reached the stage
of abject and unreasoning worship An early
critic speaks of the "Life" as 'the imitable
folly of a Boswell ambitious of universal ab
surdity" An Italian writer compares Johnson
"to some uncommon bear, and Boswell to the
Savoyard who goes showing him about ' Some
twenty years after, another book taster declares
that ' the world cannot speedily hope to receive a
similar gift, for it is scarcely more probable
to find another Boswell than another Johnson '
Forty years after its publication Lord Macaulay
wrote of the work in these terms —"Homer is
not more decidedly the first of heroic poets,
Shakspeare is not more decidedly the first of
dramatists, Demosthenes is not more decidedly
the first of orators, than Boswell is the first of
biographers He has no second He has distanced
all his competitors so decidedly that it is not worth
while to place them ' Amongst the critics of our
own day, we find the late George Henry Lewes
writing thus of this marvellous production —
"Boswell's Johnson is for me a sort of text book,
according to a man's judgment of it I am apt to
form my judgment of *him* It may not always be
a good test, but it is never a bad one " And, to
complete our list, Leslie Stephen speaks of ' the
quaint, semi conscious touches of character which
make the original so fascinating '

So much for this immortal book, but what of its
author? The vilest language cast at him by his
contemporaries could not be more scathing than the
terms in which Macaulay describes him —' Servile
and impertinent, shallow and pedantic, a bigot
and a sot bloated with family pride, and eternally
blustering about the dignity of a born gentleman,
yet stooping to be a tale-bearer, an eaves-
dropper, a common butt in the taverns
of London; so curious to know every-
body that was talked about that, Tory and
High Churchman as he was, he manœuvred, we
have been told, for an introduction to Tom Paine
—so vain of the most childish distinctions that,
when he had been to Court, he drove to the office
where his book was being printed without changing
his clothes, and summoned all the printer's devils
to admire his new ruffles and sword—such was this
man, and such he was content and proud to be "

Even when we make some allowance from
the severity of this sketch, on the ground
that it is the picture of a Tory drawn
by an ultra Whig, we are forced to confess
that there is some truth in it James Bos
well's own family seem to have smiled at his
vagaries and frowned upon his follies with mono-
tonous regularity It is related that when his
father, Lord Auchinleck, heard of his intention of
bringing Dr Johnson to Scotland on a visit to him,
he held up his hands in astonishment, and ex
claimed—"Our Jeemy's clean aff the hooks now !
would onybody believe it ? he's bringing doun a
dominie wi' him—an auld *dominie !*" Nor was his
wife—Margaret Montgomerie, a cousin of his own
—more tender to his frailties though she was
compelled to endure in silence his frequent
desertions of his home for the avocations of
pleasure, of literary converse, or dissipation The
description of his life given by Dr Carruthers is,
we fear, only too true —"He forced himself into
society, and neglected his family and his profession to meet his friend, and he was content to be
ridiculed and slighted so that he could thereby add
one page to his journal, or one scrap of writing to
his collection "

In such a home, and under the desultory training of such a father, what regularity of thought or
circumspection of conduct could be expected from
Sir Alexander Boswell? He was born in 1775,
and was twenty years of age when his father died
He had thus reached a stage at which it was likely
his convictions would be formed He would have
been taught from his earliest days to look upon
ultra Toryism as the only political creed worthy of
support, and to abjure the Whigs and Nonconfor-
mists in the same breath with that which denounced the Pope, the Devil, and the Pretender
The literary fame of his father made him acquainted
with the leaders of thought in Edinburgh, and he
would thus find that the country was wholly
under the control of the Tory party, and
that Divinity, Law, Physic, even Civic
Government were within their power It was
natural, therefore, that he should come to look
upon Whiggism as a veritable manifestation of the
Evil One, to be annihilated by any means, and at
whatever cost, by the followers of the creed of the

" Heaven born Minister," William Pitt Sir Walter Scott was the lion of literary circles in the early years of this century, and young Boswell became one of his intimate friends and was introduced by him to the Tory ring which then governed all Scottish affairs Amongst the younger members Boswell took a prominent place as much because of his easy, reckless, genial disposition, as for any special glory which he could be expected to shed upon the Tory cause He could write a good song, and sing it if required, had made some sensation by his clever comic sketches in the Scottish vernacular—"The Fast Neuk o' Fife " " Jenny Dang the Weaver," "Jenny's Bawbee,' &c —many of which are still familiar throughout the country, and was regarded by the sanguine Tories as the rhymster whose pungent satire should exorcise the demon of Whiggism from the land His picture as sketched by the able pen of the late Lord Cockburn, though drawn by a political opponent, seems life like and real, and is couched in these terms —

" Boswell was able and literary, and, when in the humour of being quiet, he was agreeable and kind But in general he was boisterous and overbearing, and addicted to coarse personal ridicule With many respectable friends, his natural place was at the head of a jovial board, where every one laughed at his exhaustless spirits, but each trembled lest he should be the subject of the next story or song "

We trust we have made as clear as possible the character of one of the principals in this memorable Fifeshire duel It shall now be our task to trace the antecedents of his opponent, James Stuart of Dunearn

OLD DUNEARN HOUSE.

PART III

Bobadil—' Faith sir so it is this gentleman and myself I have been most uncivilly wronged and beaten by one Downright a coarse fellow about the town here, and for my own part I protest being a man in no sort given to this filthy humour of quarrelling he hath assaulted me in the way of my peace despoiled me of mine honour disarmed me of my weapons and rudely laid me along in the open streets when I not so much as once offered to resist him
  —*Every Man in His Humour* (Jonson)

The third Earl of Moray was married to a daughter of the Earl of Home, and his third son was Archibald, founder of the family of the Stuarts of Dunearn The great grandson of the latter was Charles Stuart of Dunearn, who was married to a daughter of John Erskine of Carnock, and their eldest son was that James Stuart of Dunearn who forms the second party in the story of this famous duel He was born in 1776, and was thus one year younger than Sir Alexander Boswell His marriage in 1802 with a daughter of Lieutenant Colonel Robert Mowbray of Cockairny linked him doubly with the shire of Fife, and he settled down at an early period in his career to the retired and equable life of a gentleman farmer But the latter years of the eighteenth century were seriously perturbed, and the wave of Revolution which had originated in France in 1789 soon overspread the Continent of Europe and reached even these British Isles Long before the French Revolution had developed into the bloody massacre of innocence which it latterly became, the demand for " Liberty, Equality, and Fraternity" had commended itself to the leaders of the middle and lower classes in Scotland

E

The difficulties with which Liberalism had to contend at this time were very great. The press was gagged through fear of prosecution, and its circulation limited by the excessive taxes placed upon each issue. Even public meetings were looked upon with suspicion by those in authority, and the moderate Scottish Whig, who sought to establish only a moiety of "the Rights of Man," was denounced as a traitor, and ostracised from good society. As the French Revolution developed, the feeling against those who had sympathised with the aspirations of its initiators became more pronounced, and the mildest Whiggism, which sought merely a reform of flagrant imposition on the rights of the people, was denounced as the wildest Jacobinism. In these milk and water times of ours, when toleration reigns supreme it is almost impossible to appreciate the Tory opposition of this period at its full value, yet there can be no question that the form of thought comprehended under the title of "Anti Jacobinism" then became a perfect mania in society, and led its devotees to adopt absurdly extreme measures. The leading Scottish burghs at this time were in a state of almost hopeless political corruption, yet the persistent efforts of the Whigs under Lord Archibald Hamilton to effect some measure of reform in this department were denounced as the first step towards a new Reign of Terror. The country was kept in a constant ferment by the political disputes of the leaders of society, and the people were taught to look upon the advocates of Liberalism as the disciples of Rousseau and Robespierre—the enemies alike of religion and liberty.

James Stuart of Dunearn had been bred to the law as his profession, but had early shown himself to be so pronounced a Liberal that employment did not rapidly flow in upon him. For years he walked the floor of the Parliament House —the Westminster Hall of Scotland— without attaining to special distinction, and sharing the obscurity which then overshadowed Francis Jeffrey, Henry Cockburn, and a host of other eminent men whose progress had been retarded by their ardent efforts to establish Liberalism. Yet though unemployed he was not idle. No meeting of any kind in Fifeshire which was likely to advance the political cause he had espoused was suffered to escape his notice, and he contrived in company with his friend James Gibson, W.S. (afterwards Sir James Gibson Craig of Riccarton), to make himself thoroughly obnoxious to the Tory party. The names of Gibson and Stuart of Dunearn became as hateful to the Tories as were those of Radical Hunt and Joseph Hume in later times.

The advance of Liberal ideas in the east of Scotland under the leadership of the *Scotsman* and *Dundee Advertiser*, seemed very ominous, and even Edinburgh—thitherto the metropolis of Toryism—became alarmed at their success. To counteract this malign disposition, the power of the press was called into play, and the somnolent politics of the *Edinburgh Courant* and the *Glasgow Herald* were quickened into activity in a peculiar fashion. The younger literary men who gathered around Sir Walter Scott adopted methods of attack upon their political opponents which could produce no other feelings than those of irritation and contempt. The slashing and abusive style of writing which Professor Wilson had made famous in *Blackwood's Magazine* was imitated by mediocre writers who had neither his ability nor his good nature, and Scottish journalism of this time descended to the level of the worst kind of French newspaper literature. The lowest depths of this kind of literary depravity were reached when the Tories established a periodical print for the purpose of vilifying those who disagreed with them. This incident is thus described by a contemporary writer whose professional occupation made him intimately acquainted with all the circumstances, we refer to Henry Cockburn—

"Instead of being taught liberality by events, the Tory party was exasperated into insanity. It was under the influence of this malady that they set up a newspaper, which they called the *Beacon*. This famous publication first appeared, I think, in January 1821. Its funds and its machinery were concealed. All that was exposed was that a Mr Duncan Stevenson printed it, and a person called Nimmo was its ostensible editor. But its regular contributors were believed to be persons of a higher order, and articles were occasionally supplied by some it is very painful to think of as so employed. Scott chuckled with its reputed contributors, judges subscribed for it, it lay on the tables of reverend Christians.'

James Stuart of Dunearn was early selected by the writers of this paper as a butt for their virulent satire, and in August 1821 an article appeared in which he was grossly insulted. As it was impossible for him to discover the author of this anonymous outrage, he took the only course which he deemed open to him for the vindication of his honour, by publicly caning the printer in one of the streets of Edinburgh. Shortly afterwards another rancorous attack was made upon Mr James Gibson, and that gentleman, having had his suspicions awakened as to the actual instigators of it, wrote to Sir William Rae, then Lord Advocate, asking him whether he was not part proprietor in this scurrilous publication

Sir William replied denying all partnership, but acknowledging that he had joined with several of his fellow politicians in a bond which made them sureties for any debt incured by the *Beacon* to the extent of £100 each. He enclosed a list of the bondsmen in his letter, and to the surprise and grief of every one it was found that many of them were persons holding high state offices, and that Sir Walter Scott was deeply implicated in the affair. With this list in his possession, Mr Gibson determined to pursue the matter to its end, and wrote to the Lord Advocate insisting upon his disavowal of all concern in the attacks upon his character. Sir William Rae, after some demur, granted the desired disavowal, and Gibson next wrote to the others for a similar acknowledgment. Sir Walter, though thoroughly ashamed of the whole affair, did not so readily respond to this demand, and we believe that a duel between him and Gibson was only prevented through the interposition of Scott's friends, who engaged that he would give an assurance that he "had no personal accession to any of the articles complained of, and that the paper should be discontinued." With this engagement Gibson professed himself satisfied, and the career of the *Beacon* was thus brought to a violent termination. The bondsmen withdrew one by one from their contract, and the paper collapsed from sheer starvation.

Though thus publicly expressing their disapproval of the style of attack which the *Beacon* had introduced, it is little to the credit of the Tory leaders that they established immediately afterwards another periodical conducted precisely upon the same lines. The field of operations was now transferred to Glasgow, but the style of the new paper was in no degree improved, but rather otherwise. The name of the *Clydesdale Journal* which it first bore, was changed to that of the *Sentinel*, and J G Lockhart writes of it in these terms:— "The *Beacon* bequeathed its rancour and rashness, though not its ability, to a Glasgow paper of similar form and pretensions, entitled the *Sentinel*," and the former attacks upon the Liberals were resumed with increased virulence. The old subjects were rehabilitated, and Stuart of Dunearn and his friend James Gibson were again held up to ridicule, and made the mark for the poisoned arrows of masked and indecent satire.

Only a few weeks had elapsed from the period of the extinction of the *Beacon* until it was made very evident that some of its contributors had placed their pens at the service of the *Sentinel*. The first number of this paper published under its new name contained an article entitled "Mr James Stuart and the Lord Advocate, in which **the former was vilified in an unscrupulous manner.**

That the reader may understand the unbridled license of the language indulged in, and also appreciate the extent of the provocation endured by Mr Stuart, we may quote from this historical document. It refers, as will be seen, to the personal chastisement which had been inflicted upon the printer of the *Beacon*:—

"Our readers may recollect that we some time ago introduced Mr Stuart to their notice, on the occasion of his mean and unmanly attack on Mr Stevenson. They are perfectly aware that the subject matter of Mr Stuart's complaint against that gentleman was the appearance of a paragraph in the *Beacon* newspaper, which no man who read it could conceive to be either immoderate or untrue. At the time of her late Majesty's* threat to visit the Scottish metropolis, that publication, in descanting on the characters of the persons most likely to welcome her, stated that they (the conductors of the *Beacon*) did not think that any one above the rank of Mr James Stuart would desire to be presented to her, or words to that effect. It is true that the allusion to Mr Stuart's rank, which he is very anxious to talk about on all occasions, is highly ironical; but surely there is nothing in it wonderfully offensive. Be that as it may, the fine feelings of the descendant of the Stuarts could not withstand it. He waited on Mr Stevenson, the supposed editor of the paper, remonstrated with him, and ultimately launched forth into a correspondence on the subject, in which every body knows Mr Stevenson conducted himself like a man of sense and delicacy, and Mr Stuart in a manner rude and every way unhandsome. The sequel of his behaviour confirmed this. He attacks Mr Stevenson in the streets of Edinburgh in the most brutal manner, and attempts to belabour him with a horsewhip, while his own servants, brought from Fife for the express purpose, were employed to hold Mr Stevenson's hands from any retaliation. It is needless to offer any proof of these facts, they are perfectly notorious, and reluctantly admitted by the aggressor himself.

"What did Mr Stevenson do to take amends for this gross outrage on his person? Just what any gentleman of his respectability should have done, and what no person of the least claim to the character of a gentleman could have avoided. He sought satisfaction from his antagonist. But, oh, shame to the dishonoured blood of the house and name of Stuart, he, with a meanness only discernible in low life and in humble society, sought his personal safety in the most glaring cowardice! The blustering and the passionate are always in the rear of danger. James Stuart was consequently posted as a coward and a poltroon. The very rabble and oyster women on the streets of Edinburgh read the label, mused on the circumstances, and blushed for their patriot.

"We are not the advocates of duelling, God forbid. We would not stain our hands nor our consciences by any participation in its murderous subterfuges. But if ever there was a case that called loudly for satisfaction, it was the case of Stevenson. And yet it was scarcely worth his pains. When the heartless ruffian seeks for revenge for ideal injury by employing his minions to hold the arms of the persons he abuses, we would consider him utterly undeserving of the satisfaction of a gentleman, and we would desire to hold him up to the unalloyed opprobrium of mankind.

"Whether the *Beacon* indulged in a super-abundant quantity of personal hostility towards Mr Stuart, subsequently to his affray with Mr Stevenson, we shall leave the world to determine. But this we will observe, that, from the way in which Mr Stuart conducted himself, he could not have been too severely exposed. The man who acts unmanly—the patriot who degrades himself

like a traitor—the bullying bravado who is ever the tyrant in a place of safety, must lay his account to meet the hisses of society. The *Beacon* may possibly have overstepped the line of propriety on other subjects, and we do not defend it. It may have used a vulgar sentence where the satire of an elegant one might have been felt more poignantly, but in this case its personality was justifiable—its warmth and violence were excusable.

We opine that the "mildest mannered man" would have been roused to indignation by this gratuitous attack upon him from a quarter where he had given no offence, and his friends must have seen with sorrow and surprise that, despite to the engagement of the Tory party, the *Beacon* had merely changed its name without altering its character, and sought to revive wilfully the recollection of painful incidents which both parties had agreed to bury in oblivion. Restrained by the advice of his acquaintances, Mr Stuart refrained from any immediate action, thinking that this article had possibly slipped into the paper through inadvertence, and from no deliberate purpose to insult him without provocation. But in this belief he was not allowed to remain long, for the *Sentinel* soon assumed a tone towards him which rendered its purpose unmistakable.

THE OLD TONTINE HOTEL, GLASGOW

PART IV.

'Iago—Reputation is an idle and most false imposition oft got without merit and lost without deserving —*Othello*

Though professedly deprecating an appeal to the duel as a satisfactory way of settling the disputes between Mr Stuart and his assailants, the *Sentinel* plainly suggested that alternative is the only one open to a man of honour as may be seen from the quotation which we have given This course of invidious suggestion was pursued so systematically by that paper that Stuart could not fail to be impressed with the notion that the Tory party, or at least his vilifiers, expected him to adopt the duel in vindication of his honour Before he had lifted his hand to chastise Stevenson, of the *Beacon*, he had appealed to the Sheriff of Mid Lothian to protect him from the malicious slanders of that periodical, but he had found that the law, when administered by Tory officials was totally incompetent to save him from the injurious consequences of these attacks It was after this discovery that he had taken the law into his own

hands, and administered the punishment to which he considered the slanderer entitled Despite his former disappointment, he determined to bring this new case into a Court of law, and before the second number of the *Sentinel* was issued he laid an action for damages against its known editors He could not at this time discover who the proprietors were, and the authors of the slanderous articles were kept carefully in the background The only parties, therefore, on whom he could seize were the partners of the printing firm of Borthwick & Alexander, who were the ostensible editors of this publication

This action, it was soon apparent, was unlikely to vindicate Stuart's honour without dragging his name before the public in a most disreputable manner The case of the printers was taken up by Duncan Macneill —the late Lord Colonsay— then one of the leading Scottish Tory barristers, assisted by John Hope, the son of the President of the Court of Session, and in their reply to the averments of Stuart "they affirm that the statements in the newspaper complained of are true," and further, "they offer to prove, by the evidence of persons of high character and skill in the laws and practice of honour, that the conduct of the pursuer, in regard to the affair with Mr Stevenson, was most ungentlemanly, and deserving of every condemnation."

From this strange document it is made evident that the Tory defenders of these slanderers not only meant to uphold the incitement to duelling, which was still punishable by law, but actually to place the opinions of those skilled ' in the laws and practice of honour ' above the plain interpretation of the statutes! Surely no such plea was ever before offered to a Scottish Court of Justice.

Some delay took place in the preliminaries of this trial, but meanwhile the *Sentinel* in no degree abated the virulence of its attacks upon the unfortunate Stuart of Dunearn. Indeed, it seemed as if the most violent of the *Beacon's* contributors had gathered together so as to overwhelm him with abuse before the day of reckoning arrived. The muse of poetry even was pressed into service so as to render him ridiculous in the eyes of his contemporaries, and especially, as we shall show, to drive him to the desperate resource of an appeal to arms. It was at this period that the following famous contribution appeared —

'WHIG SONG'

' Supposed to be written by one of the Jameses, certainly not by King James the I or King James the V, but probably by one of the House of Stuart.

TUNE—' *Sheriffmuir* '

' There's some say that they're Whigs,
And some say that we're Whigs,
And some say there's nae Whigs ava, man,
But ae thing I'm sure
A pawky Whig do'er
's the Whig that out-whigifics a', man

Chorus—And they crack and we tak,
And they tak and we crack
And we tak and they crack awa' man

" For conscience the auld Whigs
Were sterlin and bauld Whigs,
And gied their oppressors a claw man
But now Whigs for siller
(Their Calf on the Pillar)
Ken nought about conscience ava, man
And they crack and we tak, &c

" The deil took the lawyer
And left the poor sawyer,
He wasna a mouse to his paw man
Ower straught was his mark man,
But a Whig Signet Clerk, man
Can onything onyway thraw man
And they crack and we tak, &c.

"They rant about Freedom,
But when ye hae feed 'em
Cry het or cry cauld and they'll blaw, man,
Tak him maist rampagant
And mak him King's agent
And hech ! how his fury will fa', man !
And they crack and we tak, &c

There's stot feeder Stuart
Kent for that fat cow art
How glegly he kicks ony ba' man
And Croson laug chiel man,
Whase height might serve weel man,
To read his ain name on a wa' man
And they crack and we tak &c

" Your knights o' the pen, man,
Are a gentlemen man
Ilk body's a limb o' the law, man
Tacks bonds precognitions
Bills, wills and petitions,
And ought but a trigger's sae draw man
And they crack and we tak &c.

Sae foul fa' backbiters
Wha rin down sic writers
Wha fatten sae brave and sae braw, man
Ilk Whiggish believer,
Ilk privileged reiver
Come join in a hearty huzza man !
For they crack and we tak &c."

There could be no question as to whom this biting satire was aimed against, even had the name of Stuart not been introduced, for shortly before this time Dunearn had been made a Clerk to the Signet ; and the pointed allusion to duelling, which we have italicised, almost amounts to a challenge from an unknown enemy. Had this been the first and last libel against Mr Stuart the very plain word "cow art" might have been excused by the exigencies of rhyme. *Master Stephen*, in Jonson's comedy, says —"My poesy was, *The deeper the sweeter, I'll be judged by St Peter*."

Ed Knowell—"How by St Peter? I do not conceive that."

Stephen—"Marry, by St Peter, to make up the metre."

But no such excuse could have been urged for the author of the "Whig Song," and the *Sentinel* proceeded to greater lengths in its abuse of Stuart. On the 14th of December the action against this paper was remitted to the Jury Court for trial, and in the next number a letter appeared signed "Ignotus," and dated "Dumbarton, Dec 17th 1821," in which the writer sympathises with the editor under his threatened prosecution. Throughout the whole of this communication the same strain of defiance to mortal combat is kept up, and Stuart is plainly referred to as a coward and a discomfited bully. The writer proceeds to beg leave to offer, "as one stud for a sevenfold shield against Whig assaults, my hearty subscription of five pounds " We shall not shock the reader by quoting more than one passage from this letter, in which a *refusal to fight a duel* is denounced as worthy of scorn

"You are prosecuted, it seems, by Mr James Stuart of Dunearn, once, certainly, a private individual, but a man now known to us because he has bustled out of his element If, therefore, you had held up to public ridicule Mr James Stuart as an itinerant orator from county to county and from meeting to meeting, who could have blamed you? Every public performer subjects himself to criticism—orators as well as players Orator Hunt has had it, why should not Orator Stuart? Orator Hunt, after threatening to thrash the lesser man, Mr Morley of the British Hotel, showed, in the cant language, the white feather, and refused to fight him, and was deservedly stigmatised and laughed at If Mr Stuart had done this, the parallel would have been perfect '

This attack was soon followed by another still more bitter, in which the duelling expedient was again deftly introduced It purported to be an account of the Pitt Festival which took place in January 1822, and was written with much humour in the form of a letter signed "Mark Tod" The Chairman, Sir Ronald Ferguson of Raith, long M P for the Kirkcaldy Burghs, the croupier, Francis Jeffrey, and the company generally, received their share of banter and scornful jesting in this epistle; but Stuart was again selected for special reference in connection with duelling The passage ran thus —

"Many of the toasts you will see in the papers The Army and Navy were given, but not another fighting man (unless you will allow the Director of Chancery, my Lord Rosslyn, who was remembered when toasts began to run dry), until the gallant and excellent croupier, whom Lord Byron has celebrated for some bold exploit with Anacreon Moore* (the seconds no doubt singing the beautiful air of 'Fly not Yet'), arose and gave the health of Mr James Stuart! Mr James acknowledged, in grateful terms, the honour which he had received from such a quarter So now he has a *feather* to stick in his cap to bear the other company '

With relentless severity the anonymous critic pursued his victim, holding up his every public action to ridicule, and suffering no opportunity of provoking his opponent to escape from his bitter, satirical pen Even the slightest incidents in Stuart's life were made the occasion for twitting him with cowardice, and suggesting that he was afraid to fight in defence of his honour For instance, Stuart had been a Deputy Lieutenant of

Fifeshire for eighteen years before this time, and held a command in the western troop of Fifeshire Yeomanry Cavalry Through some misunderstanding he had called out his troop against the orders of the Commanding Officer, and he was at once reported for insubordination to the Lord-Lieutenant, who adopted unnecessarily severe measures towards him Stuart at once resigned both his command and his Deputy Lieutenancy, though he did not cease to expose the reckless mismanagement of county affairs by those in power The nameless satirist immediately indited an article on "The Late Lieutenant Stuart," which appeared in the *Sentinel* of February 20th, 1822, and in which the writer alludes with feigned surprise to the fact that ' James Stuart was actually enrolled as a *fighting* man Surely these repeated aspersions upon the courage of a high spirited gentleman would have roused the gentlest temper to resentment; but Stuart now saw that his action towards the printers of the *Beacon* had been ineffectual, and he trusted to vindicate his honour in a Court of law

He had as yet no clue whatever to the personality of his traducer, but a curious circumstance at length disclosed this well kept secret The firm of Borthwick & Alexander were the printers and proprietors of the *Sentinel* Alexander had proposed that if Borthwick would retire from the firm he would pay him a certain sum within a fixed time On the faith of this promise Borthwick signed the dissolution of partnership, and Alexander at once published it in the *Gazette* When the time of payment arrived no money was forthcoming, and Borthwick applied to the Magistrates to be reinstated in the office from which he had been unjustly ousted They arranged to give Alexander eight days more in which to meet his engagement, but a fortnight elapsed without a farthing having been paid, or any excuse for further delay offered In these circumstances Borthwick re entered the premises and took up his old position at his former desk as senior partner, and no attempt was made to dislodge him by Alexander

But Borthwick had objected to some of the scurrilous prints in the *Sentinel*, and it would have been suicidal for Alexander to have allowed him to remain He knew that Letters of Caption had been issued some time before against Borthwick for an undue debt of £50 and he contrived to have his quondam partner arrested and thrown into prison under them These two men were now at mortal enmity, and Borthwick, as well to save himself as to annoy his partner, sent his agent around to the numerous parties who had actions for damages laid against the *Sentinel*, offering to

---

* See " English Bards and Scotch Reviewers '

disclose the names of the authors of the libels against them. Amongst others Stuart of Dunearn was applied to, and he agreed to go to Glasgow along with other two pursuers of the paper, to consult with Borthwick as to this proposal. That the latter might meet these gentlemen, his agent paid the debt and had him liberated. Meanwhile Alexander had made a very acute move—he changed all the locks on Borthwick's office desks and drawers to prevent him from having access to them without a warrant. But, conscious that he had a legal right to all the papers they contained, Borthwick broke open these repositories, and took therefrom the documents he required, and left the office in Nelson Street, Glasgow, with them in his possession.

Stuart and his two companions were waiting anxiously in the Tontine Hotel, Glasgow, for the revelation which they mentally expected. At last they were to discover the nameless satirists who had made their lives miserable, and had trumpeted their names coupled with every offensive epithet throughout the land. All their doubts and conjectures were now to be set at rest; and we may imagine with what eagerness they examined the fatal documents which Borthwick laid before them.

There are some secrets which it is ruinous to explore, and often during the latter portion of his long life did James Stuart wish that he had never disturbed the veil of obscurity which had covered his anonymous slither. Not with anticipated rage and indignation, but with unutterable grief and astonishment, did he discover that the writer who had made a plaything of his reputation, had dared him to single combat, and jeered at his caution as cowardice, was one whom he had never injured, whose talents he admired, and of whom he had ever spoken respectfully—no other, indeed, than his relative and frequent companion, Sir Alexander Boswell of Auchinleck! The proofs laid before him of this fact were incontestable, and it was with a heavy heart that he rode back to Edinburgh, taking the papers with him, that he might consult with his friends as to what course was now open to him.

SCENE OF DUEL ON BALBARTON FARM

PART V

" That thou mayest] gain among men the reputation of a discreet well tempered murderer, be sure thou killest him not in passion, when thy blood is hot and boiling with the provocation but proceed with as great temper and settled ness of reason, with as much discretion and preparedness as thou wouldest to the Communion after several days respite, that it may appear it is thy reason guides thee, and not thy passion, invite him kindly and courteously into some retired place and there let it be determined whether his blood or thine shall satisfy the injury —*Chillingworth* (1602 1644)

Feeling it most necessary that he should have a sage adviser in the delicate circumstances in which he was placed, James Stuart resolved to seek out his relative the Earl of Rosslyn, to lay the whole matter before him, and follow the course of action which he should propose The Earl was a military man occupying a high position in the army, and he wisely recommended that the safest plan would be for him, as Stuart's friend, to meet Sir Alexander Boswell, tax him with the authorship of the articles, and propose that he should apolo gise. But he warned Stuart that, in the event of Sir Alexander's refusing to do so, there was no other resource than to challenge him to fight Dunearn resigned himself into his hands, and agreed to submit to his direction.

Sir Alexander Boswell was then in London, and it was arranged that all proceedings should be post poned until his return to Edinburgh He arrived there on Saturday evening, and found a note from the Earl of Rosslyn awaiting him, in which the writer desired to have an early interview There was nothing in the language of this note to give any clue to the business which the Earl had in hand, but as Sir Alexander had already heard that Borthwick had played false with the *Sentinel* contributors, he seems to have taken guilt to him self in a peculiar manner, as the following letter will show It was written on Sunday to Robert Maconochie, Esq , brother of Lord Meadowbank, one of the Lords of Justiciary, to the latter of whom it makes allusion —

" Edinburgh, 24th March 1822

" My Dear Maconochie,—I received your very kind note, but I was so worn out and just setting out, that I could not come to see you, and it was too late to appoint you to come to me

" I must now address you on a subject of a delicate nature, which I do from a confidence in your friendship.

"About ten days ago Mr Stuart of Dunearn went to Glasgow, and by the instrumentality of certain persons, one formerly a partner in the *Clydesdale Journal* (now the *Sentinel*), broke open the editor's desk and carried off his papers, and, I understand, amongst others, some squibs in my handwriting. Last night, on my arrival, I received a letter from Lord Rosslyn that he wished me to appoint an hour, as early as possible, that he might make a communication to me, this, I suppose, is in reference to some of these squibs. I do not know who the offended party may be, but even if it should be Mr James Stuart himself I shall give him a meeting. In order, however, to obviate many of those circumstances which follow such transactions, I mean that the meeting shall take place on the Continent,—say Calais, and I wish to put your friendship so far to the test as to request you to be my friend on this occasion. I saw your brother [Lord Meadowbank] this morning, and his Lordship seemed to think that you would acquiesce. If I had deemed it expedient to meet my man here, John Douglas would have gone out with me, but if I should be the successful shot, I should not like the after proceedings of our Courts of Law, and therefore wish to pass beyond their jurisdiction. I know nothing of particulars yet, but write in prudent anticipation, and shall write again so soon as I know them.

"I know this is perhaps the greatest favour that can be asked of any man, but, by this arrangement, you will be implicated in less trouble, and you won't mind a trip to France. If my wish is acceded to, I would propose the meeting to take place about fifteen days hence, as I wish to make a slight arrangement respecting my estate, and legalise it by going to kirk and market, so that you may write on receipt of this, and if I must go sooner than I can receive yours, it is only a letter thrown away.—I am, dear Maconochie, yours very faithfully,   "ALEXANDER BOSWELL."

It will be apparent to the reader, from the tone of this epistle, that Sir Alexander had decided to refer the settlement of any dispute arising out of his connection with the *Sentinel* to the duel, *whoever might be his accuser*; and this resolution fully explains his after conduct. Yet this letter was written before he knew the nature of that urgent business to which Lord Rosslyn referred, and this affords a very convincing proof of his connection with the "Stuart" libels.

Upon the 25th of March the Earl of Rosslyn waited upon Sir Alexander, and speedily made him aware of the object of his visit. The Earl's account of this interview, as related afterwards under oath, is very interesting. He saw Boswell alone, and explained that Mr Stuart had obtained possession of several documents, apparently the originals of articles which had appeared in the *Sentinel*, and which seemed to have come from the pen of Sir Alexander. But if he could say on his honour that he had no knowledge of them, his word would be taken as conclusive upon this point, against all other evidence. Sir Alexander replied that the subject was one of great delicacy, and he would prefer to have a friend present before he replied. Leaving the Earl for a short time, he returned accompanied by his friend John Douglas, brother of the Marquess of Queensberry,[*] who remained during the rest of the interview. In his presence Lord Rosslyn repeated his statement, particularizing the "Whig Song," which we have quoted, as the most offensive of the documents in his possession. Sir Alexander and Mr Douglas retired to consult upon the proposal, and the latter returned alone to state that "he could not advise Sir Alexander Boswell to give any answer to the question, that Mr Stuart was in possession of the facts and the evidence upon which he relied, and he must thereupon exercise his own judgment. But, if this unfortunate business was to proceed any farther, there were two conditions which Sir Alexander considered as indispensable—one, that no meeting should take place for fourteen days; the other, that any meeting which might take place should be on the Continent."

As these terms distinctly agree with those stated in the letter to Maconochie, it is evident that Boswell was merely carrying out his determination to have a duel with some one. Lord Rosslyn left Mr Douglas, stating that he believed Mr Stuart would agree to the conditions, and when he met him shortly afterwards on the same day, he told him that, though Mr Stuart regretted that no alternative was left him, he was willing to meet Sir Alexander at any place he should appoint. It was then arranged that all the parties should meet in London on the 6th of April, and settle as to the time and place where the duel should be fought. Still anxious to avoid a mortal issue, Lord Rosslyn asked Mr Douglas if it was not possible for Sir Alexander Boswell to admit the authorship of these papers, especially the "Whig Song," to own that they had been written in a joking humour, and to say that he had no personal animus against Mr Stuart, but the reply he received did not encourage him to pursue the argument further, and Lord Rosslyn, after communicating this arrangement to Mr Stuart, had proceeded to Newhaven, intending to go north to his home in Fifeshire

_____

* John Douglas, born 1779 succeeded as 6th Marquess of Queensberry 1837, and died 19th December 1856.

Whilst waiting at the pier of embarkation he was overtaken by Mr Douglas, who had posted down to inform him of an important alteration. He said that Sir Alexander had consulted with a legal friend, and they had found that it was unnecessary for them to leave the kingdom for duelling purposes, but Lord Rosslyn declined to interfere with the arrangements already made, and proceeded to his domicile at Dysart House. Mr Douglas returned to report his ill success to Sir Alexander, and was sent by him to Mr Stuart's house in Edinburgh that he might see him and bring about a more speedy meeting. Stuart properly declined to deal with a second when he had already appointed the Earl of Rosslyn as his friend, but Douglas was so importunate that Stuart called in another acquaintance who happened to be with him—Mr James Brougham, brother of the late Lord Brougham and Vaux—and committed the matter to his charge. These new seconds arranged to let Lord Rosslyn know that Sir Alexander had learned from a legal friend that nothing need prevent an immediate meeting, it would be agreeable, therefore, that the parties should meet at once, either at Berwick on Tweed or elsewhere. With this understanding they parted, but during the course of this eventful night Mr Brougham sought out Mr Douglas at a party in the Royal Hotel, Edinburgh, and told him that some of Sir Alexander's friends had informed the authorities of the proposed meeting, and that both parties had been sworn before the Sheriff of Midlothian to keep the peace towards each other. Mr Brougham gave it as his opinion that the best plan would be to have a meeting at once—say in the course of the day—and Mr Douglas agreed with him. It was now nearly three o'clock in the morning of Tuesday, 26th March, and Mr Douglas set out at once for Boswell's house to make him aware of this new proposal.

With that levity of spirit so eminently characteristic of him, Sir Alexander had gone after his meeting with Lord Rosslyn to a party at Sir Walter Scott's house in Castle Street, and had appeared there the most jovial and merriest of the guests, though he had but newly agreed to suffer death himself, or to take the life of a fellow creature. To this meeting Lockhart thus alludes in his "Life of Scott"—

'That evening was, I think, the gayest I ever spent in Castle Street, and though Charles Mathews was present, and in his best force, poor Boswell's songs, jokes, and anecdotes had exhibited no symptom of eclipse. It turned out that he had joined the party whom he thus delighted immedi-

ately after completing the last arrangements for the duel!"

When Mr Douglas called at his house he found that Sir Alexander had retired to rest shortly before that time, but as his business would not admit of delay, the family was roused, and the principal and second had an interview together. Boswell expressed his annoyance at the interference of his friends, which had caused him to be bound over to keep the peace, and at once agreed to the proposal that a meeting should take place that morning. It was suggested that as it was necessary that Lord Rosslyn should be present, the best plan would be to have this meeting in Fife, so that his Lordship might be summoned from Dysart House to attend, and Mr Brougham afterwards consented to this proposal. The rendezvous was arranged to be at Auchtertool—a village on the road between Kirkcaldy and Dunfermline—and the meeting was to take place at ten o'clock on that day. Mr Brougham set out for Dysart to inform Lord Rosslyn of these new arrangements. Mr Stuart called upon a medical friend, Mr Liston, and persuaded him to accompany him immediately to Fife, without saying for what purpose, and Mr Douglas, Sir Alexander Boswell, and Dr George Wood left Edinburgh in a post chaise at five o'clock in the morning to fulfil their engagement. The latter party embarked at Queensferry, breakfasted at North Queensferry, and arrived on the ground shortly before the appointed time. Mr Stuart went to his mansion of Hillside, near Aberdour, to arrange some family affairs, and he and Liston drove to Auchtertool, meeting Lord Rosslyn and Mr Brougham near the village a few minutes after ten o'clock. The other party was already there, and the seconds proceeded to execute the grim task they had undertaken.

The meeting had been so hurried that Boswell had not been able to procure his own pistols, but Lord Rosslyn had brought his case with him, and Mr Douglas selected a weapon for his principal. The spot chosen for the rencontre was a hollow dell in a field on the farm of Balbarton, close beside the highway between Kirkcaldy and Dunfermline, and a little eastward from the village of Auchtertool. The distance was measured, "twelve long paces from station to station," and the opponents took up their positions and received the loaded pistols from their respective seconds. They were to fire simultaneously at the word of command, which Lord Rosslyn was to give. The doctors agreed that it would be best for them to turn their backs upon the duellists so that they

might not see the firing, and Mr Brougham re
tired for a short distance, holding Lord Rosslyn's
horse   The carriages had been sent away so as to
secure privacy

No attempt at a reconciliation between the
parties had been made but Mr Stuart had asked
Lord Rosslyn if he might not, when on the ground,
make a bow to Sir Alexander expressive of his
wish to be reconciled, and had been encouraged to
do so   He advanced therefore, apparently for that
purpose, but Sir Alexander turned away his head
—probably without noticing Stuart's motion – and
this amicable intention was frustrated   The
seconds, whilst conferring together, expressed a
wish that some means of agreement between the
parties could be found, but they took no steps to
further the desire   Lord Rosslyn afterwards said
that this notion of settlement was made wisely,
certainly without any hope on my part that such
an arrangement could be made, and without any
explicit proposal on either side   After what had
passed between Mr Douglas and me the day
before, when I had thrown out what I did and
made the greatest possible advance without success or hope, I considered the case as desperate

In these circumstances there was apparently no
method of appeasing the wounded vanity of the
one party and the offended honour of the other
than to suffer them to stand up in cold blood and
attempt to murder each other   The affair had
gone beyond mediation, and at the fatal word the
deadly weapons were raised and fired almost
simultaneously   When the two doctors turned
round after the reports of the pistols, they saw Mr
Stuart standing at his post unhurt, whilst Sir
Alexander Boswell was lying prostrate on the
ground   A brief examination of his wound showed
that he was in a dangerous condition, and it was
decided to remove him without delay to the house
of his relative, Lord Balmuto, which was in the
neighbourhood   Mr Douglas and Lord Rosslyn
advised Stuart to leave the ground as speedily as
possible   and he took his way accordingly towards
Edinburgh, stunned and confounded at the unexpected termination of this fatal dispute

BALMUTO HOUSE.

BALMUTO HOUSE

PART VI.

"Of them who wrapt in earth are cold,
No more the smiling day shall view,
Should many a tender tale be told,
For many a tender thought is due

—*Langhorne*

The field of the tragic occurrence which we have related was now left to the wounded baronet, the two seconds, Mr Brougham, and the two Edinburgh doctors, who had been joined by Dr Johnstone of Kirkcaldy Even a cursory examination of Sir Alexander's wound convinced the medical gentlemen that his immediate removal was necessary One of the party went with all speed to the farm of Balbarton to procure assistance and soon returned with four of the arm labourers bearing a door with them, which they had taken off its hinges so as to form a rude litter Mr Douglas borrowed Lord Rosslyn's horse and rode forward to Balmuto to warn the family of the coming of this unhappy company thither, and the Lord and the doctors walked by the side of the injured man, each taking his turn in assisting to carry him

Claud Boswell, Lord Balmuto, towards whose house they were bearing the unfortunate Sir Alexander, was a Lord of Session, and a near relative of the baronet After a long and honourable career as a senator of the College of Justice, advancing age had compelled him to resign that post, and he had retired from the bench in the month of February 1822—a few weeks before this fatal affair—and had sought the seclusion of his family seat at Balmuto House Sir Alexander had ever been a favourite of his, and the shock which he

received by the events now to be narrated was so severe that he never quite recovered from it and died in July 1824 There is therefore a very special interest connected with the letter which Lord Balmuto wrote to a friend describing the last hours of Sir Alexander, and which we shall lay before the reader The document has never been published before, and it is through the courtesy of Mrs Boswell of Balmuto that we are enabled to produce it here as an evidence of the high estimation in which Sir Alexander was held by his relatives —

"31 March 1822

' I had just finished breakfast on Tuesday about 10, when my servant told me a gentleman who would not tell his name wished to speak to me by myself He announced himself as Mr Douglas, brother to the Marquess of Queensberry, and said that a fatal rencontre had taken place near Balmuto between Sir A Boswell and Mr James Stewart, and he was afraid Sir A B was dangerously wounded, that they were bringing him to this house, and requested I would send some men to assist with carrying him here You may easily figure how dismayed and astounded I was on receiving this information, and still more upon seeing my friend stretched out on a board and motionless

"Everything was prepared for his reception under [Dr] Wood's direction, who said it was a bad case, and that he wished for the assistance of Mr Thomson, Military Surgeon He was immediately sent for, and intelligence given to Lady Boswell of the fatal event; that the husband she had parted with in health in the morning was now in great danger Thomson was not in town, but the express was forwarded to him He reached this about 2 on Wednesday morning Lady B had arrived on Tuesday evening about 3 o'clock, in deep distress, and watched by him to the last moment From 2 o'clock on Wednesday, when he expired, till 10 at night, she and her fatherless children continued to weep and lament over the dead body—a most distressing scene At one time in the anguish of her feelings she said to my wife—'Oh! this is more than human nature can bear' My dear friend, may you never have occasion to witness such a scene as I have done'

"They took their distance at 13 yards Lord Rosslyn, I understand, furnished the pistols on both sides Sir A before leaving the chaise to go to the spot told Messrs Douglas and Wood he was determined not to fire at Stewart unless he was fired at, and in that event he had a second shot Stewart's took effect, the ball piercing the collarbone after passing through his great coat and several plies of cloth The concussion had lessened its force and did not have sufficient impulse to carry the ball through to the opposite side He immediately fell, and the under part of his limbs lost all power of motion and continued so till the last This led the medical people to conjecture that the ball in its course had injured the spine, and then fallen down into the cavity of the body Little blood flowed externally, but a great deal internally, for when the body came to be moved to be laid in the coffin a stream of blood rushed out His features remained unaltered for several days, and Lady B was anxious to procure a cast or drawing of his features"

Not less interesting than the above is the description of Sir Alexander's final hours, written by Miss Boswell, Lord Balmuto's daughter, which is now published for the first time, and for which we are also indebted to Mrs Boswell of Balmuto It is of much value, as giving a faithful narrative of this affair as it appeared to an eye witness —

"About eleven o'clock on the forenoon of the 26th of March 1822, as my sisters and I were occupied in the library at Balmuto, my father came to us with the startling intelligence that Sir Alexander Boswell had been wounded in a duel by James Stewart, and was being brought to Balmuto The Honourable John Douglas had ridden forward to give us warning While he was yet speaking Dr Johnstone, Kirkcaldy (a very clever surgeon) came into the room, and on my father saying—'From what quarter do you come, doctor?' he replied—'From a very bad quarter Sir Alexander Boswell is being brought here, wounded, I fear mortally'

"Soon after, the melancholy procession arrived, Sir Alexander stretched on a door which had been wrenched off its hinges, carried by four stout ploughmen, and Drs Wood and Liston walking alongside My mother had got a comfortable bed room ready upstairs, but when they came into the entrance hall Dr Wood asked—'Is there no room on the ground floor he could be taken to? Carrying him upstairs would be terrible,' so the

LIBRARY IN BALMUTO HOUSE

library door was thrown open, into which they went, Dr George Wood lifting the picture of Lord Auchinleck off the couch to make room for his grandson Sir Alexander was deadly pale, but calm and collected He said, with a sad smile, to my father—'This is a shabby way of paying you a visit, Lord Balmuto' My father, who was 80 years of age, and looked on Sir Alexander like a son, was quite overcome, and wept, seeing which Dr Johnstone said—'You had better leave the room, my lord' I shall never forget the tone and the look which Sir Alexander fixed upon him—'And, pray, sir, who may you be, who desires Lord Balmuto to leave a room in his own house?' I brought him a glass of wine, and he said—'Thank you, Mary Anne' We left the three surgeons with him Mr Douglas had gone to Edinburgh, and was to break the intelligence to Lady Boswell, and also to send over to Dr John Thomson, Professor of Military Surgery Drs Wood, Liston, and Johnstone said the ball had penetrated near the shoulder blade, and taking a slant direction, had struck the spine, below where it hit being paralysed Dr Liston, who had come with Mr Stuart, left the house almost immediately after the examination The other two remained

"About eight or nine o'clock in the evening Lady Boswell and Teresa* arrived Lady B was

* Lady Boswell was a daughter of Thomas Cumin Esq, banker Edinburgh Sir Alexander's daughter Teresa was married to Sir William Francis Eliot of Stobs in 1826 and died in 1836

alone with Sir Alexander for a couple of hours. She wished to sit up with him, but Dr Wood persuaded her to go to bed about eleven o'clock, by saying—'Lady Boswell, well, you must husband your strength; you have a long time of watching before you.' There will be much fever. It was arranged that Dr Johnstone and one of our servants —a tall, powerful man, who had been accustomed to attend an invalid—should sit up. About midnight Dr Thomson came. He asked Sir Alexander how he felt, and he instantly replied, 'I feel a living head fastened to a dead body.' Dr T. said at once that it was absolutely hopeless. He retired, and Dr J. resumed his watch. Sir A. was speechless, but not then apparently suffering pain. He repeated pieces of poetry in a low tone to try to bring on sleep, then he said, 'This won't do.' Afterwards Dr Johnstone heard him repeating texts of Scripture. About three o'clock in the morning spasms came on, and continued at intervals for rather more than two hours, after which he sank into a sort of stupor.

"Lady Boswell came into the room about six o'clock, and Teresa soon after. I heard him say quite distinctly, "Poor boy—poor boy, only fourteen!" Evidently he was thinking of James†, who was fifteen just a few days before, and he felt that he himself would not live to watch over him. We did not like to intrude on Lady Boswell by being too much in the room. Any time after that when I went into the room he seemed to be asleep, but he woke enough to swallow some beef tea and jelly from time to time during the forenoon. At three in the afternoon of the 27th March he ceased to breathe. Teresa, who was watching, said she could not tell the moment. He sank from the effect of internal hemorrhage. Lady Boswell would not suffer the body to be touched nor anything done to it for many days, and when it was lifted to be laid in the coffin the blood streamed from the wound, and the stain remains on the floor to this day.

"Sir James arrived with Mr Mather about half-an-hour after all was over, and my brother soon after. He and Mrs Boswell‡ were at Glencorse, about 9 miles from Edinburgh, and there was some delay in their getting the letters we had sent, which prevented his being in time to see Sir Alexander alive. On another day Mrs Boswell came, and she it was who helped to support dear

Teresa during the trying scene of seeing the body placed in the coffin. My mother and I remained with Lady Boswell, who had sunk in a hysteric fit.

"Sir James and Lady Cunningham* came to Balmuto. I think it was the 7th of April when they left, Lady C. going with Lady Boswell and Teresa to Edinburgh, and Sir James accompanying the hearse to Ayrshire. My father and brother also went to Auchinleck, and were present at the funeral. Almost all the gentlemen in the county attended, and the expression of sorrow from all, both high and low, was quite universal.

'It was Dr Wood who kindly proposed bringing Sir Alexander to Balmuto. Ruth† was nearer the fatal spot, and some one said, 'Take him to Ruth,' but Dr Wood said, 'No, no, to Balmuto.' He said it was on Lady Boswell's account he was so decided. There were some patches of snow still unmelted at the side of the road, and Sir Alexander himself once or twice asked for a little snow to be put into his mouth to allay his thirst. Mr Douglas told that Sir Alexander said to him he was determined to go out with Stuart, but he was quite resolved to fire in the air. I believe (but of this I am not certain) that it was found his pistol had not been fired at all.

'I made two sketches of the spot for Teresa; it was a narrow valley, overlooked at one place by the high road from Kirkcaldy to Dunfermline. There Dr Johnstone and Mr James Brougham (Lord Brougham's brother) met at Lord Rosslyn's request. When Lord R. asked the doctor to be there at such an hour, naming it, Dr J. said, 'I hope you are not to be engaged in a duel, my Lord.' 'Not as a principal,' was the reply, 'but ask no questions, only join yourself to Mr Brougham who will be riding my bay horse.'

"Before leaving Balmuto Teresa asked to have the table spoon her father had been fed with, which of course, was given her. She said she would keep it in her own desk. It had the hawk and 'Vraye Foy,‡ so would not be known after her death.'

These letters are valuable not only because they relate the last incidents in Sir Alexander Boswell's career, but also as showing the affectionate feelings with which he was regarded by all who knew him intimately. His own writings and the opinions of him preserved by his contemporaries

---

† His son afterwards Sir James Boswell born December 1806 married to his cousin a daughter of Sir James Montgomery Cunningham (the present Lady Boswell) in 1830 died 4th Nov 1857

‡ Elizabeth sister of Sir Alexander, married to her cousin William Boswell, Esq

* Lady Cunningham was a sister of Lady Boswell. She was one of the representatives of the ancient family of Cummins of Earnside, and her husband was the lineal heir to the Earldom of Glencairn. He died in 1837

† The seat of General Sir Ronald Ferguson of Muirtown G C B long M P for Kirkcaldy Burgh's and the subject of some of Sir Alexander Boswell's most violent satires

‡ The Boswell crest and motto

show him to have been of a genial temperament a lover of conviviality in its best form, an ardent admirer of early Scottish poetry, and himself no mean poet yet gifted with that most dangerous possession, a caustic wit, which made him feared even by his most intimate friends He was ' a fellow of infinite jest but one who would not have sacrificed his joke to spare the feelings of his most revered acquaintance We do not believe that his attacks upon Stuart of Dunearn were made through any malice which he felt towards him, they were merely the outbreak of that super abundance of satirical humour which found vent by accident in this direction Doubtless the foolish applause of his Tory friends encouraged him to persevere in his savage onslaught upon their political enemies, and his violent death did more to discourage this system of tactics than volumes of argument would have done A few years afterwards those very libels which the Tories had applauded to the echo were thus described by J Gibson Lockhart —

"The violence of disaffected spleen was en countered by a vein of satire, which seemed more fierce than frolicsome The rude drollery of the young hot bloods boiled over Sir Alexander Boswell was revealed as the writer of certain truculent enough pasquinades A leading Edin burgh Whig, who had been pilloried in one or more of these, challenged him, and the baronet fell in as miserable a quarrel as ever cost the blood of a high spirited gentleman '

Sir Alexander's public career had not been a brilliant one He became member of Parliament for Plympton Earl Borough, in Devonshire, by a bye election on 12th July 1816, was re elected in the new Parliament on 18th June 1818, and again in the first Parliament of George IV on 8th March 1820 As we have already noticed, his principal Parliamentary work was the carrying through of the Act 59 Geo III, c 70, which re pealed the laws against duelling, and he shortly afterwards accepted the stewardship of the Chiltern Hundreds on 17th February 1821 He was created a baronet on 16th August of that year, and was killed in the following month of March

Though not of the same literary cast of mind as his younger brother, James Boswell the editor of Malone s Memoirs, who died in London a short time before him, Sir Alexander's poetical ability was considerable, and Sir Walter Scott bears testimony to it in his preface to the " Legend of Montrose ' His lyrics are more successful than his more ambitious efforts and with one of the finest of the former we may fittingly conclude this chapter It shows that he was master of the pathetic as well as the satiric vein, and, though keenly alive to the ludicrous, was not insensible to the more serious incidents of human life

" GOOD NIGHT AND JOY BE WI YE A
[This song is supposed to proceed from the mouth of an
aged chieftain]

Good night and joy be wi ye a
   Your harmless mirth has charmed my heart,
May life s fell blasts on owre ye blaw !
   In sorrow may ye never part !
My spirit lives but strength is gone
   The mountain fires now blaze in vain
Remember sons the deeds I ve done,
   And in your deeds I ll live again !

When on yon muir our gallant clan
   Frae boasting f es their banners tore
Wha showed himself a better man
   Or fiercer waved the red claymore ?
But when in peace—then mark me there—
   When through the glen the wanderer came
I gave him of our lordly fare,
   I gave him here a welcome hame

The auld will speak the young maun hear,
   Be cantie, but be good and leal
Your ain ills aye hae heart to bear,
   Anither's aye hae heart to feel
So ere I set I ll see you shine,
   I ll see you triumph ere I fa
My parting breath shall toast you mine—
   Good night, and joy be wi you a' !

ARMS OF THE MORAY FAMILY

PART VII

The Laws we did interpret and statutes of the land
Not truly by the text but newly by a glose
And words that were most plain when they by us were
    scanned
We turned by construction to a Welchman's hose *
Whereby many a one both life and land did lose
    Yet this we made our mean to mount aloft on mules
    And serving times and turns perverted laws and rules
        —*G Ferrers* (1559)

When Stuart of Dunearn left the fatal field of Balbarton he made his way as quickly as possible back to Edinburgh Only one person there, besides the parties immediately concerned had been made aware of the intended duel, and that was Mr James Gibson, his intimate friend and fellow sufferer from the libellous attacks of the *Sentinel* On the preceding night Stuart had told Gibson of the proposed meeting and when it had been accelerated in the manner we have described, he had sent to him such papers as would be necessary to arrange his affairs should he fall These papers had reached Gibson about eleven o'clock on Tuesday,

but Stuart himself arrived at his office about two o'clock on the same day The state of Stuart's mind at this time is well indicated by the graphic account which Gibson gave of their meeting —

"When I was coming to my chambers I saw Mr Stuart coming out, who instantly when he saw me turned short and ran up the stair I followed him into my room, and when I had closed the door I asked 'What has happened?' He ran into a corner of the room, covered his face with his hands, and burst into tears As soon as he was a little composed, he said that he was afraid Sir Alexander Boswell was mortally wounded He told me he had taken no aim and added 'I wish to God I had done so, as I am certain I should in that case have missed him I never fired a pistol on foot in my life before'

Gibson advised him to leave the country at once, not to avoid his trial should he be prosecuted, but to escape the imprisonment which he would have otherwise to endure, but Stuart was very unwilling to consent to this proposal, saying that "he would be miserable until he knew the fate of Sir Alexan

---

* Welchman's hose made to suit either leg

der" At length he consented to follow the advice
tendered to him, and to take his way to France on
assurance being given that he should be made
aware of the state of his opponent without delay
His last words to Gibson were—' Remember to
give notice that I shall be ready to stand trial
He did not wish to appear to anyone as a fugitive
from justice At Calais he learned of the death of
Sir Alexander, and was much moved by the intelli
gence, nor did he recover his peace of mind during
his protracted absence in France He waited
there, however, separated from all his relatives,
and daily expecting to be summoned to stand his
trial before the most august Scottish Criminal
Court upon a charge which might cost him his life

The intelligence of the fatal result of the duel
caused much excitement in those circles which Sir
Alexander had frequented in Edinburgh When
party feeling was at its highest, and a duel seemed
inevitable, it did not seem to occur either to him
or his friends that it was possible to terminate
fatally for him, and the surprise with which the
news was received gave place to unreasonable in
dignation "The death, writes a contemporary,
"of so valuable a partisan as Sir Alexander Bos
well, though in fair duel, by the hand of James
Stuart, threw the Tory party into a flame, the
heat of which, I fear, reached even the department
of the Public Prosecutor" Nor need this latter
assertion astonish us when we remember the
"Public Prosecutor' was the same Sir William
Rae whose disreputable connection with the
Beacon had already been exposed, and who
dreaded that his share in the proprietary of the
Sentinel would prove too much even for his party
to endure if brought under their notice
No more striking instance need be desired
of the high handed action taken in those be
nighted times by the Tory administrators than
that afforded by the conduct of this Lord Advo
cate in the case under consideration Our readers
will hardly credit that such proceedings could
take place in Scotland only sixty years ago

It was the object of the Tories to cause Stuart's
case to assume a most disreputable appearance,
and the Lord-Advocate lent them his valuable aid
The papers which Borthwick, the printer, had
taken from his own desk, and which had already
caused this unfortunate duel, were likely to im
plicate other parties, and it was advisable to ob
tain possession of them at all hazards On the 3d
of April Borthwick was followed from Glasgow,
and arrested in Dundee on a charge of theft, and
a compositor, formerly in his employment, who
had carried the papers from Nelson Street to the
Tontine Hotel, was also apprehended as an accom
plice. It was pretended that Borthwick meant to
escape to America, though no reason was given as
to why he should embark at Dundee
He was put in irons, and his manacles were so
small that they caused him excessive pain, and he
was conveyed to Edinburgh between two officers
armed with pistols, as though he had been a
desperate malefactor When brought to Edinburgh,
all access to him was denied The Public Prose
cutor refused to accept of the bail he offered, and
he was indicted to take his trial on the 24th of
April On that day Mr Hope, Advocate Depute,
and one of the *Beacon* bondholders, rose in his
place and stated that he ' did not mean to proceed
with this case at present, but would neither fix a
day for trial nor accept bail for the prisoner
Borthwick was remanded to prison for forty days,
intending then to "run his letters," and force on
his trial under the Act of 1701 The time expired,
but still he was not brought to trial, and
on his application the High Court of Justi
ciary made an order for his discharge Yet
before he could leave the precincts of the Court
he was apprehended again *upon the same charge*,
this time laid by his quondam partner Alexander,
but with the concurrence of the Lord Advocate,
and the unfortunate man was then led back to
prison once more in defiance alike of law and
justice Here he was detained until after the trial
of Stuart of Dunearn, and was at length liberated
upon the 12th of June without a trial He had
thus been imprisoned for *seventy days*, treated with
the utmost severity, and finally discharged with
out having had any opportunity of vindicating
himself or remitting his case to the judgment of a
jury It was evident that the liberty of the sub
ject was not safe whilst such unscrupulous Tory
partisans were in power

An attempt was made by Mr Abercromby in
Parliament to have a Committee of Inquiry ap
pointed to examine as to the Lord Advocate's
share in this disreputable affair, but that func
tionary, instead of courting the inquiry, as an
innocent man would have done, succeeded
in obtaining a majority of 25 against the
motion Mr Abercromby had plainly charged
him with being part proprietor of the *Sentinel*,
on the authority of a note signed by him,
which Mr Abercromby read to the House,
but Sir William boldly asserted that, "so help
him God, he had never seen the newspaper—
he had never received, never supported it, and
never in any shape had any concern with that
newspaper" Abercromby silently replied by
handing across the table to him the paper which
had been read, and the Lord Advocate was com
pelled to take back his oath, and to acknowledge
that his signature was plainly there. Despite this

miserable exhibition of duplicity, the motion was thrown out, and the matter, though frequently revived, came to nothing It served, however, to disgust the English sympathisers with Tory principles at their Scottish colleagues, and to pave the way for reform

The trial of Stuart of Dunearn took place in the High Court of Justiciary on the 10th of June 1822 The Judges present were the Right Hon David Boyle, Lord Justice Clerk, Lord Hermand, Lord Succoth, Lord Gillies, and Lord Pitmilly As Lord Meadowbank's name was to appear in the trial, he very wisely absented himself, and, with this exception, there was a full bench of Judges The Lord Advocate prosecuted in person, and was assisted by the Solicitor General, James Wedderburn and the Advocates Depute, Duncan M'Neill (the late Lord Colonsay) and Robert Dundas The leading counsel for the prisoner were Francis Jeffrey, James Moncrieff, and Henry Cockburn Mr Stuart took his place at the bar accompanied by several of his relatives, amongst whom were the Earl of Moray and Mr Erskine of Cardross The trial had excited great interest throughout the country, as much because of the political interests involved as from the position of the deceased and the prisoner, and the Court was crowded in every part

The indictment had probably been prepared under the direct supervision of the Lord Advocate, and deserves some notice It set out by declaring the crime charged as murder, and proceeded to state that 'the said James Stuart, having conceived malice and ill will against the late Sir Alexander Boswell of Auchinleck, Baronet, and having formed the unlawful design of challenging the said Sir Alexander Boswell *and others of the lieges* to fight a duel *or duels* went to Glasgow to procure some papers the better to accomplish this unlawful design These were obtained through the medium of William Murray Borthwick, who had been liberated from gaol, it was averred, by the prisoner for that purpose "Having found, or pretended to have found, among them some writings holograph of the said Sir Alexander Boswell, Stuart was charged with having wickedly and maliciously challenged his traducer to fight a duel, with having met him at Auchtertool and discharged a loaded pistol at him, 'whereby the said Sir Alexander Boswell was mortally wounded, the ball having entered near the root of the neck on the right side, and shattered the collar bone, of which mortal wound the said Sir Alexander Boswell died in the course of next day, and was thus murdered by you, the said James Stuart, and you, the said James Stuart, conscious

of your guilt in the premises, did abscond and flee from justice, &c '

This document exhibits as much malice as a political opponent could conveniently cram into a precise legal charge It suggested that Stuart had deliberately intended to challenge Sir Alexander before he went to Glasgow, though he was ignorant of the author of these libels until he saw the papers Then it attempted to make him a resetter of stolen property, by making it appear that Borthwick had broken into the office of another man unlawfully to obtain the papers. Still further, it insinuated that Stuart had procured Borthwick's release from gaol for that purpose only, and lastly, that he had absconded from justice after gratifying his malice All these points were subsidiary to the major charge of murder, but they were all likely to prejudice an unreflecting jury against the accused, *and every one of them was known to the Lord Advocate to be distinctly false* Had Stuart known that Boswell was his opponent, he never need have gone to Glasgow to confirm this notion, had Borthwick not been the legal owner of the papers, the Lords of Justiciary would not have refused to deliver them to Alexander, as they afterwards did, and Stuart could hardly be said to have absconded, when repeated announcements were made to the Lord-Advocate and his assistants that he was ready at any time to stand his trial The question of malicious murder was one for the jury to consider. When asked to plead to the indictment, the prisoner declared himself "Not Guilty"

A somewhat unusual course of procedure was then adopted by the prisoner's counsel In England trials are usually conducted by the prosecuting counsel relating the case before any evidence is led but in Scotland all the witnesses are heard before the jury has any clue to the bearing of their evidence other than is afforded by the terms of the indictment Neither of these plans was followed in this case for immediately after the prisoner had made his plea, his advocate, Mr Cockburn, rose and claimed that, "though he had no objection to the technical relevancy of the libel, this was one of those occasions on which it is the duty of the panel to avail himself of his undoubted privilege of beginning the business of the day by such a statement of facts as might enable the Court to judge of the bearing and relevancy of his defences " In a long and eloquent speech, he detailed all the circumstances connected with the trial—the newspaper libels, the discovery of their authorship, the repeated attempts to obtain an apology, the challenge, and the duel—and laid the facts so clearly and forcibly before his hearers that it was evident this innovation in Scottish procedure ha greatly simplified the case. As his statement agrees in every particular with the narrative which we have compiled from other sources it is not necessary for us to quote from it. Whilst he admitted that his client had met Sir Alexander Boswell in a duel, he emphatically denied all the minor accusations in the indictment. He maintained that Stuart was ignorant of the personality of his libeller until he obtained the papers from Borthwick, and denied that he had taken any part in the liberation of the latter. He stated that he would adduce evidence to prove that the Crown Office had been frequently assured of Stuart's intention to return to Scotland for his trial, and that the accusation of "fleeing from justice" was a malicious and uncalled for charge. He pointed out that everything had been left to Sir Alexander's own arrangement—Stuart was willing to follow him to the Continent, he agreed to meet him in England; and when at last the meeting was fearfully precipitated he was still ready to accommodate him at a few hours' notice. This conduct on Stuart's part conclusively proved that he was not the "bully," the "coward," the "mean man," the "heartless ruffian," the "white feather," the "man afraid of lead," the "poltroon" he had been falsely represented to be; and his bearing after the fatal termination of the duel as certainly showed that he bore no malice towards his unfortunate antagonist. To prove the latter point two witnesses would be called who were with Mr Stuart when he received intelligence of Sir Alexander Boswell's death, and they would explain whether he received it in the spirit of a man who was merely glad that he was himself safe, or with the temper of one who had any feeling of malice towards the deceased. They would tell the Court that they never witnessed so natural and so generous a flood of sorrow for the ties which he knew he had broken, and for the life which he knew he never could recall.

As to the necessity of an appeal to the duel in this case as the only means of reconciliation, Mr Cockburn pointed out that all other means had failed, and skilfully introduced the fact that the proposal to engage in this combat had so far received the approval of a Supreme Criminal Judge —a Judge even of that Court—that he had recommended his own brother to act as second! If one so conversant with law as Lord Meadowbank believed that law was powerless to settle this

dispute, Mr Stuart might be excused for falling into the same error, especially after his own experience of the impotence of law to protect him from slander. In concluding, he submitted that, ' instead of adding to the sufferings of him who has already borne so much, and who, let this case terminate as it may, is doomed to suffer so much more, the only legal, the only moral, the only appropriate conclusion to this day's trial must be a persuasion that he acted under the operation of a great moral necessity, and that a verdict of 'not guilty' is the result which will give most satisfaction both to law and to all reasonable men.'

This address was in every way an exceptional one. Mr Cockburn's close intimacy with Mr Stuart enabled him to speak with authority as to the sentiments of his client; and his strict adherence to tact and regard for law could not fail to command the attention alike of the Bench and the jury. Sir James Macintosh, referring to this speech in the House of Commons, said that it "had not been surpassed by any effort in the whole range of ancient or modern forensic eloquence. It was a speech characterised by calm and forcible reasoning, by chaste and classical diction, by the utmost skill, delicacy, and address in the management of the most difficult topics, and by a rare combination of zeal and ability in the cause of his client, with respect to the feelings of all the parties concerned, and a reverence for the rules of law and the austere decorum of a court of justice.'

No objection had been urged against the relevancy of the libel by the prisoner's counsel, but it was so glaringly inaccurate that the Bench took the rare course of excepting to it. Lord Gillies, one of the most cautious of judges, said—"This indictment is unprecedented. It charges Mr Stuart with having formed a design to challenge others of the lieges besides Sir Alexander Boswell. This has no connection with the case, and should be struck out.' The other Lords of Justiciary concurred with him, and the absurd phrase was deleted. The Lord Justice Clerk, in compliance with a now obsolete custom, proceeded to appoint a jury, which consisted of three Baronets, four merchants, and eight of the landed gentry. Evidence was then led, and two most important points were speedily elicited, which altered the whole aspect of the case.

THE BOSWELL ARMS

PART VIII

Pheidippides— 'Law! Pray who made the law? A man, I
suppose,
Like you or me and so persuaded others
Why have not I as good a right as he had
To start a law for future generations?'

—' The Clouds — Aristophanes

As the counsel for Stuart of Dunearn admitted
the main facts as to the duel it was not necessary
for the prosecutor to lead an elaborate proof on this
point. The Earl of Rosslyn was the first witness
examined, and he gave a clear and succinct narrative of his connection with the affair, which agrees
with our own account of it. One new and important fact was elicited, however, in his cross-
examination—it was that Mr Stuart said to him
when taking the pistol, that he thought he should
not take aim, and the Earl agreed with him, and
was certain from what he saw afterwards that his
shot was a random one. Mr John Douglas was
the next witness, and his version of the
affair, whilst agreeing with that of the Earl of
Rosslyn, contributed another important fact unknown till that time. He said— 'In the carriage
on the way from the North Ferry to the ground
Sir Alexander asked me, as a friend, what advice
I would give him as to firing. I answered he was
the best judge of that, and that he should consult
his own feelings. He said he had no ill will to Mr
Stuart—he had no wish to put his life in
jeopardy; though in an unhappy moment he had
injured him, he bore him no ill will, and therefore
it was his determination to fire in the air. I

expressed my approbation of his resolution to
do so.'

Surely the folly of duelling was never more
completely and mournfully exhibited than in this
case. The one party declares his intention not to
take aim, the other as decidedly determines to fire
in the air. It is difficult to see how the offended
honour of either could be satisfied by such insane
proceedings. Neither would make the first advance to tell the other of his purpose, and
the seconds had not the courage to interfere
and put a stop to the farce before it
became a tragedy, although Lord Rosslyn afterwards declared that had he heard of Sir Alexander's purpose he would not have suffered the affair
to proceed. A false notion of honour had forced
Sir Alexander to take the field rather than own to
Stuart what he admitted to Douglas, and an
equally false delicacy prevented the latter from
exposing his intention and saving him from death.

The evidence of the other witnesses in this case
need not be examined in detail. It is enough to
state that it triumphantly refuted the minor
charges in the indictment, and left merely the legal
question, as to whether duelling was murder, to
the decision of the jury. Even the testimony of his
most bitter political opponents—Lord Kinneder,
Dr Robertson Barclay, Messrs W. Gulland,
Francis Walker, Walter Cook, Richard Mackenzie,
Hay Donaldson, and others, who spoke in the
highest terms of his amiability and tender hearted-
ness—would have exonerated him from the charge

of malice, but it was yet to be seen whether his act in going out to fight a duel was not an infringement of the law worthy of capital punishment

The address of the Lord-Advocate was very brief, and almost apologetic in its tone. He maintained that he was justified in bringing this action before the Court, even if it were only for the purpose of allowing the prisoner to make such statements as would explain his situation in the affair. "He regretted that some of the expressions used in the indictment—especially as to the prisoner's absconding—had been used, but he had endeavoured to act in as fair and liberal a manner as was consistent with duty. It was impossible for him not to state, with respect to the charge of murder, in the broadest and most decided terms, that that charge, according to every view of the law, was distinctly proved. Without reading any law books, he would state distinctly that a person going out deliberately to fight a duel, and killing his antagonist, cannot be allowed to state himself as in those circumstances of self-defence which entitle him to a verdict of acquittal."

He was followed by Mr Jeffrey, to whom had been committed the conducting of the legal argument upon which the case now rested. His speech was one of the finest examples of what is called "special pleading" ever uttered in that Court. The point which he attacked principally was the assertion of malice on Stuart's part, and he maintained that the evidence had fully contradicted this imputation. He passed in review the principal cases of trial for duelling which had taken place for many years, and showed that in the majority of them the verdicts returned had partially exonerated or acquitted the accused. He artfully suggested that the practice of duelling, though condemned by law, was in many cases the only method whereby outraged honour could be vindicated, and quoted from the works of Dr Johnson, Lord Kames, Professor Adam Fergusson, and others, to show that it could be defended on moral grounds. He could not deny that the law was distinctly against duelling, and denounced it in plain terms as murder, but he skilfully put forth the very shallow though captivating sophism that the practice of juries in interpreting this law favourably for the accused had made it actually void. The fact that such verdicts received the approbation of the community and the sanction of the Courts in which they were offered seemed, he said, to show the lenient way in which the statutes should be understood.

Returning to the question of malice, he contended that no malice had been proved, and asserted that his client was as much justified in firing his pistol on the field as he would have been had a highwayman attacked him and threatened his life. A man might lawfully shoot another through fear of even less injuries—theft, housebreaking, &c—and in this case the mere presence of his opponent was a sufficient menace to justify Stuart in his act of self-defence. He pointed out that the law would excuse a man who killed another in defence of his own goods, and maintained that the defence of one's honour was still more necessary to one in Stuart's position.

' If a person," he said, " has done that which has placed me in the dilemma of either shooting at him, or of living an outcast from society—of being exposed to all manner of insults and contumelies—of being excluded from all honourable pursuits and professions—shrunk from by my ancient friends—the cause of blushing to my relations and sorrow to my children—the stain of an honourable name, and a hopeless outcast and exile from society—without hope, means, or chance of restoration—if, I say, a man by an act unlawful in itself has placed me in that situation, can it be said, there being no malice in my heart no means of defending my rights but this, no possibility of my subsisting on the earth without scorn, and all this by the unlawful act of another,—I ask you if, under these circumstances, I do not take my enemy off by assassination, but merely expose his life to the same risk as my own and that, perhaps, with as many chances against me, and he fall—is it possible that the law, which deals so leniently with other slaughters, should call that a murder? I submit to you that this would be a proposition altogether monstrous."

Alluding to the fact that no malice on Stuart's part could be proved *before* the duel, he contended that the conduct of the prisoner *after* it conclusively showed that he had no malicious intention to take Sir Alexander's life at any time. The character which he had received from the witnesses, separated as they were from him by political opinions, was precisely the character of one who would have acted with single-mindedness the part which he had done. Yet the jury were called on either to affirm that all his proceedings in this affair were actuated by malice, or else to reject the charge entirely and declare him not guilty. He trusted that the latter would be the conclusion to which they would come, and that they would "thus restore him untainted to that society of which he is the delight, and in which he performs so many useful offices, and, at the same time, in part at least, to that peace of mind which, with his feelings and his heart, I fear it is not in the power of your verdict or of any human tribunal ever effectually or completely to restore."

This able speech has long been considered a model of forensic eloquence. Whilst impassioned enough to charm the tender heart, it was sufficiently technical to beguile the unwary mind, and hoodwink the jury by clever sophistry. Throughout the whole of the address the speaker adroitly evades the question of law, and ventures to supersede the statutes of the land by an appeal to the practice of irresponsible juries throughout the kingdom, as though the interpretation of law and the administration of justice were safer in the hands of a jury than in those of a judge. With profound knowledge of human nature, he dwells upon the personal aspect of the case, and puts the position of the prisoner so movingly before the jury that all other considerations are dwarfed thereby.

The Lord Justice Clerk, however, could not suffer this fencing with the law to pass unnoticed, and in a speech remarkable for its lucid enunciation of the law and its masterly treatment of authorities he practically reprimanded Jeffrey for his loose and dangerous logic. Beginning with Sir George Mackenzie, who asserts that duels are but illustrious and honourable murders, he showed that every authoritative writer upon Scots Criminal Law had regarded this offence in the same light. He proved that the very latest writers—men as well acquainted with the modern interpretation of law as the learned advocate—had expressly excluded the plea of self defence as applicable to duelling, especially if some time elapsed between the challenge and the duel. He pointed out that some of the principal writers both upon English and Scots Law asserted that 'no man under the protection of the law is to be the avenger of his own wrongs, and that duelling was thus a deliberate infraction of this fundamental principle upon which all law was based.'

Having thus explained the legal aspect of the case, which had been so ingeniously shirked by the prisoner's counsel, he examined minutely all the circumstances attending this special duel, and compared them with those of previous cases. He expressed his own firm conviction that the allegation of malice on Stuart's part had not been supported by the evidence—that, indeed, it seemed all to point in the other direction. Mr Jeffrey had waived the question of the provocation given to the prisoner, but his Lordship thought that this fact was safer as a foundation for excuse than the general excuse for duelling which the counsel had put forward. The whole bearing of the prisoner in the circumstances in which he was placed precluded the idea of personal malice, and the uncommon provocation given must be allowed to have some weight with

the jury. The summing up, in its latter portion at least, was distinctly in favour of the prisoner, and the Judge, though himself a Tory, took the opportunity of denouncing the newspaper tactics of his party in language which could not have been pleasant to the ears either of the Lord Advocate or of Sir Walter Scott, then Clerk of the Court of Session.

"Gentlemen," he said, "before concluding, I must say that I am not one of those who can give the slightest countenance to such proceedings as those which led originally to this fatal business. Neither I nor any other Judge in this Court can give the slightest countenance to publications such as those which were directed against the gentleman at the bar. It is one of the greatest misfortunes and evils of the present day that we have to witness the disgraceful license of the periodical press; and I do lament from the bottom of my heart that the unfortunate gentleman deceased should have had any concern with writings of this description, for it is impossible to shut your eyes against the evidence by which it is proved that Sir Alexander Boswell was engaged in these writings, and that the prisoner at the bar was the object of his attacks."

When the Lord Justice Clerk had concluded his summing up, the jury, without retiring, after a few moments' consultation, returned their verdict in a voce by their Chancellor, Sir John Hope of Craighall —' My Lord, the jury unanimously find Mr Stuart *Not Guilty.*" The verdict was received with strong marks of satisfaction by the audience, and the presiding Judge then turned to the panel and said—"Mr James Stuart, I congratulate you on the verdict returned by a jury of your countrymen, but, in the present state of your feelings, it would be quite improper in me to say one word more to you upon the subject.'

The trial had lasted from ten A M on Tuesday till half past four on the following morning, and the Court had been crowded during all that time by an intensely interested audience.

Thus was concluded one of the most notable of Scottish trials for duelling in modern times. The strong political element which mingled with it had made it appear to many throughout the country as another battlefield upon which the interminable war of Whig and Tory was to be waged and possibly the eagerness with which Stuart had been pursued by the Lord Advocate and other leaders of the party gave some appearance of foundation for this idea. The triumphant vindication of Dunearn thus became a positive gain to the Liberal party, and they exulted somewhat savagely over it. A correspondent has sup plied a fragment of a doggerel lilt current at the time in Fifeshire, which, like the rude verse on some antique sculptured stone, exhibits the manners of our forefathers during that dark period which preceded the Reform Bill of 1832 —

> " For justice stood on Stuart's side,
> Though he's awa to France to hide,
> And justice felled the Tory's pride
> That morning on Balbarton '

For some time after his acquittal, Mr Stuart devoted his attention to experimental farming and commercial speculation, but did not succeed in either, and the monetary crisis of 1825 compelled him to abandon these occupations and embark for America While there he published an account of his travels, in which he spoke so flatteringly of the inhabitants and so hopefully of their future that he roused again the vituperative energies of his Tory enemies in this country After his return he undertook the editorship of the *Courier* newspaper, and was appointed Inspector of Factories whilst Lord Melbourne's Government was in power He remained faithful to his early convictions, " preserving to the last the character of a staunch partisan, a warm friend, and honourable man " He died of disease of the heart in November 1849, in his seventy fourth year

Now that the rancour of party spirit is gone, it is possible to examine this melancholy case dispassionately, and we imagine that no one can regard Sir Alexander Boswell, whose life was thus cut prematurely short, with other feelings than those of pity and regret He was a man of great parts and exceptional ability, but the possession of that fatal gift, a turn for satire, deprived the world of those talents which might ultimately have won for him a high position in literature Well had it been for him had he pondered upon the poet's wise counsel —

> ' But above all things raillery decline /
> Nature but few does for that task design
> Tis in the ablest hand a dangerous tool,
> But never fails to wound the meddling fool,
> For all must grant it needs no common art
> To keep men patient when we make them smart '

MALCOLM GILLESPIE—A ROMANCE OF ABERDEEN.

PART I.

" *Sergeant Kite*—If any gentleman soldiers or others, have a mind to serve His Majesty and pull down the French King if any prentices have severe masters any children have undutiful parents if any servants have too little wages, or any husband too much wife let them repair to the noble Sergeant Kite, at the sign of the Raven, in the good town of Shrewsbury and they shall receive present relief and entertainment '—"*The Recruiting Officer.—G. Farquhar.*

The name of Malcolm Gillespie, the Gauger of Skene, is still a household word throughout Aberdeenshire, and though there are few now living who could have known him personally, still fewer are acquainted with the story of his strange career It is not much over a century since he was born, yet tradition has already thrown a halo of romance around him, which makes it difficult to discover the truth concerning him Startling tales are told of his courage and prowess in the pursuit of his calling, and had his life been spent at a more remote period from our own time he might soon have been transformed into a historical myth—a Tell, a Wallace, or a "fause Menteith Fortunately we are able to examine the claims which were put forth by him with understanding, and have very complete evidence as to the latter portion of his eventful life. The story of his early years has been related by himself, and though he deals somewhat largely in the marvellous, we have no other narrative to follow. Whether we accept his statements or reject them—whether we consider him as a hero or an impostor—the tale of his adventures will be amusing, and the study of his character not wholly uninstructive.

Malcolm Gillespie had occupied the post of Excise officer at the parish of Skene, Aberdeenshire, for twelve years before 1826, when he suddenly obtained information that the Board of Excise intended to remove him to another district. For many reasons this removal did not suit his views. He had made many friends in the locality, had set up an expensive establishment at Crombie Cottage, and had so involved himself in monetary transactions with his neighbours, that to leave the district would mean ruin and exposure for him. To obviate this impending catastrophe he drew up a strongly worded petition to the Board praying them to alter their decision, and continue him in his present location. This document was accompanied by numerous letters of recommendation from gentlemen of standing, with whom he had come in contact, and who all wrote in the highest terms of esteem and respect regarding his character. Still further to enforce his claim to consideration from the Board, he sent with this petition a memoir of his life, detailing with great amplitude his services in detecting and defeating contrabandists, and relating his 'hairbreadth scapes' and loud and strange adventures in true Munchausen style. To this autobiography we are indebted for the particulars of his early life; and though we shall quote largely from it, let it be distinctly understood that we do not vouch for its accuracy. The circumstances which called it forth do not predispose us to accept it unquestioningly; and we suspect that our readers, like ourselves, will sometimes feel inclined to exclaim against the autobiographist with the character in Congreve's comedy —'Ferdinand Mendez Pinto was but a type of thee, thou liar of the first magnitude!'

Our hero was born in Dunblane probably about the year 1779. No account is recorded of his parentage, and his boyhood is passed over in silence. The earliest notice describes him as a youth of seventeen, having a particular attachment to a military life. The disturbances on the Continent at this time (1796) seemed to open up a path to wealth and fame for anyone imbued with true martial ardour; for distinction even in the Peerage laden British army might still be won by the valorous private at the bayonet's point. But Malcolm Gillespie did not care to work his way upwards from the lowest round of the ladder of fame if he could possibly be hoisted aloft through influence; so he pestered his friends to purchase a commission for him, but without avail. He had apparently learned no method of winning his bread as a civilian, and had most likely spent his time amongst those idle loafers who then gravitated naturally towards the army, and 'stood to be shot at for a shilling a day.' The demand for men of any kind, however, was great at this time, and Gillespie, having discovered a distant maternal relative in Captain Blair of the First Regiment of Foot, then stationed at Stirling Castle, enlisted with him as a private, on the understanding that he was to be detailed for recruiting duty for some time until his friends could be prevailed on to purchase his coveted commission. He was thus saved from all risk of losing his life ingloriously as a private soldier upon some foreign battlefield.

His recruiting station was in the ancient city of Brechin, and his genial manner and careless joviality made him a most successful enlister. Though he had never "smelt powder" himself, he had doubtless the faculty of inventing mendacious but thrilling adventures to captivate the simple minded Forfar lads, and kindle in their bosoms the baleful fire of martial enthusiasm. His success as a recruiting officer was great for during the three years which he spent at Brechin he enlisted no less than "four hundred fine young lads," and sent them to swell the hosts of His Britannic Majesty. The adroitness which he displayed in this capacity soon attracted the notice of the Colonel of his regiment—the Right Honourable Lord Adam Gordon—and as Gillespie's friends had done nothing towards the purchase of his commission, Lord Adam Gordon proposed that he would procure a commission for him in the Prince of Wales Fencibles, which were then being embodied at Berwick, under the care of Colonel Johnston. His three years' safe service at home would thus have brought to him the recompense for which many a brave soldier had fought for in vain on many a bloody field.

Circumstances had altered so seriously with young Gillespie, however, that he could not entertain Lord Adam's proposal with equanimity. Venus had conquered Mars as usual, and the services of Lucina, the thrice called, threefold goddess, had already been required—in short, as Gillespie prosaically puts it, "by this time Mr G had got married, and was father of a young family. He had besides run himself and his friends in debt by his exertions in the recruiting service, which is well known to be attended with con siderable expense." With such *impedimenta* hanging around him, the longed for commission was to be of little service, even though bestowed gratuitously, and he determined to try a new profession. "As he was well aware that having nothing to depend upon but his pay to support himself and his family, he proposed to his Lordship a situation in the Excise as the most eligible and beneficial to his young children. Lord Adam accordingly made intercession, and procured for him this appointment, with an assurance that if he continued to pursue the same line of conduct in the Excise he had followed in the recruiting department he would be his friend, and get him promoted as soon as the forms of the Excise would admit."

We confess that we have grave doubts as to the existence of the intense interest thus professed by Lord Adam Gordon in the welfare of Gillespie. The social positions of the two men were widely apart. Lord Adam was the fourth son of the second Duke of Gordon, and had played a prominent part amongst the military heroes of his time for more than thirty years before Gillespie's enlistment. He was member of Parliament almost continuously, first for Aberdeenshire, and afterwards for Kincardineshire, during the interval between 1754 and 1788, served in France, held a command in America, was Colonel successively of the 66th, the 26th Cameronians, and the 1st regiments, was Major General, and then Lieutenant General, was Governor of Tynemouth Castle, and afterwards of Edinburgh Castle and was Commander in Chief of the Forces in Scotland when Gillespie enlisted in the army. From this record we may judge whether so exalted a personage as he would ever hear of the merits of an obscure recruiting officer, or if one so "used to war's alarms" would care to foster the fortunes of a stay at home soldier, whose only merit lay in his aptitude for wheedling the lieges into the service. Nor is it unworthy of notice that Gillespie's claim to the friendship of Lord Adam Gordon was not made until that nobleman had been dead for a quarter of a century, and at a time when it was not worth while to contradict him. We have thought it advisable to show reasons for doubting this statement, which occurs on the very first page of his 'Memoir, so that the reader may see what an "unlimited power of assertion" he possessed, and may be cautioned as to placing implicit confidence in other dubious parts of his narrative.

By some means or other he succeeded in transferring his services from the army to the Excise, and continued in the employment of the Board during the remainder of his life. His first appointment was to superintend the salt manu-facture at Prestonpans, and he entered on his duties there in 1799. As a large portion of the revenue was then derived from the taxes upon this necessary of life, smuggling was carried on extensively and the heavy war expenses forced the Government to take extreme measures in the collection of it, and to discourage deception at all hazards. For two years Gillespie wrought faithfully for this purpose in the locality to which he had been appointed; and, according to his account, "during this period he was the means of detecting innumerable frauds, which had escaped the vigilance of his predecessors in that quarter." Indeed, he became a terror to the unfair trader there and frauds became less frequent than for many years previous to that time.

From Prestonpans he was removed, by his own desire, to Aberdeenshire, where both illicit distillation and smuggling of foreign spirits seriously impaired the revenue. His quarters were established at Collieston, a little to the north of the port of Aberdeen, and a spot which had been long the chosen landing place of foreign contributaries. So extensive was the lawless trade in this place that Gillespie states the monthly landing of foreign spirits amounted to upwards of one thousand ankers, and the valiant gauger determined to put a stop to this unpatriotic traffic. He had now come to the land of the Gordons—the place with which his patron, Lord Adam, was associated, and probably counted upon his support to secure his advancement. But that nobleman unfortunately died just at this time—13th August 1801—and Gillespie was forced to make his way solely by his own exertions. That his services did not meet with due appreciation at headquarters he attributes entirely to Lord Adam Gordon's demise. "In the death of his Lordship," he writes, "he [Gillespie] lost his best friend and benefactor, and he had to struggle with all the vicissitudes of fortune with a numerous family upwards of thirty years," that is to say, three years in the recruiting service and nearly twenty eight in the Excise, without being advanced one step since his first appointment although he had always a particular wish to be stationary in a district where exertions were necessary to suppress delinquents and offenders against the revenue laws. If the stories he relates of his superhuman exertions on behalf of the revenue are true, he was certainly an ill used man, and merited different treatment from that which he received at the hands of My Lords of the Treasury. Some of these tales, though toughish in their nature, and demanding a large amount of credulity on the part of the reader, may bear repetition, so as to exhibit the character of their narrator.

PART II.

"But what could single valour do
Against so numerous a foe?
Yet much he did, indeed too much
To be believed where th' odds were such
But one against a multitude
Is more than mortal can make good. '—*Hudibras*

The greatest difficulty which Gillespie en countered when attempting the suppression of the smuggling trade at Colliston arose from the fact that many of the merchants of Aberdeen were deeply interested in its success, and as they were "people of considerable stock and influence," the combat was an unequal one. Nevertheless, ' by Mr G.'s unwearied and persevering vigilance, he brought the delinquents to abandon their frauds, although it was attended with very great expense.'

That smuggling of foreign spirits was largely engaged in even by those moving in respectable circles need not excite wonder when we remember that at the beginning of this century, and for long afterwards, the duty charged upon brandy and geneva—the produce of France and Holland—was ridiculously excessive. From 1796 till 1806 the duty charged upon these spirits ranged from 7s 6d to 14s per gallon, although the first cost of them abroad did not exceed 4s per gallon. Be fore the Income Tax had been so largely utilised as an ingenious and convenient source of revenue, succeeding financiers looked upon the taxes on im ported spirits as affording security against a deficit, and Whig and Tory alike pursued the suicidal policy of increasing the duty, until in 1832 it had reached the absurd figure of 22s 6d per gallon! The consequences of this method might have been anticipated. The consumption of *duty paid* spirits decreased alarmingly as smuggling became more prevalent, and the highest tariff of duty actually produced the least revenue. The moral effect of this system upon the people was most deleterious, for "this abominable duty," according to one writer, "rendered the coasts of Kent and Sussex the theatre of perpetual contests between the peasantry and the coastguard, and pro cured for the smuggler, even when soiled with the blood of some revenue officer, the public sym pathy and support.' The experiences of the south of England were identical with those of the north of Scotland, and Malcolm Gillespie's boast of having terminated the frauds there is at least doubtful. His struggles with the smugglers of Colliston, however, were truly heroic, not to say Falstaffian!

One night, whilst on the lookout there, he per ceived a band of sixteen fishermen proceeding from the landing place towards the Loch of Collis ton, each bearing an anker of spirits on his shoulder. Gillespie was alone, and dared not attack them unaided, so he fired two pistols, at in tervals, in the air, thinking to terrify them into retreat. Some of the less courageous of them dropped their burdens and fled, but many of the smugglers made good their escape, carrying their contraband spirits with them. By severing the slings by which the kegs had been carried, he secured the abandoned plunder, and had thus made a valuable capture at the expense of a little powder. Whilst meditating some means of con veying the material to some place of safety, he suddenly found himself in the midst of six armed foreigners, who threatened his life if he did not depart. A happy thought occurred to him—such an expedient as is rarely heard of out of a novel, and which he thus relates—" He pulled a letter out of his pocket, and told them he received it from the owner of the goods, who authorised him to get these ankers from the fishermen. This pacified the foreigners, who immediately retired with the letter, and it saved Mr G.'s life, who must have suffered at the hands of these unmerciful banditti if this well timed policy had not been thought of. This prevented any further attempt of landing more for that night. The imaginary letter given to the foreigners was an old one Mr G. had in his pocket, and the darkness of the night, joined to the ignorance of these outlandish crew, prevented any discovery of the trick till they reached Colliston, which, when they had discovered, they returned very expeditiously with redoubled fury, determined to revenge the insult, but they were too late." Gillespie had procured assistance, and removed the spirits to safe custody in their absence.

His enemies, however, were not always so inno cently polite as these gentle and unsuspicious foreigners. Once whilst looking seawards from his post he noticed a lugger in Colliston Bay, from which a small boat had just set out and was steering for the shore. Believing that the intention was to land in a small creek at a place called Sandend, he made his way thither, and concealed himself in a natural cave beside it, which was then under eighteen inches of water. The height of his lurking place pre vented him from standing upright, and he re mained in a most uncomfortable position, watch ing the manœuvres of the smugglers by the fitful light of the winter moon. His surmise as to their purpose was correct, and they made straight for the creek upon whose margin he was concealed No sooner had the boat passed his ambush and floated up the shallow creek than he dashed forth upon the affrighted smugglers, and so startled them by merely firing his arms that they abandoned their craft and its contents, and fled precipitately To leap on board and push rapidly out to sea was the work of but a brief time, and he soon found himself the sole possessor and navigator of a little boat, well laden with foreign spirits

Meanwhile the smugglers had recovered from their scare, and saw with dismay their booty torn from their grasp by the astute daring of a single exciseman They gathered on the shore and pelted the courageous hero with stones and such other missiles as came to their hands, but he passed safely through this ordeal, and soon placed himself beyond their range He had still two miles to row before he could reach the open sea, and the easterly wind which was blowing had lashed the waters into fury It was mid winter, and his long immersion whilst he was in ambush now began to tell upon him His limbs stiffened, his heart was chilled, and only the exertion necessary to propel his boat prevented total collapse At length, after incredible exertion he reached the Ward of Cruden, where he expected to obtain assistance from friendly fishermen, and to land his prize in safety The period of his arrival there, however, was untimeous, for the fisher folk were still abed, and he dared not leave his captured kegs to awake them Running his boat well into the beach, he began to unload his cargo, and, when he had landed the greater portion and placed the ankers at some distance from the water, he went to the inn to procure aid But the smugglers had followed his course by land, and had reached the Ward of Cruden during his absence When he returned with assistance he found that the boat he had piloted so bravely had disappeared and nothing remained to him save those kegs of spirits which he had wisely exerted himself to land

The intrepidity of our hero in his resistance to illicit traffic in liquors soon made him a marked man in the locality, and his form and features were well known and dreaded by all concerned in this lawless trade Whether through economy at head quarters, or from a desire on his own part to obtain individual honour, cannot now be discovered, but it is noteworthy that his most Gargantuan exploits were accomplished by his own hand, when there was neither friend near to share the glory nor foe hard by to convict him of exaggeration Of his most desperate encounters he could, and did,

proudly boast—"Alone I did it!" And it is remarkable that a special providence seems to have watched over him throughout this portion of his career, delivering him from overwhelming dangers, and nobly seconding his efforts to preserve the revenue from fraudful diminution Not without suffering however, was his work accomplished, if we may credit his own tale

One wintry night as he was wandering upon his rounds on some road which led inland from the shore, he noticed a horse and cart laden with barrels coming towards him from the beach A nearer approach showed that the men who accompanied it were masked and armed with bludgeons, and he had no doubt whatever of their lawless calling With unsurpassed hardihood he boldly accosted them and demanded to know their business Without deigning to reply they seized him ere he could reach his arms and prepare himself for resistance A fierce struggle ensued, in which he endured most brutal usage, and he was at length overcome, bound with ropes so that he could not move, and left under a hedge by the roadside to perish from hunger or exposure The victorious desperadoes marched onward with their contraband cargo, convinced that they were secure from the pursuit of the irrepressible gauger But they had not reckoned on the luck or providence which so constantly attended him

The encounter had taken place about eleven o'clock at night, and during the prevalence of an unusually severe frost The ground was covered with snow, and the spot where Gillespie had been laid was far removed from any habitation The bruises he had received caused him extreme pain, the cords wherewith he was bound galled him excessively, and the bitter frosty night air so irritated his wounds as to drive him almost to madness Who may adequately describe the horrors, mental and physical suffered by this unfortunate and much enduring exciseman throughout that fearful night, or tell in fitting language the hopeless situation of one whose only crime was a high regard for the Moral Law as interpreted by the Government' But the darkest night must terminate, and when six lingering hours had sped away he was at length discovered and relieved by some wayfarer who was traversing that lonely road on his way to work When released from his bonds, did he, like some effeminate carpet knight, seek the shelter and protection of the nearest hostelry, or strive to evade the path which his oppressors had taken? No, where duty called he hastened to obey, and though stiff, sore, and exhausted by his long exposure, he set himself at once to fulfil his vocation The track of the cart wheels was still visible in the snow, and by follow ing it pertinaciously for nearly six miles, he came at last upon the spot where its load had been deposited. A cattle shed in the midst of an open field had been chosen as the hiding place for the smuggled goods, and Gillespie thus easily secured the prize which had seemed so thoroughly to have eluded his grasp. Truly the ways of smugglers are wonderful.

A still more romantic adventure befell him near the ancient Castle of Slains, the seat of the Earl of Erroll. He received information that a bathing-house on the beach about a mile from the Castle had been used as a "plant for depositing contraband spirits temporarily until they could be removed to their inland destination. One night in February he set out towards this place, alone as usual, to investigate as to the truth of this report, taking hammer and chisel with him lest he should have to force a passage. No suspicious appearance presented itself to a cursory glance around the interior of the bathing hut, but a more careful examination showed to Gillespie's experienced eye that some of the boards in the ceiling were supported by partially driven nails, as though they were intended to be removed occasionally. Pursuing the clue, he extracted the nails, and disclosed the fact that this strange place of concealment above the inner roof of an erection belonging to the Knight Mareschal of Scotland actually contained ten or twelve ankers of smuggled spirits! Gillespie found that with the aid of a small table he could reach the place where the kegs lay, but it was not easy to devise any method of removing them. Just at this time he noticed some people walking on the cliffs above him, and did not doubt but that they were the contrabandists who had deposited these goods. It was impossible for him to leave the hut unobserved to obtain assistance, as the snow lay deep upon the ground, and his movements would have been at once detected. He determined, therefore, to remove the kegs as far as possible from their present position himself, and wait the help of some well-disposed passer by. The method he adopted is thus described by him:— 'He contrived to lower the ankers from the roof of the hut with his shirt and the help of the small table. It will be observed that after he had taken off his shirt to accomplish this undertaking, he found that, even with the assistance of the table, his shirt and length of his arms were too short to complete his end without endangering the loss of the spirits, and he suffered severe falls before it was accomplished. The next consideration was how to get the ankers conveyed home, or to some place of security, as there was no prospect of any person passing that way. He saw

that if they could be carried to the top of the rocks there was a public road. He therefore set to work, and carrying them one by one, ten yards at a time, for he could not trust them out of his sight, he succeeded in arriving at the wished for destination. This was a task of considerable difficulty and trouble, and it was about five o'clock in the morning when he accomplished this undertaking, and it luckily happened that a person shortly thereafter made his appearance on his way to Slains Castle, whom Mr G immediately employed to watch the goods till he secured a horse and cart to convey the property to the Excise Warehouse.'

The Earl of Erroll, according to Gillespie was indignant at this breach of the law in one of his own houses, and gladly gave all the aid he required, besides causing a full inquiry to be made amongst his domestics regarding the incident, and discharging some of them whom he suspected of complicity with the smugglers. Gillespie is good enough to say that the smuggling was "altogether unknown to the noble Earl, but he was careful not to relate this affair until that nobleman had been dead for seven years.

It may easily be imagined that the unvarying success of Gillespie struck terror into the hearts of the superstitious fishermen, and made them imagine that he was in the service of the Prince of the Power of the Air, as well as in that of the Prince Regent. *Aut Gillespie aut Diaboli* was their form of thought, if not of speech, whenever he appeared to oppose them, and, *if the stories he tells be true*, their effect upon the people, as he describes it, was only a natural consequence, although its statement is not over burdened with modesty.

"He completely succeeded,' he says, "in putting a stop to the alarming and dangerous traffic of the unfair trader, which had been carried on for a long period in that quarter, to an extent unparalleled in the annals of history. The persons who had been employed in carrying the contraband goods from the landing place of the smuggler, and even the fishers who lent them boats to carry their practices into execution, were so terrified at meeting him, that they even specially agreed with their employers to surrender to him at once, without the smallest opposition. Delinquents, finding it impossible longer to carry on their malpractices at Colliston Bay and neighbourhood, next began their traffic at Skateraw and Braidon Bays, the one six miles to the south, the other six miles to the north of Stonehaven. There they carried on their depredations to a great extent, and on Mr G's learning of this, he applied to the Hon Board of Excise to be removed to Stonehaven. This was accordingly done, and he by his unwearied exertions completely succeeded in putting a stop to the nefarious traffic in these places also '

This consummation, however, was not easily accomplished, and he was destined to perform still more chivalrous deeds than those we have related in his new quarters at Stonehyve. The honourable ambition to abolish illicit traffic in foreign

spirits glowed inextinguishably in his heroic bosom, and he felt himself trebly armed against the machinations of the smugglers by the justice of his cause. War to the knife was declared betwixt him and them, and his annals of their conflict read like the most thrilling of romances.

CROMBIE COTTAGE, ABERDEENSHIRE

PART III

Falstaff—I am a rogue if I were not at half-sword with a dozen of them two hours together. I have scaped by a miracle. I am eight times thrust through the doublet, four through the hose, my buckler cut through and through, my sword hacked like a hand saw *ecce signum.* I never dealt better since I was a man; all would not do. A plague of all cowards. *—Henry IV. Part I*

Gillespie entered upon his duties at Stonehaven in the year 1807, and remained there for five years. The mighty deeds which he performed during this time in the locality are carefully recorded in the marvellous *Memoir* to which we have been already indebted, and when we have related some of these we suppose our readers will not wonder at Gillespie's own statement that he "ultimately succeeded in rendering the attempts of the smugglers abortive, and before he left the quarter it was rare to hear of any of these depredators on the coast."

On one occasion, whilst on the watch, he noticed a suspicious lugger making for Braidon Bay. With his usual promptitude he at once saddled his steed and rode alone to the spot where he suspected the smugglers would attempt to land, that he might interrupt them in their nefarious practices. By accident or design his presence became known to those on board, and they, knowing that it was useless to fight against Fate and Gillespie, immedi-

ately put about their craft and ran for Skateraw Bay, a distance of about twelve miles. The undaunted officer was not to be eluded, so he turned his horse's head and galloped towards the latter place, determined to thwart their evil purposes. By strenuous exertions he reached Skateraw before the lugger, and when the lawless crew found their enemy waiting for them upon the beach they turned their ship once more and sped southwards for their first landing place at Braidon Bay. Not to be baulked in this manner the gallant officer again set out in pursuit of them, and again gave them checkmate. And thus throughout that weary night these hapless contrabandists sailed between the two places, ever pursued by the phantom of an incorruptible exciseman, and unable to find a harbour on all that rugged coast wherein to shelter themselves from his vengeful fury.

The adventure, however, was at length to have an unexpected termination. Gillespie's horse, which had borne him so faithfully over these dreary twelve miles, "without stop or stay, for so many times, at last gave way, overcome by fatigue and unintermittent exercise. About midnight he found it necessary to obtain a fresh steed of some kind if his efforts were not to be quite frustrated, and as he was then near Stonehaven, he rode to the George Inn there to find the needful assistance The inmates had retired to rest, and as they were probably unaccustomed to late visitors, he found it impossible to awaken them Passing round to the stable he found a pony stalled therein belonging to some traveller who had taken up his quarters in the inn for the night, and as necessity compelled Gillespie to venture all in the service of the King, he took possession of this animal, leaving his own foundered horse in its stall, together with a note to the ostler explaining the urgency of his need But the pony was quite unable to endure the fatigue which circumstances entailed without suffering severely Gillespie soon found it sinking beneath him, and latterly was compelled to abandon it to die by the roadside His purposes, however, had been accomplished, and the smugglers had been kept at bay by the energy and zeal of a single hero Throughout the night he had anxiously expected some of the revenue cutters to approach and capture the lugger, but morning came and day waned to eventide ere the tardy aid he looked for arrived At last one of these cruisers bore down upon the smugglers craft and made an easy prize of it, as the crew were worn out by their long and anxious watching, and possibly disheartened and terrified at the apparition of the ubiquitous officer who had haunted them so closely

One would have imagined that such ardent devotion as had been displayed by Gillespie would have at once received the reward which it merited but this world is ruled in a haphazard manner so far as revenue officers are concerned Will it be credited that the owner of the pony which had succumbed under the unwonted labours of that dreadful night, actually prosecuted Gillespie for damages sustained by him through the loss of his pony, as well as for the value of the incompetent animal itself? Such is the case, however, and an ungrateful country and an unsympathetic Legislature suffered this brave defender of the laws to pay the iniquitous bill, though he had also ruined his own horse in their thankless service

It was not only on the coast that Gillespie distinguished himself, for it was frequently his lot to encounter contraband spirits whilst being conveyed into the interior The men entrusted with this task were usually of the most desperate character, generally armed, and not unwilling to defend their charge with extreme violence Many a "bloody fray" was fought over the smuggled casks, though Fame has left the heroes' names frequently unrecorded One such battle is related by Gillespie, and we think it is only due to his memory that we should suffer him to narrate it with that Homeric

simplicity of style and self unconsciousness which distinguish his writings

"A person of the name of Grant, of public notoriety was carrying on this nefarious traffic to a great extent in defiance of every revenue officer He was, indeed, held in such glaring colour that it was difficult to find a revenue officer that would venture to approach him, as it was reported that he always carried with him arms, and besides was supported in his illicit practices by two sons of as desperate characters as their father It was on one of Mr G 's excursions that he met these banditti about two miles from Stonehaven, they having along with them a horse and cart loaded with contraband whisky He succeeded in making the seizure, but during the whole road leading into Stonehaven a continued battle was kept up While Mr G had down old Grant, the sons were immediately upon him, and struck him many a blow, and when near the town Grant made another furious attack upon him, but he still kept his ground, and succeeded in getting his antagonist down On this occasion Grant opened a large knife with his teeth while he held Mr G down by his neck-cloth, intending, no doubt, to inflict a deadly wound It was then Mr G was obliged to extricate himself by giving Grant a severe beating It will be observed that during these different scuffles Grant's sons were not unemployed, for while one of them was busy in assisting the father and inflicting blows on Mr G , the other was active in carrying away part of the whisky out of the cart Old Grant, finding it in vain to attempt any more resistance, endeavoured to frighten Mr G by mentioning that it would be for his interest to allow him to depart, as the contents belonged to a gentleman who would get him removed if he insisted on the seizure He, however, did not regard this threat, but lodged his seizure safe in custody Two days thereafter a court was held, and, contrary to law, only one Justice was present, who unthinkingly condemned the spirits, but restored the horse and cart to Grant, and found the Excise liable in expenses Against this judgment Mr G protested—first, because it required two Justices to make a quorum, and, secondly, against the injustice of the sentence Mr G had to conduct all this business himself, as the collector was necessarily engaged on business The case was transmitted to the Board, and their Honours caused a *sub pœna* to be served on Grant The issue of this case before the Court of Exchequer was that Grant was found liable in penalties to the extent of £150 sterling "

Having quelled illicit traffic in this locality, and

' become a complete terror to these depredators, Gillespie, still inflamed with zeal for the suppression of vice longed to go

L ke Alexander
To spread his conquests further.

He had learned that the inhabitants of the parish of Skene were peculiarly lax in their observance of Revenue morality, and he petitioned for a removal thither, so that he might convert them. A similar measure of success attended him there and his residence at Crombie Cottage was the great centre of anti-smuggling energy in that locality for the succeeding fifteen years. As this spot afterwards became the scene of those lawless deeds which finally brought Gillespie's life to a tragical termination, we may repeat some of his experiences there, so that his reputation in the neighbourhood may be accounted for. Lest the reader should accuse us of exaggeration, we shall again quote our hero's own words as they are found in his *Memoir*.

' The first engagement worthy of notice and which indeed Mr G will have reason to remember all his life, was with a gang of most notorious and determined delinquents two miles from his residence, towards the Highlands. In the month of August 1814, about ten o'clock at night, while he was on the look out, he discovered a horse and cart accompanied by four men viz:—George and John Downie, M'Hardie, and another. When Mr G approached them they instantly recognised him to be a revenue officer, on which they all fell upon him. They were armed with large bludgeons, and one had a large sheet of ash wood of considerable size. He had his face towards them and continued retreating backwards, merely on the defensive as it was impossible for one individual by himself to overpower four desperate men, who were determined to carry their point at the risk of their lives. Mr G, on the other hand, was resolved if possible not to relinquish his prize, consequently he suffered many severe blows and bruises, to the great effusion of his blood; and from a stick he received on his head he was so stunned that he fell, and one or two of those desperadoes above him, who still continued their blows. By hard struggling, however, Mr G got up, and although the blood was flowing copiously both from his eyes and nose, he made towards the cart a second time, and finding that something decisive must be attempted, he pulled out of his pocket a loaded pistol and wounded the horse to prevent their escape. Although he had it in his power, and indeed, was highly provoked to wound some of them during the scuffle, yet he commanded his temper, as he did on all similar occasions, and continued in a cool and determined resolution,

G

although he many times threatened them with immediate death, did not surrender. By this time the noise occasioned by the report of the pistol brought some people to the spot consequently Mr G got assistance, and secured the two Downies whom he prevailed on to accompany him home, as he did not wish to use them harshly, notwithstanding the great provocation he had received. After the horse and cart which contained 80 gallons of whisky, were safely carried for, he lodged the Downies all night in his own house until in the morning, had them secured by constables and at trials committed to Aberdeen Jail to stand the issue of a trial for the wounds and offences conducted on him. They were sentenced by the Court of Justiciary to 9 and 12 months imprisonment in the jail at Aberdeen. Mr G received great many external wounds in this fray besides the loss of blood, for of course one was the twice severely bruised inwardly. This beating he has even to this day [1826] never properly recovered the effects of, but he however succeeded in completely suppressing the traffic of the smuggling carried on by the Downies and has ever since become a terror to some of the most formidable of these characters through the Highlands of Aberdeenshire, &c.

The Waterloo Year.—1815—was appropriately signalised by several during feats on the part of Gillespie which ought to be immortalised. On one occasion he encountered three carts carrying about 100 gallons of contraband whisky along the Deeside road towards Aberdeen. They were escorted by ten or twelve men led by the Grants, and apparently prepared for opposition; and though Gillespie was alone and unarmed he ventured to stand forth and challenge them. Without deigning to reply, they at once rushed upon him with their cudgels and mauled him so seriously that he was obliged to retreat into a planting near by to save himself from being murdered, after he had suffered a great many wounds with sticks and stones. He however, was determined not to give up his chance and accordingly followed this gang for a short distance by the noise of the carts as, it being night he could not see them.

When they had travelled thus about four miles retreating from Aberdeen lest he should have assistance in that direction, they finally deposited their burden near the Hill of ... unconscious that his eagle eye was upon them. No sooner had he seen where the material was placed than ''he immediately despatched a messenger for two assistants [he omits to mention where the messenger came from], while he watched the movements of

these desperadoes It is almost needless to add
that he "succeeded in seizing the whole of the
cargo."

It was his fortune later in the same year to come
into contact again with the Grants, and once more
to defeat them The encounter took place at the
back of the hill at Auchrome, where the smugglers
were conveying four cartloads of ankers of spirits
to the interior of Aberdeenshire On this occasion
Gillespie was armed, and a desperate conflict ensued The horse which he rode suffered severely,
one of its eyes being knocked out, and the treatment it received making death imminent The
Grants assailed Gillespie with the stones which
they picked up on the roadside and had he not
very acutely warded off by the hilt of his sword a
large stone which was aimed at his head he is confident he would have been murdered by it He,
however, ultimately succeeded in seizing the horse
and part of the goods, as it was impossible he
could by himself have got the whole

During the year 1816 this intrepid officer had a
perfect succession of triumphs over his inveterate
foes the smugglers Early in that year he appointed a party of officers to meet him near Gar-
logie in the evening, as he expected some contraband traffic to pass that way Having arranged
that his assistants should bring along his arms, he
went himself unaccompanied and took up his station
near the rendezvous He had not waited long ere
he heard the noise of a scuffle on the road and
hastening out from his concealment he encountered
six horses bearing contraband spirits wandering

up the pathway without guide or leader The road
ran through a piece of marshy ground, and Gillespie succeeded in driving these animals into the
yielding bog, so that they might be fixed there
until he had gained assistance But the frost had
been severe and the soft ground had become
sufficiently hard for the horses to pass over without
sinking Gillespie managed, however, to mark
each of them under the mane *with his penknife*, so
that he might recognise them afterwards, and was
forced to suffer their owners to drive them off,
whilst he remained alone in concealment By and by
his own party came up seriously bruised and mal-
treated by the victorious smugglers and when
Gillespie had made provision for his men that their
wounds might be attended to, he set out in pursuit of the Grants raising the country as he went
that all might assist him The delinquents were
overtaken on the Deside road, and though they
had succeeded in making their escape he captured
their booty and their horses, and bore them off in
triumph

His former luck seemed to have followed him to
Skene, and he began to organise at Crombie Cottage a band of daring followers ready to aid him,
for a consideration, in the most romantic of his exploit The morals of these men would not perhaps bear a strict investigation, but they were true
to the Government of the Prince Regent, and
sworn foes of the smugglers; and with them Gillespie hoped to free that quarter of the kingdom
from the imputation of illicit traffic which had so
long rested upon it

INTERIOR OF CROMBIE COTTAGE

PART IV

*I note—When a man is servant shall play the cur with him
look you it goes hard   one that I brought up of a puppy
one that I saved from drowning when three or four of his
blind brothers and sisters went to it   I have taught him—
even as one would say precisely Thus I would teach a dog.*
—*Two Gentlemen of Verona*

Besides the band of hardy and resolute assistants whom Gillespie had gathered around him at Crombie Cottage he found it expedient to call in the aid of the lower animals to suppress the unholy traffic of these reckless smugglers   He procured a bull dog at considerable expense, which he trained specially for this purpose, and he soon found it invaluable in his most desperate encounters with his enemies   Indeed, this notable creature was almost the only being whom Gillespie suffered to share in the glory of his exploits   and he relates some marvellous tales regarding its sagacity

In the month of February 1816, whilst Gillespie was on his rounds, accompanied by his faithful dog, he discovered a gang of smugglers driving four horses loaded with spirits near Midmar Lodge   The exact number of the men is not stated, but they were led by a notorious character named Greig, with whom Gillespie had already made acquaintance   Though far from any hope of assistance from his own men he boldly attacked the smugglers, and his efforts were ably seconded by his canine follower   " A desperate engagement ensued between Mr G   and these delinquents in which a deal of bloodshed occurred on both sides and during the scuffle the dog was not idle   He seized the horses one by one till by tumbling some, and others by dancing, in consequence of the pain occasioned by the hold the dog had of them

by the nose the mkers were all thrown from their backs and scattered up and down so that Mr G secured the cargo remaining unstaved by their being violently thrown from the horses through the exertions of the dog

The records which Gillespie has left of the skill of this animal might well startle anyone who denies the possession of reason by other creatures than man   Never before perhaps, had there been a dog able to discriminate between *contraband* and *duty paid* whisky, and intelligent enough to know the smuggler's horse from the exciseman's   With one other story of its sagacity and its master's prowess we must conclude our extracts from this romancing Nestor

On the evening of the 30th July 1816, Mr G discovered a strong party approaching the Cot Town of Kintore from the Highlands on the Don side   He and his assistants concealed themselves in a gravel pit till the smugglers came forward   At this time Mr G had his dog, but his servant had him leading in a rope   On their near approach he discovered four horses loaded with contraband goods, and a party accompanying these of from eight to nine persons   He immediately sprung forward and required them to surrender   They seemed determined, however, to resist, and while part of the gang were engaged with him and his party, others of them were driving the horses off to the hills   Mr G   fired a pistol at one of the horses, but the shot went through one of the mkers of whisky , he immediately ordered his man to let loose the dog, whom he desired to seize the horse   The **animal immedi-**

ately did so, and the horse soon discharged the cargo off his back by his jumping and kicking At the desire of Mr G he seized them all, one by one, till everything was laid on the field as correctly as if it had been done by the hands of men In deed, he was so trained, that even when any of the horses were running past them that had no load on their back he paid no attention to them, but only to those that were loaded ; and when he seized them it was always by the nose, which he would never lose hold of until the goods were either thrown off or in the possession of his master The delinquents were in complete confusion, and ac cordingly made off in different directions The quantity seized on this occasion was from sixty to seventy gallons, thirty of which, however were lost by staving, &c From the situation of Mr G and his party, and the smugglers driving away their horses, it was impossible to have made the seizure complete had it not been for the dog in question ; and the place where this encounter happened exhibited the conclusion of a battle which might have done honour to a hero—ankers lying here and there, tartan plaids, blue bonnets and curricks (used on the horses' backs for carrying tne whisky) lay scattered up and down for nearly a mile round "

———

We have thought it expedient to make these somewhat lengthy extracts from Gillespie's *Memoir*, partly because they give a sketch of his life in a unique manner, but principally because the reader may be able to form from them some idea of the amount of credence which may be given to those other statements he made during and after his trial We need not weary the reader with more of these miraculous adventures, how ever, though we may explain that we have not chosen by any means the most wonderful episodes in his career The circumstances which brought about the necessity for his writing a sketch of his life require some explanation

To conduct the suppression of smuggling in a district so thoroughly demoralised as Skene was at this time, Gillespie found it necessary to main tain some four or five assistants constantly in his employment It may easily be supposed that these men were not of the highest moral character, since their occupation caused them to be at once feared and despised by the greater number of the inhabitants ; and the irregular life which they were forced to lead, and the temptations to excess thrown in their way would certainly not improve them That he might have them constantly at his command, their leader made extensive alterations upon Crombie Cottage so as to accommodate them ; and his frank and

jovial manner doubtless led him indiscreetly to join in their revels, and to hold those 'midnight orgies' regarding which traditions still linger in the locality One writer describes him as being obliged "to keep a multitude of retainers in his employ more like a baron of the Middle Ages than the peaceful denizen of this civilised country ' Upon the courage and daring of his men he must have been able to rely confidently ; for though we may doubt many of the tales he tells as to his cap tures of contraband material against fearful odds, we cannot escape the fact that he was looked upon throughout the country is one of the most active members of the Preventive Service

Yet despite this circumstance, the Board of Excise for some cause not now precisely ascertain able determined to remove him from Skene to a distant part of the country The *official* reason given was that it was desirable to make frequent changes in the separate ' Rides or districts into which the counties were divided lest the officers should become too familiar with the inhabitants of the localities, and connive at their fraudulent dealing But it is more probable that rumours of Gillespie's mode of life had reached the Board from some unfriendly hand, and it was easier to remove him arbitrarily than to institute an inquiry This, at least, is certain that information reached him about the month of July 1826, that he was soon to be removed from the Skene district, which he had watched over for more than twelve years with unequalled success

The news came upon him like a thunderbolt. The style in which he had lately been living had plunged him deeply into debt he had a large family dependent upon him ; and his lease of Crombie Cottage had still twenty six years to run and could not be cancelled without severe loss He had already, according to his own statement expended nearly £1000 upon building and im proving of waste land, which would be utterly lost were he now removed The men whom he em ployed were engaged by the year, and he would be forced to pay them their salaries without having any work for them to perform On every hand ruin stared him in the face unless he could continue his appointment and remain at his old quarters A petition to the Board, if backed with strong re commendations, might induce them to reverse their decision, and he set at once about its prepa ration In this document—a copy of which lies before us as we write—he confesses that he is £400 in debt attributing this deficit to the great expense which he had incurred not only in keeping up his establishment of assistants, but also in paying large sums to informants He suggests that, instead of removing him from Skene, the Board should appoint him General Surveyor on the Coast and Interior of the Country, a new office for which he was pre-eminently qualified, and which would not require a change of residence on his part. Appended to the petition was an Abstract of the Seizures he had made whilst in the service, and if his figures are reliable, Aberdeenshire seems to have been in a hopeless state of moral turpitude. During his residence in Skene he had destroyed within that parish alone, "630 stills, 500 gallons aqua, and 60,000 gallons wash, besides seizing 5750 gallons of British and 291 gallons of foreign spirits, with 92 horses and 33 carts." To accompany this marvellous statement he wrote that curious *Memo*, portions of which we have had before the reader, and which he thus concludes:—

'This is but a faint outline of a few of the many severe encounters Mr G. has had in his exertions to suppress the alarming and extensive operations of a dangerous and lawless set of men carrying on an illicit trade, ruinous to the revenue and most destructive to the fair trader, and danger which however he has been the means of driving from the country, a great part of these desperate delinquents, by which he has ruined his constitution, and labours otherwise under much bodily infirmity. He has no less than forty two wounds on different parts of his body, and all inflicted by these extraordinary characters while he was employed in the execution of his duty as before mentioned; nor what is more remarkable, was Mr G. ever in one single instance, completely defeated in all the different engagements he had with the smuggler, having always in the end ultimately succeeded in making the seizure, or defeating the object of the delinquent.

Still further to support his claims upon the kind consideration of the Board he procured letters of recommendation from several of the leading noble men in the northern counties, and the tone in which these are written almost compels us to grant some degree of truthfulness to his narrative, since it is unlikely that a mere pretender could impose successfully upon such men as the Hon. W. Gordon, M.P. for the County of Aberdeen, the Right Hon. Viscount Arbuthnot, Sir Alexander Keith, Knight Marischal of Scotland, and the Hon. General Duff, M.P. for the Elgin District of Burghs, and brother of the Earl Fife. All these noblemen write in eulogistic terms of Gillespie's achievements and character and speak as from personal knowledge of his capacities.

Though the petition even when thus supported might not have been powerful enough to cause the Board absolutely to reverse the decision as to Gillespie's removal, it had at least the effect of delaying its execution. Possibly two petitions from distillers and Justices of the Peace in Aberdeenshire praying for his continuance had considerable influence in bringing about this result, and no further steps were taken for his removal in 1826. The sentence of transference, however, which had been pronounced against him was not yet withdrawn, and the later months of that year must have left him in a very unsettled state.

Many things conspired at this time to make him uneasy. He had striven to tide over his monetary difficulties by placing a number of accommodation bills in circulation, and his own safety required that these should be taken up if his credit were not to be wholly destroyed. Several of the names upon these bills were really worthless, since the quasi acceptors were men of straw who could not possibly have retired them. It was necessary, therefore, that Gillespie should remain in the district of Skene, where his share in the produce of seized spirits might greatly augment his income, as his removal would bring ruin upon many innocent friends, who had generously offered to aid him. He stood on the verge of a volcano.

BLACKHILLS THE RESIDENCE OF MR ALEX SMITH

PART V

We ll mak our maut we ll brew our drink
We ll dance and sing and re joice man
And mo ny braw thanks to the m kl bo es a al
That danced aw i wi the exciseman.

—Pitt

At the close of the year 1826 Crombie Cottage was inhabited by four men and two women, besides Gillespie and his "numerous family of young children, the greater part of whom were females His assistants were George Browne, William Jenkins, John Edwards, an old sailor and his brother George Skene Edwards who acted as a kind of clerk for Gillespie The women were Alexandrina Campbell, who had been in his service during all his twelve years' residence at Skene, and Jessy Greig, who was head of the establishment for two years The "numerous family" which Gillespie flaunted before the faces of the Board of Excise consisted so far as we have been able to discover, of two girls named Mary and May Gillespie, and their devotion to their father's interest seems to have been very thorough Indeed, the whole of the happy family at Crombie Cottage appear to have been actuated by an unselfish desire to make matters easy for the master, in defiance of the Decalogue The reck

lessness of his followers may be discovered from his own admission that "G S Edwards and his brother John were both banished the counties they last came from The simple confiding faith of Gillespie in these reprobates exceeds belief If his statements are true, he was the most pliable and injured of men , if false, the most deceiving and hypocritical It must be understood that in relating his story we have taken what seems the most reasonable version of that strange career, selecting its items from the evidence of those in immediate contact with him during this dangerous time

The transaction of monetary affairs was usually entrusted to George Skene Edwards , for though Jessy Greig latterly acted as clerk, and kept note of Gillespie s bills Edwards met the acceptors and procured their signatures An aged farmer in the neighbourhood—Mr Alex Smith of Blackhills—had taken a sudden interest in Gillespie, and had come forward to assist him when his finances were at low ebb His reasons for doing so are not very clear but it is probable that he expected to reap some monetary advantage from the misfortunes of the gauger It is certain that he wrote

to the manager of the Aberdeen Town and County
Bank in Aberdeen asking him to discount any bills
bearing his endorsation which Gillespie might
present, and as he was a man of means this request
was complied with. In a very short time a large
number of these accommodation bills were put in
circulation, having been presented by Gillespie
who received the proceeds and applied them to his
own purposes. In the early part of the year
1827 there were no less than twenty two of these
bills on the circuit, representing a sum amounting
to £554 10s. They were invariably drawn in Gillespie's name, and generally upon three or four
persons who accepted the bills "conjunctly and
severally," and the bank manager seems to have
had no hesitation in discounting them when they
bore the endorsation of Mr A Smith of Blackhills.
Gillespie made an arrangement with the bank
that notices of these bills falling due should be sent
to him instead of to the acceptors, and as long as
this plan was followed they were regularly retired
and handed over by Gillespie to Smith of Black
hills.

This plan of "raising the wind" was successfully carried on for some time, but at length a
fatal slip was made which exposed the whole transaction. One of the bill notices had by mistake
been sent to the apparent acceptor, as in the regular course of business it would have been. And this
man denied all knowledge of the bill, protesting
that he had never signed it. The important
document was in these terms —

        "Crombie Cottage Shore 9 July 1826
£38   10s st,

    "Nine months after date pay me or order with-
in the Bank office, Aberdeen the sum of thirty
eight pounds ten shillings sterling for value received off   "M Gillespie

"To Messrs Joseph Low, Farmer,
    Bogfurley   John Lawson
    Farmer, Kirimundu,   the
    Troup, Farmer, Longcairn
    and John Troup, Blackhall all
    in Newhills, conjunctly and
    severally"

Joseph Low described as a farmer was nearly
a crofter at Bogfurley and as he could neither
read nor write it was manifestly impossible that
he could have admitted his name to this paper.
When the bank notice reached him by post he
kept it till his son came home on the following
Sunday, and then learned for the first time what
its meaning really was. He repudiated the transaction at once and soon spread the matter
throughout the district. As Bogfurley was only
about three miles from Crombie Cottage, Gillespie

was not long in receiving word of Low's action
and he went down to the place, accompanied by
George Brownie, one of his own men, and
besought Low to own that he had signed the
bill. But the crofter was obdurate, and refused to admit the doubtful signature. It was
suggested to him that he had signed the paper
when drunk and forgotten about it, but he
stoutly denied the allegation. A second attempt
was made to persuade him to "tak wi it," but
without effect and at length he received the
following strangely worded letter from Gillespie.
The reader will notice the marked difference between the style in which it is written and that of
the *Memoir* from which we have quoted —

'   Crombie Cottage, 25th April 1827

Dear Sir —I was very sorry to hear this day
that you had neglected that you signed an
accommodation Bill to me along with a few
friends which bill you had no value for
or me, but nearly to turn my mind
with some pressing things at the time, the Bill was
cashed in the Town and County Bank, and
uplifted by the Laird of Blackhills and me and
you got no trouble about it—although you had a
glass extry at the time you obliged me with your
name, and might have forgot. Yet your wife must
recollect of the circumstance, as I told her about
it, which I have been as good as my word. Begs,
therefore, you will be so good as ask your wife regarding this, and Oblige, Sir yours, &c,

            "M GILLESPIE "

The importunity of Gillespie failed to move
Low and he adhered unflinchingly to his
statement that he knew nothing about the
bill. The affair now assumed a serious
aspect for the gauger. The Board of Excise
had issued strict rules prohibiting their servants
from having any dealings in the way of business
with those in their neighbourhood, but as it was
known that Gillespie had seized whisky in
Low's possession the fact of his holding a bill
from the latter could not be looked upon as other
than a suspicious circumstance. Thus even if the
signature were genuine, Gillespie's situation was
in danger, while his credit at the bank was im-
perilled and the other bills in circulation
depreciated in value. In this crisis he had re-
course to his steadfast friend Mr Smith of Black
hills.

A curious transaction had taken place between
them but a short time previous to this period.
Gillespie had insured his furniture at Crombie
Cottage with two Life Insurance Offices in London
for what seems the extravagant sum of £830—in
the Palladium Life and Fire Assurance Society to

the amount of £530, and 1 in the Phœnix Assurance Society for £300—and on the 21st February 1827, while he was away on business at Edinburgh, his tenant opportunely took fire, and was partially destroyed. A charge of arson was afterwards raised against some of his servants in consequence, but that need not at present concern us. We have only to notice that the occurrence of the fire at this time put Gillespie in apparent possession of a very large sum of money. On the 23d March he assigned these two policies to Mr Smith, and received the following rather strange letter in acknowledgment thereof:—

'Aberdeen, 23d March 1827.

'Sir,—As you have of this date granted an assignation in my favour, in security of the debt owing by you to me on the Phœnix and Palladium Fire Offices, London, to the extent of Eight Hundred and Thirty Pounds Sterling, as due by them to you, I hereby become bound to hold accounting with you on receiving said sum, or whatever part thereof I may receive in making up a statement of accounts between us.

'It being understood that I am to retire all the Bills in the Banks in Aberdeen which I have signed on your behalf, preceding this date; and that I am to retain the same, so as I may place them to your credit in accounting with you, but still I am at liberty to do Diligence thereon if necessary; and declaring that the sum I am to retire shall not exceed four hundred and fifty pounds sterling.

'Although eight hundred and thirty pounds sterling is stated as due by you to me, it is not to be understood that my claims against you are limited to that amount.

'I am, Sir,
'Your obedient servant,
'ALEX. SMITH.

'To Mr Gillespie Skene.'

In consequence of this arrangement Smith retired Gillespie's bills, and amongst others the document said to have been accepted by Joseph Low. Besides the provision thus made for retiring the bills in circulation, Gillespie resigned the whole of his furniture, together with his lease of the lands of Cromme Cottage, into Mr Smith's hands, obtaining a back letter acknowledging that Smith agreed to account to him for the further sum of £450. The interests of Smith were thus amply secured provided the Assurance Societies did not dispute the claim upon the policies.

The laird of Blackhills was at this time nearly ninety years of age, and said to be somewhat deficient in memory; and his young wife—barely twenty years old—was naturally annoyed to see so

much of her husband's money paid out to clear Gillespie's debts, as she supposed, without any protection. She arranged a meeting between her husband, Gillespie himself, and an uncle of hers to consult on this matter, and in the course of conversation she said that if Gillespie would not retire the bills himself she would give information about them to the Procurator-Fiscal. He implored her not to do so; but she carried out her threat shortly afterwards by placing several of these doubtful bills in the hands of the authorities. A very brief examination showed that many of the names they bore were manifest forgeries, and Gillespie and his clerk, G. Skene Edwards, were apprehended and thrown into prison on a charge of forging and uttering false bank bills.

In his first declaration dated April 30th, 1827, Gillespie avers that the bill, value £38 10s, on Joseph Low and others, was signed by him as drawn and discounted by him for his own accommodation; that he did not see the acceptors sign; that he desired George Skene Edwards to get some of his (Gillespie's) acquaintances to sign the bill, *without telling Edwards to whom he was to apply*; and that Edwards brought the bill back to him, signed by Low, Lawson, Alexander Troup, and John Troup. He also admitted that he had written the letter we have quoted to Low.

His second declaration, dated May 6th, 1827, gave a different version of the affair. In it he stated that before Edwards went to get the bill £38 10s, signed by Low and the others, *he gave him a note in writing of these persons' names*, as the persons to be applied to. Edwards returned all the bills to him as having been regularly signed by the acceptors. It was pointed out that two of the bills bore the names of men who were dead at the date of the acceptance, but he explained that *Edwards must have made a mistake* as to the Christian names of these men.

Edwards in his two declarations professed total ignorance as to how the signatures to the bills had been procured. He had written out the bills and addressed them by Gillespie's orders, but had always left them unsigned, nor was he sent to the parties to procure their signatures. He knew nothing about the way these names were adhibited, except that he had seen Gillespie forging bills, and had found fault with him for doing so. As these declarations directly contradicted each other, and by no means exculpated the accused, Gillespie and Skene Edwards were both remitted for trial to the ensuing Circuit Court at Aberdeen.

At this time, and for long afterwards, the penalty denounced for forging bank bills was capital punishment. Sir Samuel Romilly, the first law reformer who effected any mitigation of the severity of our criminal laws, had suggested an alteration with reference to forgery, but his ideas in this respect were too far in advance of his time, and he died long before this reform was accomplished. Even the eloquent voice of Sir James Mackintosh though raised repeatedly in the House of Commons on this subject, did little towards a thorough reform; and the first step in that direction was not made until after Gillespie's trial. In 1830 Sir Robert Peel carried a Bill consolidating the laws against forgery —11 Geo IV, and 1 Will IV cap 66—by which the punishment of death was limited to forgeries of the most serious kind. This law gave little satisfaction for even the bankers who were likely to be most affected by this crime, confessed in their petitions against the Bill that the extreme penalty rather increased than repressed forgery. At length in 1861 an Act was passed—24 and 25 Vic cap 95, sec 1—repealing a portion of the Act of 1830,

and enacting that forgery should be punished with "Penal Servitude for life, or for any term not less than Three years, or to be imprisoned for any term not exceeding Two years with or without Hard Labour, and with or without Solitary Confinement." This is the present state of the law in this matter.

It will thus be evident that the trial of Gillespie and Edwards for forgery in 1827 was a much more serious affair than it could now become. It involved the lives of those two men and even escape from punishment would mean total ruin and degradation for one at least of the accused. The prominent position which Gillespie had occupied, and the many enemies he had made by his strict enforcement of his preventive power made the approaching trial one of great interest to the whole neighbourhood of Skene and Aberdeen, and many of those who had suffered at his hands openly rejoiced at his melancholy situation.

SKENE CHURCH—GRAVE OF GILLESPIE (*Marked* *)

PART VI

Thus men go wrong with an ingenious skill
Bend the straight rule to their own crooked will
And with a clear and shining lamp supplied
First put it out, then take it for a guide
Halting on crutches of unequal size
One leg by truth supported one by lies
They sidle to the goal with awkward pace,
Secure of nothing—but to lose the race.
                                        — *Cowper*

Gillespie and Edwards were brought up for trial at the Circuit Court held at Aberdeen on 26th September 1827. They had already been five months in prison, and the case against them had been carefully prepared, but as the Court was pre-

sided over by Lord Pitmilly and Lord Alloway—
two of the calmest and most cautious Judges on the
Bench—they were sure of obtaining substantial
justice. The Council for the Crown were Archibald Alison, Advocate Depute — afterwards
well known as the Sheriff of Lanarkshire,
and author of 'The History of Europe' —
and the Hon. Alexander Leslie Melville, advocate.
Gillespie was defended by Alex M'Neill and
Charles M'Dougall, advocates, and the counsel for
Edwards were Charles (afterwards Lord) Neaves
and William Dauney, advocates. Three indictments had been prepared and served upon the prisoners, accusing them of forging and fabricating as
well as using and uttering certain bills or notes,
specified accurately in each indictment. The first
of these accusations included eight bills bearing
twenty-five forged names, the second embraced
seven bills with twenty-three false signatures and
the third gave details of seven other bills with
twenty alleged forgeries, making in all twenty-two
bills bearing sixty-eight separate acts of forgery.
The total sum of money thus procured amounted
to £554 10s. Both prisoners pled Not guilty,
and as the relevancy of the first indictment was
maintained the jury was empannelled and the case
went to trial. The eight bills specified in this indictment amounted to the sum of £230 16s.

The prosecution was conducted very ably by Mr
Alison, but the evidence need not be exactly detailed. Mr Simpson, Procurator Fiscal, had confronted the prisoners with all the alleged acceptors
of the bills—with the exception of the two who
were dead—and Gillespie had averred that
they were the men who had signed these
papers. Ample evidence was brought to show
that Gillespie had himself received the proceeds of
the bills, and that they were not retired by the
quasi acceptors. One by one the latter were
brought into the witness-box, and all with unvarying uniformity, declared that they knew nothing about these bills, and had never signed them.
Some of them admitted that they had signed bills
previously to oblige Gillespie, but utterly repudiated those in the indictment. During the course
of the examination of these witnesses, the lines of
defence adopted by the prisoners' advocates came
into collision, and it was soon apparent that both
men could not be saved. Mr M'Neill, in defending
Gillespie, asserted that all the signatures had been
forged by Skene Edwards, whilst Mr Neaves
maintained that nothing brought out by Mr
M'Neill's cross-examination should be allowed to
prejudice his client. The difficulty was thus cast
upon the jury of discriminating exactly betwixt
the evidence relevant only to each case.

For some reason which we cannot discover, one
important witness—Mr Alex Smith of Blackhills
—was not summoned at all, nor were the two
"Back letters" which he had granted to
Gillespie put into the process, though they
would have served to explain some of the darker
parts of the case. Mrs Smith, however, was examined as well as her uncle John Smith of Lister
Ord, and they both testified to the terror that
Gillespie displayed lest the Fiscal should hear of
the bills which were in the hands of Smith of
Blackhills. The postmaster at Upper Banchory
identified George Browne, Gillespie's servant, as
the man who had obtained a letter from him
addressed to one of the acceptors of a bill, and
which contained a bank notice regarding it, and
Browne himself admitted that he had done so. At
this time Browne was in custody upon the charge
of fire-raising at Crombie Cottage and his evidence cannot be taken as of much weight, yet he
distinctly charged George Skene Edwards with
having several times put down other folks' names
to bills. The declarations of the prisoners were
read and this closed the case for the Crown.

The exculpatory evidence was of a most dubious
kind. Two engravers from Edinburgh deposed
that they had examined the bills before coming into
Court, and were of opinion that all the forged
names were in the handwriting of G. S. Edwards.
The only other witnesses were Jessy Greig and
Alexandrina Campbell who were both in prison
on the charge of the arson at Crombie Cottage.
The grave doubts which had already been cast
upon the morality of their relations with Gillespie
must have seriously affected their credibility, and
though they both testified that Edwards had
forged the bills libelled in their presence, the Court
did not seem inclined to receive their evidence at
all. Campbell declared that she had seen Edwards
repeatedly signing bills for other people, and that
the method he took was to place a genuine signature on the window pane, put the bill over it, and
trace the letters in this fashion. No evidence
whatever was adduced in defence of Edwards.

Mr Alison carefully analysed the criminatory
evidence in his speech for the prosecution, pointing out that the names on the bills were undoubtedly forged; that they had been uttered by
Gillespie though he knew that they were not
genuine, and that he was thus a participator in
the crime even though he was not the actual
forger. No part of the proceeds of these bills had
gone to Edwards, and there was therefore no adequate motive to account for his committing such
a crime without Gillespie's knowledge. The only
reason for such conduct on his part that had been
suggested was that Edwards was too lazy to go
round to the parties named as acceptors by Gil-

lespie to procure their signatures, and had written these himself without informing his master, but was it credible that this man would not only risk his own life, but that of his employer, to save him self so slight a trouble? It was proved, however, that he had drawn out the bills, and, in some in stances, had signed them for other parties without their consent, and had afterwards allowed them to go into the hands of Gillespie, knowing them to be forged. He was thus distinctly implicated in the forgery, and it was impossible to hold him guiltless.

Nothing could be clearer than Gillespie's connec tion with this crime. He had confessed that he concocted the bills, that they were for his accom modation solely, and that he believed the acceptors had adhibited their names willingly so as to oblige him. Yet when a bank notice regarding one of them is sent out a fortnight before it falls due, and he hears of this, he sends at once to intercept the letter lest it should fall into the acceptor's hands. If the signature were genuine he need not have troubled himself to do this—if he even believed it to be genuine he would not have done it, but his action distinctly implied that he knew the signature to be false, and dreaded the exposure of his crime. That he knew the dangerous position in which he stood was shown by his conduct upon several occasions. When Gillespie was urging Low to take with the signing of the bill, he said "it would save him from the rope" if he would do so, when Mrs Smith threatened to inform the authorities about the bills, he said "he might as well blow out his brains as let the matter reach the Fiscal," and when he was first apprehended, he said to Fyfe, the messenger, "I m a gone man!" and asked to be allowed to escape till the matter was settled. These ex pressions plainly implied that he had a guilty know ledge of his turpitude. Mr Alison concluded by asking for a verdict of guilty against Edwards as actor of forging the bills, and guilty art and part of uttering, and of guilty against Gillespie as actor, of uttering, and guilty art and part of the forgeries, all as libelled.

Mr M'Neill, in his eloquent address on behalf of Gillespie, made strenuous efforts to fix the crime solely upon Edwards, and endeavoured to exonerate his client by a skilful course of special pleading. But his case was essentially weak, and he had not been able to adduce witnesses to give it even the semblance of truth. Mr Neaves was not more successful in his attempts to clear Edwards of the crime charged against him, and he had the double task of combating both the prosecutor and the counsel for his client's fellow-prisoner. He admitted that the bills libelled were forged, and that they were dis

counted, but he denied that any credible evidence had been led to show that Edwards had done more than write the body of each bill. These bills were drawn out by Edwards by order of his master Gillespie, and he knew nothing more of them— either as to their acceptance or discounting— afterwards. That he should be held responsible for these bills because he had written out the formal part of them was an absurd doctrine. The concluding portion of his speech was the most effective. He said:— "When the public pro secutor brings two prisoners to the bar, and attempts to prove that it was one or other who committed the crime that will not answer. He is not entitled to place you, gentlemen of the jury, in such a dilemma—he is not entitled in this way to leave you to grope in the dark, and if you are not certain of laying your hand on the guilty man, you must allow both to escape. I maintain that my client is innocent, and my client's innocence is perfectly compatible with the guilt of the other prisoner."

The case was summed up by Lord Alloway[*] in a plain and common sense fashion which fully justified Lord Cockburn's estimate of his character as "an excellent and most useful man, kind in private life, and honest in the discharge of his public duties, without learning or talent, and awkward in expressing himself either orally or in writing, he was a good practical lawyer and re markably knowing in the management of the common business of life, and having more sense and modesty than to aim at objects he could not reach, experience and industry gave him no com petitor within this not very high, but most useful range." In his summing up Lord Alloway re viewed the evidence very skilfully, yet in a manner thoroughly intelligible to an ordinary jury. He pointed out that there never was a case of forgery in which the evidence on this point was more com plete. The forgeries could not have been com mitted except by one or other of the prisoners, or perhaps by both. Gillespie had discounted the bills, and received the whole of the proceeds, and had contradicted himself in his two statements with reference to his knowledge of the acceptors. As to the names upon the bills, it was shown that two of the persons were dead, and a third could not write, so that forgery must have been resorted to ere their names could have appeared. It had been urged that Gillespie had no motive to adhibit these names, since the Bank would have discounted the bills upon Mr Smith's endorsation, but the jury must consider whether Mr Smith had not been induced to endorse the bills by seeing the

---

[*] David Cathcart, Lord Alloway, died in 1829.

signatures of apparent acceptors The evidence for the defence he considered entitled to no regard, as it could not overturn the indirect evidence afforded by other points in the case He distinctly expressed his own opinion, though he said it was ' contrary to his usual practice to do so,' that both prisoners were guilty of the charges libelled against them

The jury retired about one o'clock in the morning to agree upon a verdict The Court sat for three quarters of an hour afterwards, but as the jury had not then made up their verdict, the Court was adjourned When it reassembled on the following morning, a written verdict was given in by the Chancellor of the jury, Mr Knowles of Kirkville It was read amidst profound silence, and was in these terms —The jury, ' having considered the criminal libel raised and pursued, at the instance of His Majesty's Advocate for His Majesty's interest, against Malcolm Gillespie and George Skene Edwards, pannels, the interlocutor of relevancy thereon pronounced by the Court, the evidence adduced in support of the libel and the evidence in exculpation, they, by a plurality of voices find Malcolm Gillespie guilty of the crimes of forgery and uttering, actor or art and part, of the first, second, third, fourth, sixth, seventh, and eighth charges libelled †, and George Skene Edwards guilty of the crime of forgery, actor or art and part, of the first, second, third, fourth, sixth, seventh, and eighth charges libelled

Mr M'Neill, on the part of Gillespie, objected to the verdict, as its grammatical construction rendered it nonsense, the strict interpretation being that the panel was guilty of *forging* and *uttering* the *charges* libelled, but the objection was overruled Mr Neaves on the part of Edwards, also moved an arrest of judgment stating that his client had not been found guilty of *uttering*, but only of *forging* the bills though it was necessary that the latter should follow the former so as to constitute a crime This objection seemed plausible, and their Lordships certified the case to the High Court of Justiciary for the opinion of their brethren Mr Allison then moved for judgment against Gillespie

Lord Pitmilly, whose simple and impressive eloquence upon solemn occasions gave his words great weight, addressed his brother judge in these terms — ' My Lord Alloway, the duty which it now remains for us to discharge towards the prisoner at the bar is at all times a distressing duty, but I must say that I perform it in the present instance with feelings more than usually painful I do not at this moment forget the

various occasions on which I have seen that unhappy man in this Court in a very different situation from that in which he is now placed, and that on these occasions I have had to express my approbation of his zeal and activity as an Officer of Revenue The recollection of these things has not been absent from my mind a single moment since this trial commenced, and I could scarcely make myself believe that so sad a reverse had taken place However, I listened to the evidence which has been led, I listened to it with the greatest attention, and certainly I could come to no other conclusion than that at which the plurality of the jury have arrived The evidence is clear and satisfactory, and it rests with us to pronounce sentence on the verdict I need not state to your Lordship nor to the unhappy man before us that we have no alternative in regard to the sentence to be awarded We are merely the organs of the law No choice is left to us We have no power to do anything else than to award the punishment which the law attaches to the offence '

Lord Alloway, putting on his hat then addressed the prisoner pointing out that he had been "found guilty of one of the highest crimes which can be committed in a great commercial country ' He was a man possessed of talents which might have raised him to an eminent place amongst his contemporaries ' But sir he said, " your fate will be a warning to the present generation Your case will show them that persons must not trust to talents, however great, to save them from conviction Sooner or later punishment will overtake the guilty The sentence upon Gillespie was then read —

" In respect of the foregoing verdict, the Lords Pitmilly and Alloway decern and adjudge the said Malcolm Gillespie, panel to be carried from the bar back to the Tolbooth of Aberdeen, therein to be detained till Friday, the 16th day of November next to come, and upon that day between the hours of two and four o'clock afternoon to be taken from the said Tolbooth to the common place of execution in Aberdeen, and there, by the hands of the common executioner, to be hanged by the neck upon a gibbet until he be dead, and ordain his whole moveable goods and gear to be escheat and inbrought for his Majesty's use, which is pronounced for doom "

The devotion and zeal which Gillespie had shown to the interests of the Government led many of his friends in Aberdeen, as well as himself, to expect a mitigation of this severe sentence, but the weeks flew away without bringing any prospect of release, and on the Tuesday preceding his execution he abandoned all hope of reprieve He then be

---

† The fifth charge was abandoned by the Advocate Depute The jury divided 14 to 1

gan to draw up in writing what he called 'The Dying Declaration of Malcolm Gillespie'—a lengthy document in which he endeavours to criminate Edwards, who was still unsentenced and seeks to explain away his own guilt by several specious arguments which cannot now be accepted as tenable. We fear that the romancing vein which had been developed by him a short time before when preparing his *Memoir*, was still rampant within him, and his dying declaration is as mendacious as the record of his life. It is with regret that we have reached this conclusion since we know that he uttered his declaration whilst on his way to the scaffold, protesting that 'he would not die with a lie in his mouth,' and 'solemnly declaring, as a dying man that he was innocent of the crime for which he suffered.' We have laid the evidence fairly before the reader; let him judge.

The execution took place in accordance with custom, before the old Tolbooth of Aberdeen, and the culprit to verify an old saying in the city was made to 'look down Marischal Street.' The crowd assembled before the scaffold, we fear, would contain many who had suffered at the hands of the rigorous exciseman, and execrated his incorruptible devotion to duty. His body was committed to the care of his relatives, and buried in the churchyard of Skene. Even yet the tradition of the locality asserts that his grave mound is rising instead of falling, as successive winters pass over it, and the spot is known by report to the youngest villager as the burial place of the 'Gauger of Skene.'

We must now dismiss briefly the minor characters in this strange life drama. George Brownie and Alexandrina Campbell were tried at the same Circuit at Aberdeen for wilful fire raising at Crombie Cottage, and after evidence was led to show that deliberate means had been taken to ensure the destruction of the cottage, the panel's counsel interrupted the examination of the witnesses by proffering a plea of guilty of fire raising without intent to defraud the Insurance Companies, in short, that they acted according to their master's orders in setting the house on fire, but they knew nothing of his views or reasons for wishing it done. This plea was accepted by the Advocate Depute, and sentence of seven years transportation was pronounced against them.

The case of Edwards had been certified to the High Court of Justiciary, and when he was finally brought up there for examination he pleaded Guilty, and was sentenced to banishment for life. The *quondam* inhabitants of Crombie Cottage were thus dispersed throughout the world.

To analyse and explain the development of such a mind as that of Gillespie would be a most delicate task. There are some minds to whom deceit is so habitual that it becomes part of their nature, and a defect in their moral character makes them unconscious of this failing, and incapable of appreciating truth. Such, we fear, was Gillespie and the end of his life shows the danger into which a talented man may be led if careless of his moral conduct.

CLYDE STREET, ANDERSTON—(*SCENE OF SMITH'S MURDER)

THE GLASGOW COTTON-SPINNERS—A TRADES UNION TRAGEDY

PART I

Quel fut ce tribunal abominable institué par Charlemagne en Westphalie, tribunal de sang appelé le Conseil Veimique tribunal plus horrible même l'Inquisition tribunal composé d'un juges inconnus, qui jugeaient à mort sur le simple rapport de ses espions?

What became of that abominable tribunal instituted by Charlemagne in Westphalia, that bloody tribunal called the Vehmic Council, more horrible than the Inquisition composed of unknown judges who condemned to death on the simple charge of their spies?—*Voltaire—Dictionnaire*

On Tuesday, the 25th of July 1837, the inhabitants of Glasgow were startled by the appearance of a placard posted upon the most prominent positions in the busiest thoroughfares of the city, intimating that a brutal murder had been perpetrated before midnight on the preceding Saturday. The crime had been committed in the throng of a crowded street upon the person of an unresisting member of the working class, and was marked by all that treachery of purpose and cowardliness of action which we are accustomed to consider as foreign to the Scottish character. The placard to which we refer was issued in the form of a proclamation by the Magistrates, and was printed at the office of Peter Mackenzie, the well known editor of the *Loyal Reformer's Gazette* It was couched in these terms:—

"ATROCIOUS MURDER

"WHEREAS, on the night of Saturday last, the 22d July current, between the hours of 11 and 12 o'clock, John Smith, cotton spinner, while peaceably passing along Clyde Street, Anderston, with his wife, on his return to his dwelling house, was wickedly and maliciously FIRED at by an ASSASSIN, armed with a pistol, two balls of which entered the body of the said John Smith, and he immediately fell, MORTALLY WOUNDED, and is since dead

"AND WHEREAS, there is reason to believe that this MURDEROUS ASSAULT has been committed by one or other of the *Turn out Cotton spinners* And the master cotton spinners of Glasgow being determined to use every means in their power to bring to condign punishment the perpetrator of this cold blooded murder, hereby offer

"A REWARD OF £500

to any person or persons who will give such in formation to George Salmond, Esq., Procurator Fiscal, as will lead to the apprehension and conviction of the guilty party or his associates.

"P. Mackenzie & Co., Printers.

"Glasgow, 24th July 1837."

The unfortunate man, whose life had been prematurely cut short in this cowardly fashion was a native of Ireland about fifty years of age, and had been employed in the factory of Messrs Houldsworth & Sons as a cotton spinner about four years before his death. In the April preceding his assassination a serious strike had taken place amongst the cotton spinners of Glasgow in consequence of a proposed reduction in their wages by the masters, and as their Trades Union was then very powerful all the spinners in Glasgow left their work so as to compel their employers to accede to their demands. For a long time this pressure on the part of the workmen was ineffectual, and as the managers of the Union had large sums of money at their disposal, they succeeded in keeping up the opposition vigorously for some time by giving large weekly allowances to the idle operatives. There were about 800 spinners in Glasgow, and it soon became evident that the resistance of the master spinners would rapidly exhaust the Trades Union treasury. To obviate this difficulty the allowances were gradually reduced until they reached the starvation point of eighteenpence a week, and then the strike suddenly collapsed, and the spinners were glad to obtain work to keep them from absolute penury. But meanwhile the Trades Unionists, driven to desperation by their bankrupt condition, began to adopt violent measures of intimidation both towards employers and spinners, that they might drive the former into an unwilling compliance with their demands. Incendiaries were despatched by the leaders of the Union throughout the city to fire the mills and to attack the overseers houses, to terrify the women and maltreat the men who dared to take work in the factories under strike without the permission of the autocrats of this trade, though it were to save their families from absolute want and privation. The climax was reached, however, when these reckless men sent hired assassins through the streets of Glasgow, to shoot down in cold blood the wretched imbeciles who had dared to be independent, and had taken work from the employers whom the Unionists had denounced.

Amongst their victims was this hapless Irishman, John Smith. About a month after the strike had begun he had been offered some of the empty wheels in Houldsworth's factory, and impelled doubtlessly by want, he had professed his willingness to work for his subsistence, and had accepted the proffered boon. He entered upon the working of wheels in the factory which had been abandoned by a Unionist, and from that moment he was a marked man. No one molested him, no one warned him of his danger, but "the old hands passed him without speaking," there was the averted head, the scowling look, the frigid silence which too plainly tell the thoughts that the tongue may never utter. For about two months he led this irksome life, oppressed by a weight of indefinable foreboding, shunned by his former companions, occasionally jeered at by the idle spinners who loafed like evil spirits around the gate where they were wont to enter, yet never actually injured by upraised arm or threatening hand, whilst he was still spared to earn his living. But at last the end came, and while he was calmly returning to his home, thinking no evil —as old indictments phrase it—he was ruthlessly shot down like a cur in the streets by a cowardly ruffian who had dogged his steps and lurked behind him, biding his time.

Who were the authors of this outrage, and what was their object? These were the questions with which the citizens of Glasgow were confronted when they read the startling proclamation. No crime worthy of death could be laid to Smith's charge, for his life, so far as we can discover, was blameless, and he had been pistolled by the side of that wife who showed long afterwards how tenderly she dwelt upon the memory of him. He had been raised on a litter and borne to the Royal Infirmary, and with his dying breath he had said —"I am convinced that the old spinners would have injured me, if they could have got the opportunity, and it is on account of my having taken work from Houldsworth & Sons that I was shot last night." Within a few hours of his having made this declaration he died, leaving the personality of his assassin undiscovered. The cause of his death—that is, his conduct in resisting the dictates of the Trades Union—had never for a moment been doubted, and immediately after his decease, the proclamation which we have quoted was printed and published, carrying fear and consternation into many a Glasgow household.

We are so accustomed in these days to look upon the Trades Unions with which we are now surrounded as peaceful combinations of law abiding craftsmen, constituted for the protection of the interests of each trade by legitimate means, that it is difficult for us to realise the steps whereby their present liberty was won, or to understand the fearful condition of affairs between master and servant in Scotland less than half a century ago Few can have an intelligent remembrance of these events at this time and it is our purpose briefly to sketch the history of Trades Unionism in Scotland during the earlier part of this century, so that the reader may properly understand the Trial of the Glasgow Cotton Spinners

Combinations of craftsmen for the protection of special trades have existed throughout Europe for a very long period, although latterly they were considerably altered both in constitution and purpose The old Guilds, whose history may be traced back to mediæval times, appear to have been the first form which trade protection assumed, but these Guilds were really combinations of the employers for resisting the encroachments of the nobles, and took no care of the workman unless the interests of the masters were endangered by his wrongs Despotic rulers soon discovered that they could keep the nobles in check by utilising the Guilds, and obtain a cheap popularity by cultivating the affection of the lower orders, hence the munificent gifts and lavish charters of immunity bestowed by the kings upon these corporations soon made them a political power in Europe Trades were converted into exclusive monopolies, and placed under rigid protection and it took centuries of warfare and suffering to break down the barriers by which they were surrounded, and establish the principle of Free Trade The march of progress, however, was irresistible, and the Guilds, having played their part in securing the political liberty of the lower orders, quietly sank into a state of impotent and senile existence The Reform Bill of 1832 deprived them of the last vestige of political power, and swamped them entirely by introducing the "Ten pound Householder" The power of directing the nation thus passed in a large measure from the hands of the masters to the workmen

Long before this time, however, the workmen had found it necessary to establish combinations amongst themselves to resist the encroachments of the masters Though not forbidden, they were unprotected by law, and existed as Secret Societies, spreading their ramifications throughout all classes of operatives Their object in every case was to dictate to the masters the rate of wages, the number and kind of employés, the hours of labour and even the very methods of working which they preferred Their success in separate efforts for the raising of wages soon suggested the idea that a combination of different trades in assisting each other would enable the workers to control the labour market, in defiance

of the inexorable law of supply and demand, and the mutual aid thus afforded ultimately made the workers almost independent of their employers Until the year 1824 they were liable to prosecution for conspiracy, but by Mr Joseph Hume's Act passed at that time, their association for trade purposes was made legal and their existence tardily recognised

They had discovered their power before that period, and availed themselves of it in a dreadful manner When the French nation in 1789 shook off the chains of slavery which had so long bound it, the feeling of new found liberty led the people into all the horrors of frantic excess, and in much the same fashion the Trades Unions had abused their privileges, and prostituted their power to base and ignoble purposes The battle which they waged in the earlier years of this century was not a *political* but a *social* conflict, and its area was so rapidly extended that it threatened to destroy the whole fabric of society Their efforts were directed towards an artificial forcing of the rates of wages, which they sought to produce either by limiting the number of apprentices, or by causing the members of the Union to abandon their work, thinking by adopting a short sighted policy to increase the demand for their labour by limiting its supply Finding their struggles to bring about this phenomenon totally ineffectual, they resorted to inexcusable methods of coercion directed against the fundamental principles upon which society is erected An elaborate system of espionage was established, whereby the leaders of the Unions knew the sentiments of each member in their Association regarding their actions, and issued their unchallengeable edicts accordingly The Trades officials selected their Secret Committees, and sent them forth to molest, to intimidate, to maim, and even to murder the contumacious workmen who dared to defy them Ere long the Unionists found that their professed friends and defenders were their hardest taskmasters

When the Parliamentary Trades Commission sat in 1867 to inquire into the Sheffield trade outrages, the confessions of Broadhead and his associates, Hallam and Crookes, as to their "rattening," intimidating, and even murdering obdurate workmen who refused to join the Union were looked upon, and spoken of, as "unparalleled in history" We regret to find that Scotland had afforded a parallel, painfully similar, nearly fifty years before In Glasgow alone the dastardly outrages that culminated in the murder of John Smith exceed in atrocity the worst deeds of the Sheffield artisans To some of these acts specially connected with this trial we may shortly refer.

Mr Hume's Act of 1824, though designed to assist the Trades Unions by legalising their meetings, really had the effect of bringing the worst features in their character to the surface. One writer adverting to it says:—"The repeal of the Combination Laws was imperiously demanded as a concession due to natural justice; but owing to the ignorance and perverseness of the workmen, that which was designed by the Legislature as a boon to them was converted into a curse to themselves and the country. The period of their emancipation they seemed to regard as a *Saturnalia*, during which they were entitled, like the Roman slaves of old, while that season lasted, to indulge in all sorts of freedom with impunity; and many of them rushed into the most hideous excesses. They construed the liberty they had acquired into a power to dictate to and oppress their masters; and confederacies were everywhere formed, extremely well organised, at the head of which generally were turbulent individuals who acted the part of tribunes of the people—taking it upon them to denounce masters who had become obnoxious to them, and singling them out as objects of vengeance. Disobedience of their mandates was sure to be punished by personal violence, and not unfrequently, in Glasgow especially, by assassination."

We have incontestable evidence before us that this picture is not overcharged. In 1825, barely a year after the passing of Mr Hume's Act, a Committee of the House of Commons, under the presidency of Mr Huskisson, was appointed to inquire as to the administration of the Combination Laws. Evidence was led before them to show the fearful power which the Trades Unions had assumed to protect their own interests. One of their favourite methods of persuasion was to throw sulphuric acid upon the face of any independent workman who dared to disobey the dictates of the omnipotent Union. The members of the Trades Administration met in secret, and chose by ballot the man who should commit the horrid deed of cruelty or murder. They had no proof before them save that of their paid spies, nor did they call the offender to their bar to answer or deny their charge. Like the Mediæval *Fehmgericht*, they received the reports of their emissaries, and sent forth their judgments immediately, whether these were maimings, mutilations, or death, without hearing one word of excuse or in mitigation of sentence. Some of these sentences may be recorded.

In September 1824, whilst Charles Gurney, cotton spinner, Glasgow, was returning home from his work, a large quantity of sulphuric acid was thrown in his face, evidently with the purpose of maiming or destroying him. The doctor's report written after the unfortunate man had been more than five months in the Royal Infirmary, pronounced him as incurable. We need not horrify our readers with the medical details of this brutal outrage. Two months afterwards, while Neil M'Callum, Glasgow, was going out to his work at five o'clock in the morning a fluid afterwards proved to be sulphuric acid (vitriol), was dashed in his face whereby his sight was utterly destroyed, and he was rendered totally blind and incompetent for his work during the remainder of his miserable life.

Amongst the witnesses examined before Mr Huskisson's Committee in 1825 none was more damaging to the interests of the Unionists than Mr Robinson, then Sheriff of Lanarkshire. The startling revelations which he made almost exceed belief. He said that "there was a conspiracy in 1823 among the powerloom workers to assassinate one powerloom master and five cotton masters. There was also at the same time and by the same operatives, one of the cotton mills attacked with the view to an assault upon the persons working therein. The number of persons who did so amounted to a mob. There was one life lost in consequence of a shot from the mill; and such was the appearance generally, that after trying to get matters restored to quiet without the military, I was under the necessity of calling the military with a view to protect the lives and properties of the proprietors and workers in the mill."

It was distinctly shown that these lawless deeds were the direct acts of the Secret Committee of some of the Trades Unions, yet little was done to restrain their malignant influence. Their edicts went forth silently but surely, and the victims whom they condemned never escaped the penalty which they imposed. A new despotism had been established in the country, and no one could say what its end would be. Thirteen years afterwards it decreed the murder of John Smith, and attempted to cast its impervious cloak around the murderer when he fled from justice. In this case, however, punishment lay in wait to overtake the guilty.

H

OAKBANK MILL—SCENE OF THE RIOTS

PART II

Priuli—' We stand
　　Upon the very brink of gaping ruin
　　Within this city's formed a dark conspiracy
　　To massacre us all, our wives and children
　　Kindred and friends our palaces and temples
　　To lay in ashes , nay the hour too fixed
　　The swords for aught I know, drawn e'en this
　　　moment
　　And the wild waste begun   From unknown hands
　　I had this warning but if we are men
　　Let's not be tamely butchered but do something
　　That may inform the world in after ages
　　Our virtue was not ruin'd, tho we were
　　　　　　　Venice Preserved—Otway

The state of terrorism into which Glasgow was plunged between the years 1822 and 1837 by the domination of Trades Unions is matter of history No occupation where trades combinations had been attempted was secure from the contagion of law lessness which swept over the country , and the firebrands who deluded the poor workmen into a suicidal opposition to their employers alone reaped a rich harvest from the misfortunes of their fellows In 1825—a year of abnormal prosperity—the miners in the coal and iron mines of Lanarkshire found that they could force the employers to aug ment their wages and limit their hours in an ex ceptional fashion , and when the increased price of the minerals brought with it an inevitable de crease in the demand, the masters found starving weavers and unemployed operatives eager to obtain employment in the mines to keep themselves from absolute want   The miners who would not work set upon and assaulted the tradesmen who were willing to do so , and the military were frequently called out to quell the disturbances which arose between these two classes The case of the Cotton Spinners was similar, though their operations were conducted with even more malignity and pur blind perversity

Our commercial system is a much more delicate organism than it appears to be to the superficial observer , and its sensitiveness may be disturbed alarmingly by apparently inadequate causes The leaders of the Cotton Spinners' Union took no thought of the certain results of their conduct, but assumed that the Capitalist was their natural enemy, and adopted every means to thwart him They counselled that the operatives should show their power over him by refusing to work when the notion of idleness came over them , and especially inculcated the dangerous doctrine that the fear of a greater loss from his unemployed sunk capital would force him to accede to their de mands, however unreasonable he might deem them   Lest our readers should think that we are exaggerating the case against the Trades Unionists of the time, we shall quote a very startling statement of their purposes from the *New Liberator*—their own special organ—of 1st February 1834, as an authorised account of their views upon strikes —

" There's will not be insurrection, it will be simply passive resistance. The men may remain at leisure, there is and can be no law to compel them to work against their will. They may walk the streets or fields with their arms folded, they will wear no swords, carry no muskets, assemble no train of artillery, seize upon no fortified places. They will present no column for an army to attack, no multitude for the Riot Act to disperse. They merely abstain, when their funds are sufficient, from going to work for one week or one month, through the three Kingdoms. But what happens in consequence? Bills are dishonoured, the *Gazette* teems with bankruptcies, capital is destroyed, the revenue fails, the system of Government falls into confusion, and every link in the chain which binds society together is broken in a moment by this inert conspiracy of the poor against the rich."

The daring boldness of such advice given thus openly to semi-educated men calls for serious reprobation, even had there been nothing more intended than the species of "inert conspiracy" towards which it points, but we are in a position to show that the leaders of the working classes had, years before this time, entered into an *active* conspiracy of the most deadly character, which finally culminated in the trial that we have now to relate —a hateful treason against the foundations of society which must have been well known to the writers of the *New Liberator*. It was believed by the Master Spinners long ere this time that some secret bond was entered into by their employees whereby the "nobs," or men who took employment during a lock out, were threatened with corporal punishment of some sort so as to intimidate them, but for a long time every attempt to discover the conditions of this secret treaty proved abortive. At last Sheriff Robinson of Lanarkshire came into possession of a copy of the oath administered by the Cotton Spinners' Union to each new member, and quoted it before Mr Huskisson's Committee on Combinations in June 1825. This impious and immoral declaration was couched in the following terms —

" I, A B, do voluntarily swear, in the awful presence of Almighty God, and before these witnesses, that I will execute with zeal and alacrity, as far as in me lies, every task or injunction which the majority of my brethren shall impose upon me, in furtherance of our common welfare, as *the chastisement of nobs, the assassination of oppressive and tyrannical masters, or the demolition of shops that shall be deemed incorrigible,* and also that I will cheerfully contribute to the support of such of my brethren as shall lose their work in consequence of their exertions against tyranny, or renounce it in resistance to a reduction of wages, and I do farther swear, that I will *never divulge the above obligations* unless I shall have been duly authorised and appointed to administer the same to persons making application for admission, or to persons constrained to become members of our fraternity."

The existence of such a fearful oath not only accounts for the protracted series of trade outrages which took place in Glasgow from 1822 till 1837, but also explains very clearly why it was found so difficult to procure evidence against the ringleaders of the Cotton Spinners' Union. The member of the Union whose sense of justice or humanity revolted against the terrible deeds which his oath bound him to perform knew that if he disclosed the dread secret to the authorities he might himself become the next victim of their lawless violence, and thus the fear which closed his lips made him a silent participator in their crimes. No Jesuit under a vow to resign himself 'as a lifeless corpse' (*perinde ac cadaver*) to the commands of his General could be more impotent than the slave of this bloodthirsty band of Unionists. We have already mentioned some of the heartless outrages sanctioned and paid for by the Cotton Spinners' Union, and need not linger over them. It is only necessary that we give some details of the strike of 1837 which brought about the murder of John Smith in the circumstances related. To avoid all chance of unfairness we shall adhere closely to the account given by the *New Liberator*.

The year 1836 was one of exceptional prosperity, and the manufacturing interest was fully employed throughout the country. The Master-Spinners, though able to purchase wool at nearly the same rate as formerly, were receiving an advance of almost 35 per cent upon their selling prices, and the employees considered themselves justified in asking an increase of wages. As the state of trade seemed to warrant the demand, it was granted very readily, and the spinners found themselves enjoying wages ranging from 35s to 42s per week of sixty nine hours.*

*This rate of wages is quoted from the *Edinburgh Review*, Vol LXVII, p 244. A witness at the trial, however, gives the wages prior to the strike as 26s to 28s and after it as 24s. The difference probably arises from the fact that some of the spinners employed their own piecers.

A sudden reverse overtook the manufacturers in the early part of 1837, and by February of that year prices had fallen so considerably that they found they could not continue the advanced rate of wages. They proposed that the employees should be put upon the footing they had formerly occupied, which would still leave them a remuneration of from 26s to 36s per week—a sum greatly in advance of the wages earned by other tradesmen. The perverse way of looking at trades' questions which was then prevalent is shown by the remarks of the *New Liberator*. Though the writer admits that in the spring of 1837 "a frightful and every way alarming stagnation of trade had set in—the manufacturer had little demand for the productions of the looms, and the weavers were thrown idle in thousands, he condemns the employers for attempting to reduce the wages, stating that "this step was promptly and decidedly opposed by the operatives, who struck work on 8th April 1837." "In consideration," he continues, "of the deplorable circumstances of the times, the multitudes of unemployed people who were wandering in destitution about the city, and the many thousands of females and of little children employed in the factories to be thrown idle—the strike was far from being popular, and perhaps was exceedingly ill timed, but the fault, it must be admitted, was entirely attributable to the masters. Nothing was left to the workmen but to submit to this aggression on their comforts, or resist it."

The enormity of this strike will be better understood when we state that at this time there were 38 mills in Glasgow, employing about 800 spinners, each of whom required the assistance of from five to eight women and girls as piecers, carders, pickers, and reelers, whose work was all subsequent to that of the spinner, and who could not be employed whilst he was idle. From a credible statement which we have before us we learn that the refusal of the spinners to accept the reduction, which their own organ admits to have been legitimately caused, actually forced the alarming number of 5600 workers of both sexes into unwilling idleness, to swell the ranks of the unemployed in other trades throughout the city. Nor must we omit to notice that whilst the Union provided a strike fund to support the 800 spinners who were members, it offered no assistance whatever to the 4800 women and girls who depended upon them for existence, and who had no alternative but beggary or crime to save them from starvation.

In these circumstances it is not to be wondered at that the streets of Glasgow became the scenes of continual violence. There were more criminals tried by jury in Glasgow during the year 1837 than had ever been before, and the total number of deaths had increased about 300 per cent in this year as compared with that of 1822—only fifteen years before. Disease had spread with alarming activity amongst the working classes, and the fever patients in the Royal Infirmary, whilst this strike continued, far exceeded any number recorded during its existence. The description of the state of the city given under oath at the trial by Sheriff Alison—afterwards Sir Archibald Alison—shows unmistakably the condition of danger into which it had been thrown, and his evidence leaves no doubt whatever that this had been brought about by the strike of the Cotton Spinners. On the 8th of May he received information that large bodies of men were assembling and parading through the town, and that Oakbank Mill had been especially chosen by the mobs as a rendezvous. The proprietors of this mill had made themselves obnoxious by employing several spinners who were not Unionists, and the oath which we have already quoted condemned both the employers and these "nobs," as they were called, to condign punishment. There were nearly 800 people assembled on the road at Oakbank, and though the police had escorted the twenty or thirty new workers to a place of safety, Sheriff Alison saw some ten or twelve of them with bleeding faces, disfigured and abused by the mob. A proclamation had been prepared, but the Sheriff saw that it was hopeless for the small number of police to cope with the multitude, and he was forced to apply for military aid. A party of Lancers was brought from Hamilton, but ere they arrived on the scene the mob had dispersed. A week afterwards the rioting was resumed at Mile-end—about three miles from Oakbank—which was not then under the supervision of the Glasgow police, and an attempt was made to prevent a renewal of these lawless courses by apprehending some of the rioters. One Keddie was tried before the Sheriff, and was about to be sentenced to three months' imprisonment, when his agent stated that if sentence was deferred Keddie would be able to influence the Union to desist from further acts of violence. On this condition, he was released on bail, but he failed to perform his promise.

A great meeting of operatives was held in Glasgow Green on 14th June, and so apprehensive were the authorities of an outbreak that the military were kept in readiness, though fortunately they were not required. From that time up till the 29th of July incessant complaints were made of isolated outrages. Several attempts were made to set fire to the mills. A bomb was thrown in at the window of a manufacturer's house with the intention of destroying him, and some mill managers received threatening letters warning them of impending death should they continue to take "nobs" into employment

During this terrible period frantic efforts had been made to stem the torrent of distress and starvation within the city by the establishment of soup kitchens, and a Glasgow paper of the time states that in one day twelve hundred families were temporarily relieved. No prospect of a termination of the strike was yet apparent and it had continued for four months when the murder of John Smith startled the community. Information was sent to Sheriff Alison, who immediately communicated with the Home Secretary, and received authority to offer a reward for the apprehension of the murderers. Three days after the man's death the Procurator Fiscal told the Sheriff that several persons were willing to give evidence if they could be protected in the meantime, and he met them clandestinely and received their statements. From them he learned the name of another person who was to be murdered, and got him sent out of the way. So plainly had the Committee of the Cotton Spinners'

Union been involved in the outrages that the Sheriff saw no other course for him than to arrest them in a body, and he at once put this bold stroke into operation. He learned that they met in a public house in the Black Boy Close—now entirely demolished—and at 10 o'clock on the evening of Saturday, 29th July, he went with twenty police under the charge of Captain Miller to this spot and apprehended the whole fifteen of the Committee and took possession of their papers. Three active members of the Union were captured during the same night, and by this courageous move the organisation was paralysed. After a brief detention these men were all released, with the exception of the four chief officials, who were committed for trial upon the charges of conspiracy and murder. Within three days after this arrest the spinners of Glasgow held a meeting, at which they resolved to return to their work upon the terms the masters had offered, and on the 5th of August the strike, which had lasted for eighteen weeks, was happily terminated. Great revelations of the tactics of Unionism were expected from the forthcoming trial.

HOULDSWORTH'S MILL, CHEAPSIDE STREET

PART III

'*Menenius Agrippa* —   You slander
    The helms o the State who care for you like fathers
    When you curse them as enemies
2d Citizen —Care for us ! True, indeed ! They ne er cared
    for us yet Suffer us to famish and their storehouses
    crammed with grain make edicts for usury to support
    usurers , repeal daily any wholesome Act established
    against the rich and provide more piercing statutes
    daily to chain up and restrain the poor If the wars eat
    us not up they will and there s all the love they bear
    us   —*Coriolanus*

The five members of the Cotton Spinners' Union who were detained for trial were Thomas Hunter, President of the Association , Peter Hacket, Treasurer , Richard M'Niel, Secretary , James Gibb, Assistant Secretary , and William M'Lean, member of the Guard Committee M'Lean had not been apprehended at the same time as the others, having disappeared from Glasgow , but during the following week he was traced to Kincaid, in the parish of Campsie, and taken into custody on a charge of conspiracy and murder The prisoners were confined in the Bridewell of Glasgow, whilst elaborate preparations were being made for their prosecution.

No sooner had the strike of the Cotton spinners been terminated in the precipitate fashion we have described, than the operatives began to look with some degree of commiseration upon the unfortunate men who had been apprehended Meetings expressing indignation at their treatment were called together throughout the country, and whilst the Unionists wished to effect the liberation of the accused, lest they might be criminated by the prisoners' confessions, the mob—rarely vindictive or revengeful—were willing enough that they should be released, since the mills whereby the people lived were once more open The agitation in favour of the Cotton spinners was kept up in a still less reputable fashion by the Ultra Radicals of the time, who did not scruple to denounce the apprehension of these men as arbitrary and tyrannical, and to utilise this case as a text for the advocacy of Universal Suffrage, Vote by Ballot and the Abolition of the Corn Laws The *Glasgow Liberator* was then in the hands of the notorious Dr

John Taylor, and he did his utmost to instigate the working classes, whose ear he had gained, to rise in rebellion against the Tory Sheriff and his myrmidons who had made the capture The manufacturing districts of England were over run by agitators of the same class, and contributions towards defraying the expenses of the forthcoming trial flowed in to Glasgow from all quarters

Never, since the trials for sedition in the early part of the century, had any case raised such an amount of feeling throughout the Scottish working classes, and the sufferings through which they had lately passed made them ready to listen to the inflammatory speeches of any demagogue who would abuse the capitalists unstintedly The Radicals had expected that Queen Victoria, who had newly ascended the throne, would have been willing to listen to their demands for further reforms in Parliament, but when they found that she retained the services of Lord Melbourne and the Moderate Whigs their rage was turned against what they denominated "the base Whig Ministry, and every means adopted to bring obloquy upon them Even the Cotton spinners' case, long before it came to trial, was selected as a weapon wherewith to attack Her Majesty's advisers, who probably knew little about it. To prove that we are in no degree exaggerating the excitement caused by this trial we shall quote from one of the speeches delivered on this subject by the Reverend Mr Stephens, of Ashton under Lyne—a peripatetic politician of the most advanced stamp, who had won by his eloquence the hearts of the artisans The Trades Unionist of our time, though placidly enjoying full freedom of speech, will hardly believe that such language could have been used effectively upon any of his predecessors during the reign of our present Sovereign

At a large meeting held in the Bazaar, Glasgow, for the purpose of considering the conduct of the Government at home and abroad Mr Stephens took up the question of the factory system His words, as we find them reported, were these — "At the present moment a civil war was raging in Glasgow, in proof of which he referred to the disputes between the manufacturers and their workmen, and to the Cotton spinners trial He roundly charged the manufacturers of Glasgow with being systematically guilty of child murder and robbery, declared the Cotton spinners innocent, and asserted that if they were sent beyond seas all the manufacturers would be sent after them If the factory system were not reformed he observed, then the factory system must be destroyed The working men of Glasgow and Manchester would be called upon to come out, with a torch in one hand and a

dagger in the other, and level every factory to the ground 'The system,' he continued, 'must be either ended or mended We have sworn by our God, by heaven, earth, and hell, that from the east, the west, the north, and the south, we shall wrap in one awful sheet of devouring flame, which no army can resist, the manufactories of the cotton tyrants, and the palaces of those who raised them by rapine and murder, and founded them upon the wretchedness of the millions whom God—our God—Scotland's God—created to be happy !' In another part of his speech he contended that even if the Cotton spinners were guilty of the murder with which they were charged, the crime would not be so much theirs as it would be th crime of the manufacturers of Glasgow, who had begun and practised the accursed system under which the crime had been committed '

Unmoved by the violent language used against them, the authorities proceeded with their investigation of the affairs of the Cotton-Spinners' Union, slowly, but surely, unravelling their plots, and gathering up the most damning evidence against them Witnesses were more willing to speak than formerly, having the assurance of legal protection, and the books and papers which had been seized threw much light upon the matter To expedite their trial the accused took advantage of the Act of 1701 by "running their letters," but, through some unaccountable error, these letters were directed against Mr Salmond, the Procurator Fiscal, instead of the Lord Advocate, who alone could prosecute for the crimes charged against them This mistake was rectified, however, and the Lord Advocate—afterwards Lord Murray—was forced to have their case brought into Court in November.

The indictment, which was served upon the prisoners on 23d October 1837—nearly three months after their incarceration—was a most formidable document, consisting of twenty six quarto pages, and giving the names of seventy six witnesses for the prosecution The history which it gave of the Cotton Spinners' Union was a startling one, and, as its accuracy was never called in question during the trial, we may assume that its truth was unassailable It was stated that several years before that time an Association of Operative Cotton Spinners was formed at Glasgow, for the purpose of raising or keeping up wages The members came under a secret oath to support resolutions, orders, or directions, and to execute every task or injunction of the majority, and not to divulge the oath Great numbers, comprising almost the whole Cotton spinners in Glasgow and adjoining districts, had joined The Association had resolved at various times that its members, or certain of them working at certain mills, should strike work on account of disputes with the masters, and on these occasions had illegally and feloniously conspired, confederated, and agreed together, for the purpose of *forcibly* and *illegally* raising or keeping up wages or prevailing in their dispute by using *intimidation, molestation,* and *threats* to operatives working, or willing to work, upon different terms from those stipulated by the Association, and also to *perpetrate acts of violence* against the persons or property of such operatives. In furtherance of this conspiracy, a GUARD COMMITTEE was appointed, as occasion required, to watch the cotton mills, and by means of terror and alarm caused by such demonstrations of force, and by molestation and threats of violence, and by actual assaults committed by the Guards, to prevent operatives from working there —these Guards being paid and rewarded by the Association. In cases where Guards had been apprehended and committed for trial on such charges, the Association, in order to *frustrate the ends of justice,* and that those Guards might *elude trial* and punishment by absconding, procured law agents and others to become cautioners in the bail bonds that the Guards would appear at trial, placing the amount of the bail bonds in the hands of the cautioners to meet the forfeiture. The Association had directed *threatening letters* to be addressed to masters and managers, and mills, warehouses, dwelling houses to be *set fire to* the *dwelling houses* of workmen to be *invaded,* and themselves to be *assaulted and murdered*—all in order that by the *terror and alarm* thereby created the masters and managers might be compelled to submit to the demands of the members of the Association. To manage these things the Association occasionally appointed, by ballot or lot or other secret mode, a SECRET SELECT COMMITTEE, whose names were kept secret from the *ordinary members* of the Association, but the latter knew that the functions of this Committee were to enforce and obtain the object of the strike by organising and preparing the means, making choice of and engaging, hiring, or rewarding the persons whom they employed for *firings, writings, invasions, assaults, murders, &c.* Various such acts during strikes had been so planned, committed, and rewarded, and the Committee were not bound to explain the special application of monies paid therefor, and did not. The Association, it was asserted, had caused the Strike of 8th April 1837, and had appointed a Guard Committee to watch the mills for the purpose already stated, and the prisoners, as mem-

bers of the Association, were parties to this strike, and responsible for the results of it.

The specific charges brought against the accused were limited to eight criminal acts consisting of conspiracy by them as a "Secret Select Committee," hiring persons to assault workmen, sending threatening letters, invading the dwelling of a spinner at midnight—the crime known in old Scots Law as "hamesucken"—and forcing him to swear not to work, incendiarism, and finally, the murder of John Smith. In the last charge, though the prisoners were all included as participators in the crime, it was distinctly stated that the assassination of Smith had been committed by M'Lean.

The trial was appointed to take place at the High Court of Justiciary on 10th November 1837. The prisoners had now been kept in close custody for nearly three months, and their seclusion without having been brought to a public trial naturally created a strong feeling in their favour amongst their fellow workmen. Their crimes—if crimes they were—became to some extent forgotten in the presence of the fact that their forcible detention seemed a glaring infraction of the personal liberty of the subject, and meetings of sympathisers were more frequent and demonstrative than formerly. To avoid the danger of escorting the prisoners under a military guard to Edinburgh, it was arranged that they should be removed from Glasgow by coach early in the morning. From the *Dundee Advertiser* of Friday November 10th, we learn that "the five cotton spinners who have been indicted to stand their trial before the High Court to-day, for being accessory to the assassination of the unfortunate man Smith in Anderston, arrived in Edinburgh on Wednesday in the Red Rover, driven by a coachman, postilion, and four horses. Their legs were heavily fettered."

The latter precaution seems a strange one to be taken with men who were as yet only *suspected* of crime, and it gives some ground for the oft repeated assertions that the accused had been subjected to severe privations during their incarceration. One evident effect it had in favour of the prisoners—the contributions towards their defence flowed in uninterruptedly, and their friends soon found themselves in possession of not less than £1000 sent from all quarters of the kingdom for this purpose. In these circumstances it was more than probable that they would secure the aid of the foremost leaders of the Scottish Bar in having a fair and impartial trial.

THE GLASGOW COTTON SPINNERS

PART IV.

" THIS IS TO GIVE NOTICE !—Whoever shall seize
   And such person, or persons to justice surrender
Shall receive—such REWARD—as his Highness shall please
   On conviction of him the aforesaid offender

And in order the matter more clearly to trace
   To the bottom his Highness the Prince Bishop
   further,
Of his clemency, offers Free PARDON and Grace
   To all such as have *not* been concerned in the murther

" Done this day at our palace—July twenty five—
   By command,
       (Signed)
            JOHANN VON RUSSELL '
            —*Ingoldsby Legends*

On the morning of Friday, 10th November 1837, the High Court of Justiciary assembled in the Court House at Edinburgh for the purpose of trying the five cotton-spinners The Lord Justice Clerk (Boyle) presided, and the bench was occupied by Lords Mackenzie, Moncreiff, Medwyn and Cockburn Lord Advocate Murray prosecuted in person, and was assisted by Solicitor General Rutherfurd (afterwards Lord Rutherfurd) and John Shaw Stewart (afterwards Sheriff of Stirlingshire) and R J Handyside, Advocate Depute The prisoners were defended by some of the leading members of the Bar, their case having been taken up by Duncan M'Neill (afterwards Lord President of the Court of Session), Patrick Robertson, Alex M'Neill, James Anderson, and Henry Glassford Bell (afterwards Sheriff of Lanarkshire) When the indictment was read the panels severally pled *Not Guilty*, and special defences were lodged for them in these terms —

" The defenders are not guilty of any of the charges contained in the libel

' In regard to the alleged murder of John Smith which seems to be more particularly charged as having been committed by the defender M Lean, the prosecutor has not specified the precise hour it which it is said to have been committed It is proper to state that during the whole or greater part of the night of the 22d July M'Lean was in the public houses of Angus Cameron in Saltmarket Street, and Gilbert M Ilwraith in Bridgegate Street, and in the vicinity of these places '

Mr Duncan M'Neill then took exception to the phraseology of the indictment, founding his objections to the relevancy of the libel upon some minute grammatical forms employed An elaborate debate followed, in which Mr Handyside the Lord Advocate Mr Robertson and the Judges took part but which would be quite uninteresting to the reader, and need not be detailed For four hours the discussion was continued upon the question whether the prisoners should be charged with conspiracy *or* murder, instead of conspiracy *and* murder, and the Judges afterwards took other two hours to deliberate upon the arguments At length they returned to Court and announced that they repelled all the objections, and found that the case must go to a jury As the day was far spent, and other cases to be called would fully occupy the following day, it was decided to postpone the trial till the 27th November This adjournment was made almost necessary from the fact that a list of fifty witnesses for the prisoners had been lodged with the Clerk of Court *on the night before the trial* (9th November), and the Lord Advocate was ignorant of the rebutting evidence thus to be brought against him In any case, therefore, he could have insisted upon an adjournment , but to prove that he intended that the accused should have a fair trial, he took the unusual course of granting expenses to all the witnesses whom they had summoned

That this adjournment was really judicious and in the interests of justice was soon made evident, for the precognition of the prisoners' witnesses by the prosecutor disclosed unsuspected ramifications of the plots in which the Cotton Spinners' Association had been engaged The *Glasgow Chronicle* of 24th November 1837 records that "the Authorities, in their arrangements to meet the evidence for the defence, have obtained such information as they can make the grounds of several new charges relating to the Union throughout the kingdom, and to the assaults and intimidation some time ago at Oakbank Factory " In consequence of these new discoveries, the Lord Advocate found it necessary to ask for another adjournment , and intimation was sent three days before the proposed trial to the counsel for the prisoners directing them not to summon their witnesses, as the case could not go on At a formal meeting in the Robing room of the Court, Lord Cockburn postponed the trial till 18th December

Meanwhile the friends of the cotton-spinners were not idle, and took advantage of these repeated delays to attempt a diversion in their favour At an overflowing meeting held in the Lyceum Rooms, Glasgow, on 27th November—the evening of the day on which the trial should have taken place—it was "Resolved, that *since justice cannot be obtained by law*, application be immediately made to Parliament for the immediate trial or liberation of the Committee of the Glasgow Cotton Spinners "

In pursuance of this resolution the matter was brought before the House of Commons on 8th December, but the Lord Advocate, whilst declining to discuss the merits of the case, assured the House that no undue delay had taken or would take place. Indeed he had already caused a new indictment to be served upon the prisoners, under

Criminal Letters, on 2d December, appointing their trial finally to take place on 3d January 1838 This document, though couched in similar terms to its predecessor, contained fuller information as to the charges against the accused It was stated that they had offered £10 as a reward for an assault upon two spinners, which assault was executed , that they had paid £10 each to three of their associates for breaking into the house of a "nob," and forcing him to swear to give up his work , that £20 were offered for setting fire to the house of a master spinner in Bridgeton, which fire raising was attempted , and that M'Lean was offered £20 as his hire for assassinating John Smith, and had undertaken the work and committed the deed The list of witnesses had swelled to the large number of ninety one, besides the fifty whom the prisoners had summoned

The Glasgow cotton spinners' trial had now gained Parliamentary notoriety, and was kept constantly before the public for the succeeding four months On 12th December many petitions for the liberation or speedy trial of the prisoners were laid on the table of the House of Commons— one from Glasgow and the neighbourhood bearing no less than 20,000 signatures The *London Dispatch* and the *Glasgow Liberator*, then the wildest Radical newspapers, were loud in their complaints against the law officers, but failed to move them in the least, and at length the important day came round which was finally to dispose of this protracted case

On 3d January 1838 the bench of the High Court of Justiciary was occupied by the Lord Justice Clerk, and Lords Mackenzie, Moncreiff, and Cockburn The counsel for the Crown and for the prisoners were the same as formerly The first indictment had been held relevant, and the prosecutor might have proceeded with it , but as he had issued new Criminal Letters these had to be read, and it was open to the prisoners' counsel again to object Of this advantage they at once availed themselves, and a long debate took place on the point whether the words "or otherwise" should not have been used instead of ' as also " After considerable delay this profound question was settled, and a jury was balloted for Numerous challenges of the jurymen were made for the prisoners—two accounts say seventeen, and another twenty five—and a jury was at length empanelled and the trial proceeded

The declarations of the prisoners were proved by Sheriff Moir and Mr Salmond, Procurator Fiscal, the latter witness describing the arrest of the prisoners in Smith's public-house, Black Boy Close , and corroborative evidence was given by two

officers who had been engaged in the affair Be
fore introducing his principal witnesses the Lord-
Advocate said "that he wished to state that he had
experienced the greatest possible difficulty in procuring persons to give evidence in this matter,
and he had given to the witness about to be
examined, and to the others, an assurance of the
fullest protection which the law could give, both
before and after the trial He had already been
compelled to confine four of his chief witnesses in
jail, both at Glasgow and Edinburgh, to protect
them from insult and injury, and he wished the
Court to renew his assurances of their future safety '

James Moat, operative cotton spinner, was the
first witness called, but before he was sworn, Mr
Anderson, on behalf of the prisoners, objected to
his evidence being admitted "This witness,' he
said, "has received a promise of reward for giving
his evidence Your Lordships may perhaps be
aware that two rewards were offered, and I wish
to call your attention to the terms in which the
offers are expressed The first reward is an offer
by the master cotton spinners of £500 to any
person or persons who will give such information
to the Procurator Fiscal as will lead to the ap
prehension or conviction of the murderer of Smith
The other by the Sheriff, on the part of the
Crown, is conceived in terms more objectionable
It is in the form of a proclamation issued by the
Sheriff, by authority of Lord John Russell, and
offers, in Her Majesty's name, a reward of £100 to
any person who shall give such information
and evidence as shall lead to the discovery and
conviction of the murderer or murderers That
comes clearly and directly under the objection in
the law of Scotland that a reward promised to any
person for any evidence that he shall give must
disqualify him as a witness He is not to get it
for merely giving information or evidence, but
only in the event of discovery and conviction
And the effect of this offer has been that differ
ent parties in the Crown list of witnesses who
think they have been most instrumental in leading
to the discovery of the alleged perpetrator or
perpetrators of this deed have entered into a
newspaper controversy as to which of them is en
titled to the reward offered in respect of the infor
mation given by them "

Such an objection to a Royal Proclamation had
never been urged before, and was quite unexpected
by the Crown Counsel The Solicitor General re
plied, pointing out that the public interest must
not suffer by the fact of a reward having been
offered The terms of the Proclamation were
these —'That Lord Russell will advise the grant
of Her Majesty's most gracious pardon to any
accomplice, not being the person who actually

fired the pistol, who shall give such information
and evidence as shall lead to the discovery and
conviction of the murderer ' If the objection
offered were tenable it would exclude any accom
plice even from giving evidence, and applied to
the witnesses already examined as well as to those
yet to come The reward might affect the credi
bility of the witness, but could not exclude him
from examination The Lord Advocate observed
that "instead of any one coming forward to give
evidence, the remarkable feature in this case is
that a person was murdered in a public street in
Glasgow, and no one came forward to give infor
mation, even after the offer of reward "

The matter was debated at length, all the
judges giving their opinions, and agreeing that the
promised reward could not exclude the witness
"No atrocious deed, said Lord Moncrieff, "was
ever committed without some such reward being
offered by the Crown or public authorities, and it
has never been the law in this country that that
created an objection to the testimony of a witness '

"It is not a bribe said Lord Cockburn, in his
usual lucid style, "for giving false evidence that
may lead to a conviction by unjust means, it is a
reward for speaking the truth For example, if a
witness were to be convicted of perjury he would
not be entitled to the reward It is a fair and
honest reward, given for a public object, to aid in
the discovery of the truth "

The objection was over ruled, and the witness,
Moat, was recalled Before he took the oath
Lord Moncrieff assured him that he would receive
the full protection of the law, and he proceeded to
give his evidence in a calm and deliberate manner
He stated that he had been a member of the Asso
ciation for upwards of twenty years In 1822 23—
two years specially marked by trade outrages —he
was a member, and had been sworn to conceal the
proceedings of the Union, and to stand by the
resolutions of the majority The Association was
divided into three districts, and each returned
four members as a Committee He could
not tell how the President was elected,
but he nominated three to be a Secret Com
mittee The remaining nine were all sworn
not to reveal who this Secret Committee were
A new method was adopted in 1837 The delegates
were enjoined to bring in one name from each
shop, and these were put into a hat, and the parties
whose names were drawn out became the Secret
Committee men Moat was a member of the
Supply Committee about 1823 Shortly before this
one Cairnie had been burned with vitriol,* and

---

* The date of the burning of Cairnie was September 1824—
see Part I of this present account -but Moat stated that he
could not give the exact year

though the Supply Committee, including several of the prisoners, were averse to such measures they had given aliment to the three men—Milne, Macdonald, and Kean—who had done the deed. The members of the Committee were instructed to tell these men that they only gave them aliment ' for God's sake'—meaning thereby, as witness understood, that they did not approve of their action.

Witness was a member of the Supply Committee in 1837 when the last strike commenced, but as he was not in very good health, and was opposed to the strike, he did not attend regularly. He knew that there was a Grand Committee appointed to manage the guards placed upon the mills. The duty of these guards, he knew from their invariable practice, was, if occasion offered, to reason with individuals who took work at reduced wages, and, if necessary, to threaten intimidate, and offer violence to them. Members of the Association were fined if they did not execute the duty laid upon them. The prisoners were on the Finance Committee, which afterwards became merged in the Supply Committee. About seven weeks after the strike began a mass meeting—to which we have already referred—was held in Glasgow Green, and addressed by Dr John Taylor, of the *Liberator*. The Supply Committee of the Cotton Spinners' Union met in the Black Boy Close the same evening, together with the delegates, in all about forty members, under the presidency of the prisoner Gibb. Hunter introduced the subject of appointing a Secret Committee. His language was ambiguous, and he used what witness called " sophistry ,' but his object was to show that some more efficient means were necessary if the Association was to be successful in the strike. He did not come to the point nor mention a Secret Committee, but John Davies proposed that such a Committee should be appointed, and the motion was seconded, and carried almost unanimously. Witness and another man opposed it, the latter saying he would have nothing to do with it, as it was disgraceful, and the former stating that it would do no good, and only make the masters more determined against them. All who had been any time in the Association knew the object for which the Committee was appointed. *Q* ' What was that object?' *A* "Its chief design was to destroy life and property according to my understanding and belief at the time. That was the ground upon which I refused to go into the resolutions. I did not argue on the ground of *injustice*, but on that of *inexpediency*, the former argument would have been laughed at.'

From this time witness ceased to attend the meetings. Some weeks afterwards he met Gibb,

who said he had once been against the appointment of a Secret Committee, but the conduct of the masters was so bad that he would now go upon it. Shortly after this Smith was murdered. Hunter and Hacket had been connected with the Association for many years, Gibb for about eight years, and M'Neil for a shorter time. It was usual in the trade when a member left one mill to go to another to send to the Committee what was called a 'free line," signed by three belonging to the mill he was leaving, saying whether he was free of debt or not. Witness shown a certificate (No. 23 of process), in the following terms :—

"*Committee Rooms, July* 11, 1837.—This is to certify that William M'Lean is A Clear Member of the Glasgow Operative Body of Cotton-spinners. He has always done his duty, and we recommend him to all our friends.—(Signed)—Thomas Hunter, James Gibb, Peter Hacket, Richd M'Neill."

The document, witness averred, was in M'Lean's handwriting, and he supposed that these four formed the Secret Committee, and had given M'Lean this certificate in that capacity. Several of the books of the Association which had been found in their Committee room were shown to Moat, and he explained them as far as he could. One of these contained a minute, dated June 15, 1837, which throws much light on the methods of coercion adopted by the Union. It runs thus :—

"Moved at the general meeting by William Johnston, and unanimously carried, that the name of every nob at present working, and the districts they last wrought in, should be enrolled in a book, and, at the end of the strike, unless a change in the list takes place, they be printed ; but, at all events, the names of all who remain nobs at the termination of the strike shall be printed and sent to all the spinning districts in Scotland, England, and Ireland, that they remain nobs for ever, and a *persecuting* Committee be appointed to *persecute* them to the utmost."

Referring to an entry in one of the books of "expenses for nobs, £10," Moat said that " the expense might be incurred by reasoning with them, and giving them drink, or the money may have been given as rewards for maltreating them."

When the evidence of this witness had been completed, it was proposed that the trial should be adjourned until the following day in justice to the prisoners, so that the jury might be able to continue the investigation of this complicated case without exhaustion. The prisoners consented, and the jury were lodged in the Queen's Hotel for the night. The first day of the trial had merely lifted a corner of the curtain which shrouded the dark deeds of the Secret Committee.

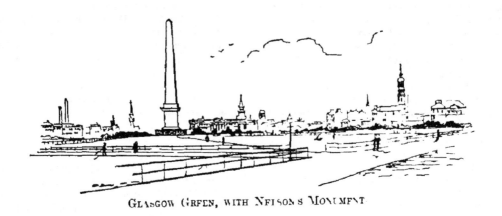

GLASGOW GREEN, WITH NELSON'S MONUMENT

PART V

Glanville—   Say quickly
                  Is our first work achieved ?
Ragozin—   Successfully
          With two bold ruffians whose assisting hands
          Were hired to make the business sure I traced
          His steps with care and in the darksome path
          Which leads beside the ruined Abbey's wall
          With furious onset suddenly attack'd him

                              Clone—Dodsley

When the Court re-assembled on Thursday, 4th January, the first witness called was James Murdoch, a cotton spinner, and at one time an official in the Association The Court renewed to him the assurance of protection which the Lord Advocate had given—an assurance not unnecessary since he had been secluded in the jails of Glasgow and Edinburgh already, to save him from the vengeance with which he had been threatened His evidence was of the highest importance to the prosecutor

He deponed that he came to Glasgow from Renfrewshire in 1816, and went to work in Hussey's mill, Dale Street, Bridgeton, where his brother in law was employed He was told that he could not remain there unless he joined the Association, and paid his share He was afraid, though the Association was not then general, that the men would use the influence they possessed to make him uncomfortable He joined the Union, therefore and went through the necessary ceremony, which he thus described —

'An oath was put to me, I can't remember its words, it was divided into two branches One an oath of secrecy to keep secret my taking it, and after the administrator had explained the good of it, the other branch was to abide by the majority in all cases regarding the trade A Bible was used in administering the oath It was put under the right oxter during the time the oath was taken, and the word 'Ashdod was used It is in the 20th chapter of Isaiah, 1st verse Signs were used so that each might be known to the other members of the Association A change was made in both the oath and the word, I think, about 1822 The new word was 'Armageddon' taken from Revelations xvi chap, 16 verse, and both words were given after that time The change in the oath was a great deal for the worse, it became more vicious in its nature, introducing something about punishment and abhorrence of *nobs* I can't recollect more I understand a *nob* to be a man who enters at a reduction of wages during a strike, but it may be understood otherwise A person who revealed the names of the Secret Committee was considered the greatest nob, the speaking to anyone so doing is also nobbing

The reader will notice from Murdoch's evidence that the oath which he could not precisely recollect was similar to the formula which we have already quoted (Part II), but the exact words of the oath, as we have given it, were probably not adopted until about 1824, for the witness continues —" The last time I was present at the administration of an oath was about nine or ten years ago, and a third oath, worse than either of the former two, was then administered There was something in it with respect to masters that was not in either of the two before " This date brings the concoction of this latter oath within

Hunter's term of office, and makes him responsible for it The absurd use of the two Scriptural words is not without parallel amongst other Secret Societies They were possibly chosen for their sesquipedalian sonorousness, rather than for any meaning which they expressed , from the same feeling, in short, which gives a mysterious influence to "that sweet word, Mesopotamia," and which prompted the country members of Walpole's time to cheer loudly at the mention of Moldavia or Wallachia The acute critic might find an involuntary confession of crime in the adoption of the second word, since, according to Dr Wordsworth, "Armageddon is not any spot in Judæa or Italy, but *wherever men associate themselves in a league of ungodly polity*'

Murdoch's evidence as to the functions and deeds of the Secret Committee was of a most startling character, and will be best understood from his own simple language —

"The first Secret Committee that I recollect was appointed in 1818, when a factory called Broomward was started by Mr Dunlop, and women instead of men put into it to work , and the object of appointing this Secret Committee was to get them put out The first attempt that was made was to set fire to the mill I know that from the public newspapers and from the money that was paid for it appearing in the schedules, which were handed round every fortnight It was inserted '*Colliery*,' which was a term perfectly well known by the whole Association, and I understood it to be money paid for attempting to burn the factory , but it was a word which then for some years implied mischief generally The object of the Committee at that time failed Several other acts of violence to person and property were committed by that same Committee before another was elected A widow woman named M'Pherson, who had a daughter that worked in Broomward Mill, lived in the Calton, and her house was entered and her life taken—that is, the mother's life was taken, as we considered, in mistake for her daughter I could not exactly say the year this occurred, it might be in 1820 or 1821 Two men, Patten Dunlop and Bernard M'Kenny, were sent to America at the expense of the trade I believe the sum paid to them for going out of the country was on account of their concern with Widow M'Pherson, and no other reason was ever assigned for it among the trade

"There was one Macquarrie shot at and wounded in 1820 I recollect of three different payments for 'Colliery' made to Andrew Darroch, Owen O'Callaghan, and Stephen Campbell, for shooting at Macquarrie O'Callaghan was afterwards transported for shooting John Orr at Paisley Campbell remains at Bridgeton or thereby The payments were entered in the schedule as 'Barr's Strike Colliery'—Barr being the name of the proprietor of a mill then on strike The individuals' names were not entered I was an eye witness of the shooting of Macquarrie. It took place near the Green of Glasgow on an afternoon in the summer season, in clear sunshine I was told in Bridgeton that there was to be an attack upon the nobs at the skailing of Barr's mill, and I went down to see it, along with some others I found a good many spinners standing, gathered in a hollow in the Green towards an entry that leads to the mill We remained there a little, and the work stopped and the nobs came down the street There were two brothers named Kerr who went along by the Green Dyke towards the town, and they and Macquarrie entered the Green near the Monument [the memorial obelisk to Nelson] Darroch walked a few steps across the Green, and fired a pistol at the Kerrs ; but the shot did not take effect Macquarrie came along the Serpentine Walk, and Stephen Campbell came out from the trees and fired a pistol at him, which wounded him, though he did not fall He recovered afterwards, and there was no trial about this matter I gave no information as to this, because I was afraid of similar consequences Campbell was a member of the Association A reward of £300 was offered for information regarding this assault '

The prosecutor proposed to ask witness whether Campbell had told him that he had received £15 as a reward from the Association , but the prisoners' counsel objected, and the question was not pressed Murdoch proceeded, therefore, with his startling revelations

"I recollect one John Graham being shot at A dispute in the trade took place after the shooting at Graham, and a Select Committee was appointed to act openly to the trade only, so that all might know who were in the Committee, that the like thing of shooting might not take place again One John Kean was tried for shooting at Graham, convicted, and transported for life, after being whipped publicly at Glasgow I know, as a member of that Committee that payments were made A claim of £20 was made by one Daniel Orr, and five referees, of whom I was one, were appointed to investigate as to it His claim was that he was hired in a house at Barrowfield Toll, along with Kean, Lafferty, and another man, to shoot Graham He produced one Thomas Paterson as a witness, and the referees were satisfied and awarded Orr the sum claimed I know of payments being made to Kean's wife after his trial.

She got 12s a week for eighteen months out of the funds of the Association I know payments were made to Lafferty's wife—she received the same sum for the same period Lafferty got eighteen months' imprisonment in Bridewell, and after he came out he was sent by the Association to America The expenses of Kean's trial were paid by the Association

"I remember one M'Dade He was not convicted or tried, so far as I know, but he was paid £4 16s, I think, for maltreating Margaret Banks in 1825 or 1826 because she was a nob

"I know of the shooting at the house of William Brown, and one Walker was tried for it—in 1827, I think Walker was a member of the Association I was present at a private consultation before his trial at a shop meeting in Hussey's with members as to his defence It was proposed at the meeting to get men to swear that Brown had hired persons himself to shoot at his house Walker had not then been tried, and they did not know that he would plead guilty When this proposal was made to get these witnesses to swear I knew it to be false Walker was tried, pled guilty, and was transported

"I recollect the case of Cairnie, the spinner, who had an eye burnt out with vitriol He had been a nob, but was not at that time There was a trial Peter Mellen was tried for this and acquitted Four men received aliment for this burning, one of them being James Macdonald who was impeached with the action, but was not tried for it, as he fled on account of that business to Catrine Works, in Ayrshire

"I have known Hunter to be a member of the Association for eighteen years, Hacket since 1823 or 1824 (twelve years), M'Neil for nine, and Gibb for twelve years M'Lean has been a member for ten or twelve years to my knowledge"

Referring to the mysterious certificate which M'Lean had received from the other four prisoners, witness said, "The office bearers have no authority to give certificates or *free lines* This is not in the usual form, and I never saw such a line given unless where the person has done something for the Association which compels him to go away, and such I understand this to be" In cross examination he stated that he had once signed a

line similar to this one when he was a member of the Secret Committee, and he believed it was sent to Patten Dunlop, the supposed murderer of Widow M'Pherson, after he had been sent to America Besides, he pointed out as a matter of fact that the books of the Association showed that M'Lean was in arrears at the date of this certificate, and was not entitled to a free line

Henry Cowan, cotton spinner, gave evidence principally corroborative of that already led as to the method in which the affairs of the Association were conducted During the strike of 1837 he was employed in Hussey's mill, and though he was averse to the strike he was forced to go out along with the rest As to the obscurer officials of the Union, he said "it was very well known in the trade what a select, or secret Committee was When a select Committee was appointed, it was generally understood that some party was to be shot, or vitriol thrown, or some property destroyed, and that those things required a select Committee It was perfectly understood that the select Committee hired persons to do all these things either directly or indirectly It was quite general in the morning for the members of the Association to ask one another if they had heard any news, and the answer was 'No, nothing done yet,' meaning to express surprise that the delay was so long after the Committee was appointed We expected some person to be shot, or burnt with vitriol, or maimed in some way or other"

Sheriff Alison gave evidence as to the origin and progress of the riots in Glasgow, and described the apprehension of the prisoners in the manner already related The latter portion of his evidence was confirmed by Henry Miller, Superintendent of Police in Glasgow, who made the capture Alexander Arthur, manager of the Adelphi Cotton Mill, detailed the molestation to which his new hands had been subjected by the guards placed on the mill during strike, and also read two threatening letters which he had received, plainly menacing his life John Bryson, manager of Mitchell's Mill, reported similar experiences, and three engravers concurred in declaring the handwriting of these letters to be M'Neil's At this stage the declarations of the prisoners were read

CLOSE IN SALTMARKET—SITE OF ANGUS CAMERON'S SPIRIT SHOP —(*Now demolished*)

PART VI

"'Vell said Mr Weller 'now I s pose he ll want to call some witnesses to speak to his cl aracter or p raps to prove a allybi I ve been a turnin th business over in my mind, an l he may make hisself easy Sammy *I ve got some frier ds as ll do either for him but my advice ud be this here—never mind the character an l stick to the alleybi Nothing like a alleybi Sammy no*thing *ck Papers*

The treatment of suspected persons differs con siderably in this country from that adopted on the Continent In France and Germany the accused is submitted to frequent and prolonged examina tions, and plied with questions cunningly devised to entrap him into a confession of his supposed g ilt In Germany trials are sometimes pro tracted for years in the expectation that the person charged will admit his crime, such an admission superseding all evidence which may be brought in his favour The Scottish law provides that an accused person shall be informed of the charge against him, and asked to give an explanation which will exculpate him, but before he is permitted to reply to any question or make any statement he is warned that whatever he says may be used against him He may decline to answer any query put to him or to criminate himself in any way, and whatever de claration he may make must be emitted volun tarily The tenderness with which British law regards the prisoner prevents such declarations from having undue weight attached to them, and they are often overborne by the evidence of wit nesses or valued only as showing the state of mind into which the prisoner was thrown by the accusa tion brought against him

The declarations of the Cotton spinners, however, were really of more importance than such docu ments usu illy are All the prisoners had been examined twice, and the versions which they gave as to the rules of the Association were in direct opposition to those advanced by the three witnesses whose evidence we have quoted On 1st

August Thomas Hunter emitted his first declaration, in which he made the following statement —

Aged forty one, a native of County Antrim, Ireland, and came to Scotland twenty four years ago. For many years he has been a member of the Cotton Spinners Association, the object of which was that its members should have a fair remuneration for their labour, by all lawful means. Entry money is £1. No ceremony at initiation, and no oaths of secrecy imposed. A strike in April, when Committee of twelve appointed to find supplies. Was elected Preses. No minute book was kept. Met daily—no meetings on Sabbath. No oath imposed on Supply Committee—no Sub Committee—no ballot. Guard Committee appointed to watch factories, and report as to persons employed, but the Guards were withdrawn several weeks ago, and the Committee dissolved. Not aware of any list of names. Never heard of a Select Secret Committee, appointed by ballot or otherwise. Never heard of one assaulted for opposing such a measure. Never heard of resolution to murder masters. Never proposed the appointment of a Select Secret Committee. Guards had no allowance from funds. Never saw books shown him. (These had been found in the Committee room.) Never heard of a *Persecuting Committee.* Never heard of violence to masters or hands. Never heard of offer of £20 to assassinate a master or a new hand or *Nob.* Knows nothing of entry of £15 1s paid Guard Committee. Heard of Smith's murder on Sunday, 23d July. Left Committee previous night at 5 p.m. Saw offer of reward of £500 for discovery of assassins, and insinuating that the deed had been committed by turn out Cotton spinners. Every one of Committee deprecated this act, but no resolutions or steps taken. Heard of an attempt to burn Hussey's factory. Does not know James Murdoch, cotton spinner. Heard of combustibles thrown into Wood's house, but this was never talked of in Committee. Declarant innocent of all. Does not know who proposed Guard system. They were never supplied with arms or money. Never saw the Bible in Committee room."

When re examined on 1st September Hunter affirmed that his first declaration was true, and declared that he had signed the certificate for William M'Lean, dated 11th July 1837. It was a clear line showing that he had paid up his accounts, but Hunter signed it on information, and without examining the books.

The declarations of the other prisoners were couched in similar terms, and it is not necessary to detail them. Peter Hacket stated that he was thirty six years of age, and professed that he had

never heard of Guard Committee, Select Secret Committee, or of any Committee to effect objects of the Association by force and violence. No oath was administered on entering the Union. He was unable to explain entries in minute books referring to cash affairs, and did not know what some of the cant expressions used really signified. On re examination (1st September) his attention was directed to the entry "Expenses with Nobs, £19 ' and he asserted that ' the figures had been put in the pound column instead of the shilling column by mistake." He did not know the meaning of such entries as "Fugitives, £5 1s 6d, and ' Guards and Expenses £24"

Richard M'Neil, aged twenty eight, did not so roundly declare his ignorance of the affairs of the Society, but took the safer though more suggestive plan of declining to answer. After stating that he was not aware of a Guard Committee, he was shown an entry, ' 12th June—the following names have been added to Guard Committee' and he admitted that the entry was in his handwriting, but could not explain it. When re examined (5th August) he denied that he had written any of the threatening letters, and when interrogated at a third examination (1st September) as to certain letters signed "Richd M'Neill, which gave some strange particulars as to the expenditure of the funds, he declined to say whether they were written by him or not.

James Gibb, aged thirty three, declined to say when he became a member, and also refused to tell whether there was any ceremony gone through at initiation, or any oath administered. He had not only heard of a Guard Committee, but gave the names of several who had served upon it lately, and knew of their having received sums of money, not exceeding £5 at a time. The most striking part of his declaration was that where he stated that it was formerly the practice of the Association to take bills from members of whose adherence they were doubtful, bearing to be "for value received, but for which no value was given, that these bills were protested when they fell due, and decreet in absence obtained from the Sheriff, so that the Association could hold bogus warrants over the heads of recusant members, and persecute them by process of law '

As William M'Lean was the person charged with the actual perpetration of the murder of John Smith, his declaration was necessarily of great importance. He was examined on 9th August, and declared—that he is aged twenty six, a native of Glasgow, son of Archibald M'Lean, lately a cotton spinner, a member of Association for twelve years. Cannot remember where he was initiated, nor if put upon oath. Understood all were to

Obey the majority Has had aliment since the strike varying from 8s to 8d per week Knew of both Supply Committee and Guard Committee being appointed Never acted as Guard himself, but knew several who had done so Never heard of Secret Select Committee to destroy cotton spinners or new hands Knew the deceased Smith, they worked at the same mill Does not know if he was a member Two or three years since he saw him Since the strike heard that Smith was working at Houldsworth's Does not know where he lived Never heard of his being complained of as nobbing On Sabbath, 23d July, heard that a cotton spinner had been shot, and on Monday learned that it was Smith Has no knowledge or suspicion who did it

Declarant next gave a detailed account of his proceedings on the evening of Saturday, 22d July, from six P M till midnight He went to Glasgow Green for the purpose of receiving his weekly aliment, but as the persons who were to pay it had not arrived, and it was raining heavily, he went along with about a dozen spinners, to the spirit shop of Angus Cameron, in the Saltmarket, where they all remained till their allowance —1s each—was brought to them The party had three or four mutchkins of whisky, and nine of them remained together in Cameron's till after twelve o clock When they separated four of them went with him to the spirit cellar of Gilbert M'Ilwraith, in the Bridgegate, where they had more whisky He was the worse of it After one o'clock all the party went home except himself and another, and these two met several cotton spinners at the Cross, who took them to Brassbell Entry, where they got more drink. Recollects leaving this place and going along Main Street of Calton, but after that his senses forsook him, and he remembers no more until he found himself on awaking in his father's house at King Street on Sunday afternoon, and learned that he had been brought home at 7 A M Did not leave home till Monday morning Interrogated as to why he had shaved off his whiskers? Declared that he had whiskers until one day in the middle of last week, when he happened to be cropping them with a pair of scissors, but having made a "gaw" in them, he shaved them off altogether, with the intention, however, of letting them grow again

From these statements it will be seen that M'Lean had fully prepared an *alibi* as the time when Smith was shot was accounted for in his declaration as spent in Saltmarket, more than a mile from the scene of the murder He had still to explain why he had absconded after the apprehension of the other four prisoners, and this

he did in a manner surely never before attempted He declared that he remained at home during the week after Smith had been shot, but on Monday, 31st July, he went to reside with his cousin, Ann Cameron, who was married to one Smith, a printer at Kincaidfield, Campsie, because he had got information from James Walker, cotton spinner, that some persons had given false information to the Fiscal that he had several years ago committed a violent assault on Mr Miller, a spinning master at Lancefield, and £100 had been offered for the depredator By advice of friends he went out of the way till he should have an opportunity of proving that he had nothing to do with that assault Never knew till Sunday evening, 6th August, that he was accused of Smith's murder On the day he went to Kincaid he wrote out a certificate telling where he had been on Saturday, 22d July and put down on it the names of the persons who had been with him Declares that he was induced to write out that paper from his friends saying that if false information were given in against him as to Miller's assault, it was just as likely the same thing might occur as to the murder of Smith, and it was therefore better to prepare for the worst, as it was considered that his going out of the way, as to the assault on Miller, might strengthen the suspicion that he was accessory to Smith's murder, supposing false information was given in against him His own impression was that he was in England during the time when Miller was assaulted Had an intention on 11th July of going to England, and applied for a travelling card, which he got from the Committee, who also advanced him three shillings, but he spent the money and abandoned the design

On re examination (12th August) he adhered to his former declaration, and stated further that dozens of his friends had advised him to go out of the way, but this was after the Committee was seized, no one advised him to do so before that time Heard of their apprehension on Sunday, 30th July, and his father and friends then advised him to go away, but this was relative to the assault He went to Kincaid the following day Heard whisperings of a Select Secret Committee, but not from an authentic source Interrogated and desired specially to explain how it happened, if he was wholly unconnected with Smith's murder, that the intelligence he received of the apprehension of the Committee on the night of Saturday, 29th July 1837, should have led him to apprehend danger to himself, not from anything connected with that murder, but a crime of which he says he was suspected, committed many years ago, under the direction of a totally different Committee, and of which, he alleges, he was equally innocent as of Smith's murder? Declares that he merely went out of town for a few days on this occasion until his friends could ascertain in which year and at what time the old crime with which he heard he was charged had been committed, in order that he might be able to prove his innocence.

Although the prisoners' declarations were read in portions during different stages of the trial, we have thought it the most intelligible method to bring their principal statements together. The reader will thus be able to perceive how far these varied, and will understand better that portion of the evidence for the Crown to which we must still refer. To make the inconsistencies of M'Lean's declaration thoroughly apparent, one word may be necessary at this point.

Smith was murdered about twelve midnight on Saturday 22d July. M'Lean states that at this time he was helplessly drunk at a considerable distance from Clyde Street. He remains in Glasgow all the following week whilst search for the murderer is ineffectual, but when the Committee of the Cotton spinners—the probable hirers of the assassin—are apprehended on Saturday, 29th July, and he hears of this on Sunday he flies away on Monday morning to a country district some fourteen miles distant because he says he had heard that *he was to be accused of another crime of which he was not guilty.* By his own account he did not know that he was suspected of Smith's murder till Sunday evening, 6th August, when he was apprehended, yet his first work on arriving at Kincaid on the previous Monday is to draw up a certificate as to where he was when Smith was killed. This certificate had no bearing upon his connection with the assault upon Miller—the reason he gave for absconding—and he thus showed the influence of a guilty conscience in a most singular manner.

The witnesses for the Crown, who were examined after the first portions of the declarations were read, gave evidence as to the special outrages charged in the indictment. The most peculiar case of social tyranny was that related by Thomas Donaghey, a cotton spinner, who took work with the Mile End Spinning Company at reduced rates during the strike. He had been asked to give up work

ing, but had refused, and on the night of 30th June, when he had retired to rest an attack was made upon the house where he resided by a number of people. He would not open the door, and the panel was broken in, and one of the men, Thomas Riddle, came into the room by the aperture. 'I stood in the middle of the floor, said Donaghey, 'having a pistol in my hand, and threatening to fire if they did not go away. Riddle was for going away, and some of them behind urged him on. He asked me if I would give over working, and I said if they went away peaceably and quietly I would be out next day by eight o'clock, meaning I would leave the work. He desired me to give him my hand then, and I gave him my hand. He said, 'Now promise me you will come out at eight o'clock,' and I said 'I promise.' He said, 'Say I declare to God,' and I said it. They then went away. I changed my lodgings next day and went to my work, and have continued there ever since.'

After this outrage the ringleaders had absconded, but Riddle was apprehended in Bolton in the month of December, and was awaiting his trial at the Circuit Court in Glasgow at the very time this witness was giving his evidence. When brought up for trial on 11th January 1838 he pleaded guilty, and was sentenced to seven years' transportation. The prosecutor averred, in his indictment against the Cotton spinners, that the Association had paid £30 for the commission of this daring crime.

Several witnesses were examined as to the attempts to set fire to the house of Mr James Wood and to Hussey's Mill by throwing canisters filled with combustibles through the windows, and four cotton spinners described how the men on strike had violently assaulted them. Two of the latter asserted that they had been sworn to secrecy when admitted to the Society, and one of them mentioned *hlod* as the word used. On both occasions the oath was administered by Gibb.

The prosecutor had almost exhausted the witnesses whom he had summoned to give evidence to the first eleven charges in the Criminal Letters, and had now to lead the evidence at his command as to the murder of John Smith. The Court adjourned at ten o'clock P.M. to meet on Friday morning.

HOULDSWORTH'S BARRACKS, CHEAPSIDE STREET

PART VII

' Thou little wotest what this right hand can
  Speak they which have beheld the battailes which it wan '
                              —*The Faerie Queen*

The proceedings on the third day of the trial were opened by a long and desultory debate as to the admissibility of a certain letter as evidence, and considerable delay was caused without advancing the trial in the slightest degree. Several officers of the police gave evidence as to the riots at Oakbank and Mile End. At length Margaret Lochrie or Smith, the widow of the murdered man, was placed in the witness box, and gave a simple and affecting narrative of the incidents upon the fatal Saturday night :—

"My husband was working in Houldsworth's mill after the strike. I recollect going out to make markets on Saturday night with him. We went into Clyde Street about eleven o'clock. The watch was crying ' past eleven ' as we went into a shop at the head of Washington Street, next to Clyde Street. Then we went into a flesher's shop near the head of Clyde Street, in Anderston Walk. We went down Clyde Street intending to go round to Cheapside Street, where we lived, by the Broomielaw. We passed Mrs Cross's shop, and then my husband was shot while I was at his side walking together with him. The shot came from behind our backs. My husband fell forward, and I started, my senses having nearly gone from me, but I saw like four persons behind me, but could not say more than that they were dark bodies or objects. I stooped to lift up my husband by the arm. I did not know where the persons went, they did not come to my assistance. When I rose the first thing I saw was a man coming from the foot of the street to help me. I had screamed out 'Murder' two or three times, and when this man came the length of me there were more around me. I ran up the street before them, when my husband was lifted and carried away. When I went to lift my husband he said he was shot, but said nothing then to me as to the cause of it. He was what is considered a 'nob.' He never expressed to me any fear of being injured for being a nob. I have no recollection of having observed any persons following me or my husband, and nobody whatever spoke to me or him in the streets."

The circumstances of the murder, as Mrs Smith detailed them, effectually prevented her from identifying any of the prisoners as being concerned in it , and though she had some faint recollection of having seen M'Lean acting as a guard at Houldsworth's mill, she could not connect him with the assassination

Peter M'Quiston, land-surveyor, had made plans of the streets about Cheapside Street for the use of the Court, and as it became evident from the cross examination of this witness that it was intended to advance an *alibi*, the Lord Justice Clerk directed the special defences to be read at this stage These were in similar terms to those produced at the first trial in November, and asserted that none of the prisoners was near the place where the murder was committed at the time stated in the indictment

Dr Pagan, of the Glasgow Royal Infirmary, gave evidence as to the date and cause of Smith's death and the unfortunate man's dying declaration, from which we have already quoted, was read He stated that he was unable to say who shot him, and had no suspicion of any one nor had he heard any footsteps behind him at the time the deed was done But he was clearly convinced that he had been made a victim solely because of his reputation as a nob

The most important witness for the prosecution so far as Smith's murder was concerned, was Robert Christie, at one time a cotton spinner, but latterly spirit dealer in the Gallowgate of Glasgow, since he deponed upon oath that M'Lean had confessed to him that he had committed this atrocious crime The testimony which this witness gave threw still further light upon the baneful system of terrorism under which the members of the Union were held by the Committee Having received the assurance of full protection from the Court, he stated that he had been a member of the Association for nine years, and had been sworn to secrecy on the Bible, the word *Armageddon* being used He was acquainted with all the prisoners, but knew M'Lean best, as he was frequently in the spirit shop of witness, and he related a curious incident which occurred upon the Wednesday before Smith's murder, tending to show M'Lean's sentiments regarding assassination

"I remember a conversation,' Christie said, "in my house with M'Lean about Arthur, the Adelphi manager The strike at that time had lasted a good while On this night M'Lean came into my shop, and said he was going an errand to the other side of the water I said if he would wait I was going to close my shop in a few minutes, and I would accompany him He waited, I closed, and we went on together. Before we reached St Andrew's

Square he spoke to me several times concerning Mr Arthur I did not understand at first what he meant, but when he came the length of St Andrew's Square he said he was going direct across the water to *death* Mr Arthur I trembled when I heard the words expressed, and I began to flatter him and to put him off the notion He said he was determined to do so, and he gave a wee bit stagger to a side, and put his hand into his pocket and said, 'It is here that will do for him ' I still continued to coax him and to put him off doing it , but he still persisted, with an oath, that he would I saw the butt end of a pistol, as I thought, in his pocket '

With considerable difficulty Christie prevailed on M'Lean to forego his purpose at this time , but the assassination of Mr Arthur was alluded to on more than one occasion The witness gave a strange piece of evidence with reference to M'Lean's connection with the Committee It appeared that M'Lean was in Christie's debt to the extent of twenty five shillings, and *early on the Tuesday morning after the murder of Smith*, M'Lean told him that 'the Committee would pay every fraction of this debt ' The portion of his evidence, however, which related to M'Lean's confession to him was of most importance, and ran in these terms —

' On the Tuesday after the murder, at my shop in the Gallowgate, I saw him for the second time of that day about eleven o'clock M'Lean then said to me, 'I've made one sleep' I said, 'O, William, what's that you are saying ' He said, 'I made one sleep,' and turning round pointing to a placard on the street, asked if I saw you and I said, 'Yes , it is £50 of a reward offered ' No,' said he, 'it is £500 I was agitated at the time, and just said £50 as being confused On his saying this I took him by the breast and said, 'For the love of God, William, make your escape, or you will be apprehended immediately ,' and he turned about and said to me, ' There's nae *down* on me , they are awa' after another man to Liverpool,' meaning that the suspicion was not on himself He went into the room to the rest, where they were drinking spirits In a few minutes he asked for a light to his pipe When going out for one, I was standing at the side of the counter, and he put his hand into his pocket and then put his right hand out and said, 'That's the wee paw that did the trick He was going out, but before he did so I asked if any person saw him do it, and he said he took good care of that , and he put his hand into his breast, as if pulling out a pistol, and put himself in a position as if firing a pistol, and then, putting his hand into his breast again, said, ' I walked off, I did not run , I just walked across the street' That day, in the afternoon, M'Lean came into my shop alone, and said he had done for one, and would do for some more of them He said he had done for Miller in Lancefield, when no other person would take it in hand, and that he had got £50 or £100 or a reward for it I think that he referred to Miller getting a terrible beating 'I wish to God' he said, 'that there were three days of darkness that I might do for them all' Next day M'Lean began to speak about America, and said he was meaning to go there I asked if he had got clothes and all things in readiness, and he said, 'The Committee have supplied me with them things I spoke about friends I had there, who wanted me to go and that I should like to do so, and he said, Let who will go, I *must* go' On another occasion, when speaking about Smith's death, he said that Houldsworth and Salmond had asked Smith if he knew who had done the deed, and that Smith had answered no He swore an oath, and said, 'Little did they think I did it'"

If perfect credence could have been given to this story the guilt of M'Lean would have appeared indefensible, and the prisoner's advocate, Mr P Robertson, tried to upset Christie's evidence by a severe cross-examination, striving to make it seem that Christie had become an accomplice by hiding the criminal from justice But the Solicitor General overturned this acute device by eliciting the following startling statement from the witness —

"I was examined six or seven times before the Sheriff before I told all I have now disclosed I was reluctant, knowing that I was under an oath not to reveal anything about the Association, and knowing that many individuals had been shot at and burnt with vitriol by that Association It was a scrupulous fear of my oath and of that danger which made me keep silence to the Sheriff until I became persuaded by his strong assurance of protection and safety I did not tell, though it was a right thing to disclose a murder until that I saw I was in safety; and I did not refuse to speak out, because M'Lean's statements had left any doubt upon my mind of the truth of what he told me It was the breaking of the oath and the fear'

James Hamilton, partner of a firm of shipping agents in Glasgow, spoke as to M'Lean's calling upon him on 20th July to arrange about a steerage passage to America, and his clerk corroborated his evidence Adam Dixon, cotton spinner, though apparently inclined to favour the prisoners by denying statements that had been made against the procedure of the Association, really confirmed Christie's evidence in some of the particulars as to

M'Lean's conduct after the murder of Smith He underwent a very severe cross-examination, which ultimately left his testimony of little use to either side The Court adjourned after a prolonged sitting

On Saturday morning the first witness examined was Archibald Campbell, cabinetmaker at Kirkintilloch, who deponed that on the night of Saturday, 22d July, he had been in a spirit shop in Stevenson Street, Calton, where he overheard some spinners say, 'Smith will be shot to night' As he could not identify any of the prisoners his evidence was of little value John Sheriff stated that on the Tuesday or Wednesday before Smith's murder he had sold some leaden bullets of a size similar to those extracted by Dr Pagan from the body of the murdered man; but he could not swear that any of the prisoners had purchased them William Smith, cotton spinner, gave evidence of a kind which was probably never before accepted in a Court of Justice When under cross-examination he made the following statement, which the reader will notice was 'hearsay evidence of the very worst description' —

'I knew Mary Wilson wife of Allan M'Donald, who died of a fever shortly after Smith was shot I had heard that she had seen Smith shot, and went to her I asked her if she had seen it, and she told me she had I asked what like the person was that had fired the shot, and she told me that he was a little set man with dark moleskin clothes on, jacket and trousers of the same I asked where he went She said she saw the direction he took, and followed him about, and he went into the first through going close in Clyde Street, going into Piccadilly Street She said he went at a quick pace, after adjusting his hat on his head, and she followed him a bit I spoke to her twice, and she told me the same story both times She was quite well at the time, but she died of typhus fever about a fortnight after our last conversation'

More than one witness had described M'Lean's attire on the day of the murder as being "a dark green coat light trousers, and black hat, and if Mary Wilson was correct in her description of the man whom she took to be the murderer it would be difficult to prove his identity with M'Lean But so unsatisfactory was this evidence considered by the Prosecutor that, though the wife of the last witness had been summoned, he did not call her to the box Mr Robertson, as counsel for M'Lean, took advantage of this fact, and placed her on his list of witnesses for the defence, thus adroitly defeating the Lord Advocate with his own weapons

John M'Manus, a brother in law of the

murdered man, gave evidence to show that Smith was unpopular as a "nob" amongst the turn out spinners, and stated that on the night of the murder Smith had spoken of himself as being apprehensive of foul play at their hands David Thorburn, a fellow workman in the mill, who lived beside Smith, had left him at the head of Clyde Street about half an hour before he was shot At that time, with a strange premonition of his approaching fate, the unfortunate man "ex pressed fear and anxiety to get home He was afraid of being ill used on account of working at Houldsworth's factory, and he said he had some things to buy yet This witness, having received assurance of the protection of the Court, confessed that he had been hired by the prisoner Hunter to assault a nob some seven years before He had received money to enable him to leave the country after the crime had been committed, and he remained away from Glasgow for six months; but when he returned he was apprehended, tried for the assault and convicted, his sentence being sixty days in Bridewell The testimony of this witness was given with evident reluctance, and an apparent desire to screen the Committee if possible

Four men who had been passing down Clyde Street when the shot was fired were examined, and stated that they saw two men pass hurriedly up the west side of the street immediately after the report One of these fugitives was described as being "gey and tall," and having a long black coat on, which agreed with the appearance of M'Lean; but though these men could easily have arrested the two suspicious looking characters, they made no attempt to do so The officer who had apprehended M'Lean at Kincaidfield narrated the circumstances, telling that the prisoner had given a false name at first, and was much agitated when he heard that he was charged with murder

Two certificates upon which M'Lean had founded his *alibi* were read, and were in these terms —

"This is to certify that William M'Lean was in my house till twelve o'clock on Saturday, 22d July, from about ten o'clock —*Angus Cameron*"

"William M'Lean was in our company from nine o'clock on Saturday, the 22d July, till about two o'clock Sabbath morning —*Thomas Loag, Alex Stevenson, John Thom, James Grieve, James Corrigan, John Miller, John Lockhart, John Andrew*"

From the evidence of Thomas Loag, the first of these certifiers, it was made perfectly plain that

the *alibi* was a pure concoction. He stated that he had left M'Lean at the Cross at *nine o'clock* on the Saturday, and had not seen him again till the following Monday He had signed the certificate at the request of M'Lean's father, but had afterwards drawn back, as he could not truthfully swear to the hour written on the paper

Robert Macome, writer, Dumbarton, had been employed in 1836 to defend three cotton-spinners concerned in an assault upon some nobs at Duntocher The Committee had lodged money with Macome so that he might get the accused out on bail, and he had done so. One of the men absconded, and the money—£20—was forfeited Peter Hacket was the principal party in this transaction This concluded the parole evidence for the prosecution, and when the last portions of the prisoners' declarations had been read the Solicitor General announced that he passed from all further proof It was now the task of the counsel for the prisoners to rebut the very weighty charges which had been brought against them by adducing more credible testimony than had been offered to the jury

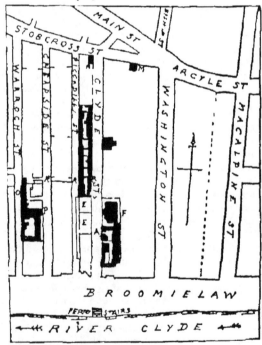

PLAN OF CLYDE STREET, ANDERSTON, AND VICINITY

A Spot where Smith was shot E Woodyards F Church C Shop of Mrs Cross M Flesher's shop N Doctor's shop O Houldsworth's Mill I Houldsworth's Barracks R R R Communications between Clyde, Piccadilly, and Cheapside Streets

THE BRIGGATE OF GLASGOW IN 1837—(*From a contemporary print*)

PART VIII

" Does not in Chancery every man swear
  What makes best for him in his answer '
  Is not the winding up witnesses
  And nicking more than half the business '

For witnesses, like watches go
Just as they're set—too fast or slow
And where in conscience they're strait-laced
Tis ten to one that side is cast '

—Hudibras

Seldom has there been a case brought into a Court of Justice which more evidently shows the worthlessness of a judicial oath than that of the Glasgow Cotton spinners. Those witnesses for the prisoners who had been connected with the Association made solemn statements upon oath, which were not only irreconcilable with the evidence for the Crown, but contradictory, in some points, of the declarations made by the prisoners themselves. There was, besides, such a suspicious similarity betwixt these statements that it is almost impossible to escape the notion that their stories had been pre arranged, and the miserable failures which they made under cross examination prove that there was collusion between them, and an understanding amongst them to deny everything of which the prisoners were accused. We have reached this conclusion after a careful analysis of their evidence as detailed in four different reports of the trial, and to avoid the tedium of reciting all this mass of contradictory testimony, we shall lay merely a slight narrative sketch of it before the reader.

Seven members of the Cotton spinners Association were called to give evidence as to the procedure of that body. They all agreed in saying that no oath was administered on entering the Society, that they had never heard the words "Ashdod" or "Armageddon" used, that the object of the Union was merely to get the rate of wages which they thought they were entitled to by legitimate means, and that though the decision of a majority was to form a guide to the trade in all disputes, the minority were suffered to act as they deemed expedient without molestation. A nob, they all asserted, was in perfect safety to walk about the streets either by day or night during the whole time of the strikes. On the latter point a question was put to each of these witnesses, and they all replied to the effect that they would not themselves have been afraid of violence had they been nobs.

Upon these matters they were unanimous; but on several important subjects they differed widely. Some of them had never heard of Guard Committees or Secret Select Committees, whilst others confessed that they had acted as Guards during more than one strike. Some were ignorant of any Debt or Decreet Committee—as the junto which held the false bills we have spoken of was called—but others said that though they did not remember of this lawless institution, they knew it as intended to organise such a Committee. Hunter admitted that he was present at the meeting after the demonstration on the Green, but one of the witnesses swore that not one of the five prisoners was there. Even the question of entry money was dif

ferently described, some asserting that it was £5, and others maintaining that it was £10, and various opinions being expressed as to the custom of admitting repentant nobs to the sacred privileges of the Association. The ominous entry "expenses with nobs," so frequently repeated in the cash-books of the Union, was explained by one witness as referring to money spent in treating nobs to whisky, &c.; and by another as meaning aliment given to nobs who had agreed to leave their work and join the Association. Another witness asserted that he never saw "expenses with nobs" entered on the schedules; and though one of the rules in the Constitution of the Association was read to him, stating that idle men were "to get £5 for every one they unshop," he declared that he had never heard of such a rule. One witness—Archibald Mackay—who had entered the Association in 1823, and had therefore been through all the dreadful periods of assassination and assault in 1825, 1832, and 1837, calmly made the following statement upon oath:—

"I have heard of violence being laid to the spinners, but I did not believe this. I do not believe, and I never knew of any Cotton spinner having done violence to a man, because of a man working contrary to a strike. I believe there was vitriol once thrown, but I don't believe this was done by spinners." On cross examination this witness explained that he had overheard people speaking about vitriol throwing; and he confessed that he knew of several trials of Cotton spinners for molestation. These numerous contradictions and counter assertions could only be explained either on the mild supposition that the witnesses for the defence were not in the confidence of the Cotton spinners' Committee, or on the likelier one that they held themselves under a deeper obligation to the Association than to the most solemn judicial oath which could be administered to them. In either case their evidence was valueless, for it was absurd to set up the unsupported statements of mere outsiders against the coherent testimony of men like Moat and Murdoch, who were cognisant of the secret workings of the Association, even had they shown some regard to consistency and some respect for their oaths. With every desire to do justice to the accused, we are compelled to acquiesce in the decision of the Recorder of Macclesfield regarding their witnesses—"The whole defence was founded in fraud and supported by perjury."

We have already alluded to the evidence given by William Smith as to the statements made by a woman, since deceased, who declared she had seen the murder committed. This man's wife, Helen Caldwell or Smith, was examined upon this subject, and gave a story substantially the same as her husband's, but it was evident that no cross examination could overturn satisfactorily the mere repeated statements of another person No English judge would have suffered such incompetent testimony to be led in his court, and it shows an aspect of fairness on the part of the Bench towards the prisoners which almost amounts to disregard of the claims of justice Severe legal critics of this trial have asserted that this worthless evidence really turned the scale in favour of the prisoners

There still remained the important defence founded upon the *alibi* We have seen that Thomas Loag, the first man whose name was attached to the certificate, had declared it false, giving evidence against it for the Crown He stated in his evidence that he had told M'Lean's father that he declined to swear to the time at which it was said he had left the prisoner, and it appears that the indefatigable old man, anxious to save his son, had prepared another certificate, which was put in process It was in terms identical with the previous one, however, and bore only five instead of eight names, one of them—Andrew Whyte—being different from those appearing on the first paper Two of these certifiers were produced as witnesses, and never perhaps was there appearance of collusion made more evident without being followed with a prosecution for perjury

Andrew Whyte described the circumstances under which he signed the certificate thus —" I was asked to sign a certificate about M'Lean about three weeks after Smith's murder, to satisfy M'Lean's friends and acquaintances that we were with him on the night of Smith's murder till one o'clock and after it I recollected, and we all recollected, where we had been with him We all agreed that we had been with him at Cameron's from ten to within ten minutes to twelve o'clock, and that we had all come to that house from the Cross, and after we left it we went to M'Ilwraith's in the Briggate This was talked of among us when we signed the certificate "

The Solicitor General here interposed, objecting to the validity of this evidence " You have not merely the existence of this certificate," he said, " but you have the persons who sign it assembled in a room together The whole story is agreed upon The witnesses are tutored, they are examined in the presence of one another, they get a complete lesson of the sort of evidence that is required from them, and all this is done by the panel himself or his friends "

Mr M'Neill endeavoured to separate M'Lean's case from the others, and claimed that the evidence of the *alibi* should proceed, and the Judges

after consultation, agreed to allow the witnesses to be examined, cautioning the jury as to the weakness of their testimony Lord Cockburn's deliverance on this subject was very clear " Of all points in a case," he said, " the establishment of an *alibi* is the one in which the minds of the witnesses ought to be kept the most unprepared and untutored There is nothing in the world so easy to be proved If the witnesses are prepared even as to time and place, there is scarcely an *alibi*, however false, which may not be established But here, within thirteen or fourteen days after a crime has been committed, while one of the prisoners is in hiding and accused of that offence, some person acting for him gets individuals into a room together, and there a certificate is prepared, and they are all tied down to what they are to say, in expectation of a trial, and this certificate is so expressed that, while it binds them down to the fact that the prisoner was with them in the places mentioned at a certain time, they are left as to all minute particulars to the invention of their own fancy Is it to be expected after this that you can get from these witnesses free and unconstrained evidence?" The Lord Justice Clerk was still more precise in his condemnation of this *alibi*, and said, " I have never in all my experience seen witnesses offered and received under such disqualifying circumstances "

As might have been expected, these witnesses contradicted each other as to the minor details of their story when under cross examination One stated that the room in Cameron's where they first met on Saturday, 22d July, had neither fire nor fireplace, another averred that there was a fire burning in the grate " M'Lean sang a comic song," says one ; " No songs were sung by any one," says another, whilst a third " Cannot recollect whether any songs were sung or not " James Grieve confesses that he left M'Lean before twelve o'clock on Saturday night, and Andrew Whyte says he was home at half past one ; yet both sign a paper stating that they were with the prisoner till two o'clock on Sunday morning Still more serious was the slip made by Whyte in saying that when the party met to sign the certificate M'Lean was in custody Lord Moncrieff pointed out to him that M'Lean was not apprehended for two days after the date of the certificate, and asked him how he had come to connect M'Lean with the murder before he was found? " I could not be certain, but I *thought* he was in custody," was the blundering reply

The shopmen in the spirit shops of Cameron and M'Ilwraith gave evidence as to M'Lean being present in these two places on that Saturday night, but as they had no special marks by which they could identify him, and as they stated that the shops "were very throng that night" their testimony was not worth much. This closed the exculpatory proof. It had been begun upon Saturday afternoon, and had lasted till the following Tuesday at half past two o'clock P.M. The intervening Sunday had been spent by the jury under the close surveillance of the two Macers of Court, though some of them had been permitted to attend public worship, and others had driven to Musselburgh Links for an airing.

The Lord Advocate's address to the jury occupied upwards of five hours, and was principally directed towards a recapitulation of those points in evidence which told most strikingly against the prisoners. In opening he defended himself from the charge of unduly interfering with the rights of labour. So far from considering it unlawful in workmen to take all proper means to raise their rate of wages, he thought it was the dearest, the most sacred right that any man possessed—that of using his labour in any way he thought fit. But still, they were not to interfere with others in preventing them from taking what wages they chose. He considered the rights of all men equal and free with regard to the produce of their labour, and that no man had a right to control another.

"The deeds of violence and atrocity that took place in Glasgow for many years," he said, "surprised and astonished the country. The throwing of vitriol, the assassinating harmless and innocent persons, the shooting at individuals in open day are acts that certainly took place, but which are so unlike anything that we are acquainted with anywhere else that it could hardly be believed that they had taken place in Scotland. They appeared still more extraordinary from taking place without any apparent motive. The perversion of moral feeling which gave rise to them is now explained by this important and extraordinary trial—unprecedented in the history of the kingdom."

In a very masterly manner the Lord Advocate detailed the secret history of the Association, pointing out the hidden manner in which its operations were conducted, the oaths of secrecy, the squandering of money in support of strikes throughout the kingdom, and finally the state of desperation into which it had fallen during the last protracted strike, driving its members to the committing of assaults, to attempting fire-raising, to sending threatening letters, and at last to cold blooded assassination. The contradictions between the prisoners' declarations and the statements of their own witnesses told strongly against them,

and M'Lean's conduct especially seemed inexplicable on any other supposition than that of guilt. He concluded by stating that the whole charges were, in his apprehension, proved, and he trusted that by this trial the whole mystery would be exposed, and those proceedings—so atrocious, so disgraceful, so abhorrent to the feelings of Scotsmen—would be for ever put an end to.

Mr Duncan M'Neill was charged with the defence of the four prisoners, Hunter, Hacket, Gibb, and M'Neil, and rose to address the jury on their behalf in a speech which lasted nearly four hours. His address was ingenious though sophistical, and well calculated to deceive an impressionable jury. He pointed out that the charge of murder in the case of his clients depended wholly upon the conviction of M'Lean. They were charged with having hired M'Lean to commit the deed, but if his advocate could show, as he believed he could, that M'Lean was not concerned in it, the charge against the other four prisoners must fall. But even if M'Lean were convicted of the murder, was there anything to connect his clients with this crime? It was asserted that they had hired M'Lean, but no proof of this was adduced, no evidence brought to suggest that they had more to do with it than any other of the eight hundred spinners in the Association, all of whom, with equal justice and propriety might, and still may, be put upon trial for their lives for this capital crime. The prosecutor had made a point as to the Association proposing to take a passage for M'Lean to America. The murder was committed on the 22d July, the vessel was to sail on the 24th from Liverpool. Nothing could be more opportune. Why, then, was his passage not taken in that vessel? This story turned against the prosecutor, for it showed that the Association had the means, and knew they had the means, of sending M'Lean away if they had the disposition to do so. Had M'Lean been the instrument of the Association, would they not have sent him away? Assuredly they would—and as assuredly they did *not* send him away.

The peroration of Mr M'Neill's speech was one of those gems of forensic eloquence which are really worthy of preservation, as showing how art may make "the worse appear the better reason," and impose by rhetorical solemnity upon an unwary jury. We make no apology, therefore, for quoting it entirely.

"I can believe that some individual cotton-spinner, oppressed and goaded on by want and despair—acting under the impulse of desperate and misguided feelings, or perhaps having some cause of personal enmity against the unfortunate man Smith, may of himself have perpetrated this deed It was not a deed which required many heads to contrive it, and a separate hand to execute it It is possible that one who was connected with the particular work in which Smith was employed may have both conceived and accomplished it Breathes there the man so confident in his own powers of discernment as to say that this case is free of doubt ? Are you, then, to seal the doom of these prisoners in the dark, or to accept of suspicion as a substitute for proof ? Are you so impatient of blood that you cannot wait till the truth is revealed, as it must one day be ? Or are you so weak as to dread that when it shall be revealed you may, perhaps, be exposed to the reflection of having allowed the guilty to escape, and to walk abroad as living evidences of your want of penetration ? In the fulness of time the voice of Truth must be heard, and it may one day ring a fearful peal in your ears, if you act rashly now Yes, when Time the great revealer as well as the great destroyer of all things human !— Time, which brings to light the darkest transactions that the craft of man has vainly endeavoured to bury in perpetual obscurity, just as surely as it moulders into nothing the proudest monuments by which man as vainly endeavours to perpetuate the memory of his own perishable name !—when that great agent of Omnipotence shall have shed its illuminating influence over this dark transaction, and exposed its deepest depths— when each of these men, who now in vain asserts his innocence and implores justice, shall have suffered the unmerited anguish of your condemnation, the horrors of the condemned cell, and the ignominy of a felon's death, and shall have transmitted a hated and blighting name to a helpless and unoffending progeny—when the tempests of winter and the sun of summer shall have passed alike unheeded over their unhallowed graves, and the revolution of these seasons shall have brought

the return of your duties, and again placed some of you in that seat, to administer justice on the real delinquent, the true murderer, then detected —not, as now, groping your way amidst the darkness of mystery, and doubt, and error, but walking in the full, clear, and safe light of truth then made manifest -perhaps with your own ears hearing from the lips of the culprit himself the penitent confessions of a conscience become unbearable to the midnight assassin, because of his participation in the still deeper tragedy of this night, in which you too are asked to play so prominent a part—his silent acquiescence in the shedding of the innocent blood of these men, with which you too are about to stain your hands if you yield to the demand that has been made upon you—what then will be your feelings, what your reflections ? You will not, I know, have any cause to upbraid yourselves with having returned a verdict which at the time you did not sincerely believe to be in accordance with the truth Your own conscience, I know, will acquit you, and rightly acquit, of that sin, whatever may be the opinion of the world—just as their consciences now acquit them, on this their day of trial, and would do even if it was their day of doom But although you escape self condemnation on that score, you cannot possibly escape the bitter and painful and humiliating reflection that, presuming, vainly presuming, on your own penetration, you thought you could discover that which had not yet been revealed to man, and with rash and impious hands had endeavoured prematurely to rend asunder the veil of mystery which, in its inscrutable wisdom, Providence had interposed between you and the truth of this deed of blood "

The learned advocate concluded his address, amidst the applause of his audience, at eleven o'clock on Tuesday night, and the Court was adjourned immediately until the following morning

THE TRONGATE AND CROSS OF GLASGOW IN 1837.

PART IX

' The fond multitude
Hung with their sudden counsels on the breath
Of great Pisistratus that chief renowned,
Whom Hermes and the Idalian queen had trained,
Even from his birth to every powerful art
Of pleasing and persuading from whose lips
Flow'd eloquence which, like the vows of love
Could steal away suspicion from the hearts
Of all who listened —*Akenside*

On the seventh day of this remarkable trial the proceedings were opened by Mr Patrick Robertson's address in defence of M'Lean, which occupied nearly four hours in delivery This accomplished orator, afterwards well known as Lord Robertson, enjoyed the reputation of being one of the wittiest and most eloquent advocates at the Scottish Bar, and seldom did he deliver a speech so effective as this one   With the vigour of a Demosthenes and the art of a Cicero he carried his audience through every form of rhetorical figure, from the most solemn adjuration to the most humorous ridicule We have only space for a very brief summary of his address

After detailing the series of outrages regarding which evidence had been tendered, extending from 1818 up till 1837, and including crimes of the most violent description, he warned the jury that a calamity still more dreadful than any of these outrages would be the conviction and execution of an innocent man on other than the clearest evidence He counselled them not to be led away by theories of political economy questions of capital and labour, which had been unwarrantably introduced into this trial , but to confine themselves strictly to the consideration of facts, and their bearing upon the case of the accused Proceeding to analyse the evidence, he dealt with that portion which referred to the election of the Secret Committee in a strain of broad ridicule, which served to make it *appear* nonsensical, though it did not in the least affect its credibility. Having seen from the first that Christie's evidence was certain to tell most severely upon his client (M'Lean), he directed all his powers of farcical satire against that unfortunate witness, treating his evidence as a silly fabrication with which it was impossible to deal without laughter He took full advantage of that strange part of Christie's testimony which related to the threatened assassination of Mr Arthur.

"Such an appalling account of crime," he said, "and such ludicrous stories never came from the mouth of any witness This bold-faced villain—this Pierre of the conspiracy—this Pistol of the Association—this braggart is bawling out in the streets of Glasgow, 'I will do for him !' Christie answers, 'Whist ! do not speak so loud ! my character is at stake !' I am Christie the pure !' I had some intention a fortnight ago to go to America I have changed my resolution, I do not know why My character is at stake The credit of my house in the Gallowgate—the refuge for all the respectable of the trade—is it stake, and the credit of my hotel on the other side of the water is at stake Take care, do not speak aloud Arthur !' 'But I *will* do for him—here is the pistol, I *will* do for him !' rejoins the other, loudly There was no assault on Arthur 'He knew d——d well where Arthur was ' I suppose he was snug in his bed, but Pistol and Bardolph were ready to go to his bed chamber, and drag him out for the purpose of the assault—and here the tale terminates "

The dubious testimony which Archibald Campbell gave as to overhearing some cotton spinners in a public-house far removed from the scene of the murder, speaking of it as a deed to be accomplished, was legitimately ridiculed by the orator, but no prosecutor could have touched more tenderly than he did upon the case of the unfortunate victim of this murder

"Gentlemen, he said, "I cannot, I must not, I *dare* not pass this part of the case—I that am counsel for this man, unjustly, as I think, accused —I cannot pass this part of the case without shedding one tear over this deed of blood We have heard of murder done from malice—we have heard of murder done from avarice—we have heard also of murders done that the bodies of the victims might be made the subject of profit But I do not think that any of these murders is more base or more infamous than this ! It was a murder perpetrated on this poor man, who had finished his week of labour in the toilsome occupation to which Providence had destined him, and who was entitled to lay his head for one night on his peaceful pillow, and to look forward to the return of that day when even the weary artizan is entitled to repose—is entitled to repose of body and rest of mind that he may dedicate to his God one day of the week, and pass some hours without bodily fatigue, if not without mental solicitude At that moment the cowardly assassin, lurking behind, draws the fatal trigger which hurries this honest and toil worn artizan, in a very few hours, to the presence of the God who made him, and **terminates** his earthly career of toil and care But, gentlemen, the more base, the more unprincipled, the more inexcusable this deed of darkness is, the more are you called upon not to convict unless your mind be overwhelmed by evidence of which no doubt can be entertained "

Even from the worthless evidence given as to the statements of the deceased Mrs M'Donald, the accomplished orator contrived to envolve quite a dramatic scene We have already stated that such evidence would not have been tolerated elsewhere, yet the adroit advocate knew how to utilise it for the advantage of his client

"It you believe, ' he said, "a true account is given of what Mrs M'Donald stated, who had no interest in the matter, and who is now unhappily removed from your sight, I say the case is at an end What was her account of it ? *The dress and stature of the murderer in no degree corresponded with M'Lean* Mr Smith said 'She told me he was a *little stout man*, with dark moleskin clothes, jacket and trousers of the same ' This comes out when he is cross examined Then we call the wife of this witness She was in the list of the witnesses for the Crown but not called by the prosecutor, on account, I presume, of that cross examination Mrs M'Donald told her he was a little man, with dark, dirty moleskin clothes, and that he was below the common size of men M'Lean is *above* the common size of men Stand up ! [Here M'Lean stood up] He is taller, I believe, than any of the prisoners Says my learned friend, the Lord Advocate, this must have been a mistake on the part of Mrs M'Donald, she may not estimate the height of men as others do, she may have been mistaken God help us, gentlemen, will this do ? Is every thing a mistake that tells in favour of the prisoners ?'

With profound wisdom, Mr Robertson passed rapidly over the evidence in support of the *alibi*, treating it in so apologetic a fashion that its influence upon the jury must have been very much weakened He admitted that M'Lean's appearance upon his apprehension was not in his favour, and reprobated the officious urgency of those injudicious friends who had endeavoured to make a way of escape for him But all this, he maintained, was of slight avail, and he proceeded to terminate his address in these terms —

"I put it again to you to say—is this murder proved ? I confidently submit that it is not There are two things which, in a Court of Justice, never must be named but to be reprobated—the one of these is fear, the other is suspicion Fear that crime shall go unpunished is no reason for convicting without evidence Gentlemen, we have had an appalling picture drawn by the Sheriff of the state of Glasgow, and at the outset I called your attention to the number of outrageous acts mentioned and gathered together in this inquiry Gentlemen, I think he stated that there was reason to believe these dangers were now terminated Gentlemen, for the purposes of this inquiry I care not whether they are terminated or not. As a free citizen of this State, I trust in God that they are at an end. But I repeat that for the purposes of this inquiry I care not. I am certain that the fear of consequences is not to affect you in the verdict which you shall return. No, though the fabric of the Constitution itself shall be undermined—though 'temple and tower go the ground'—let the pillar of justice still stand unshaken, and, amidst the darkness, and the desolation, and dismay of revolution, let the flower of truth still blossom in the wilderness. And, as to *suspicion*, it has been said by one of the noblest of created beings, 'Suspicion sleeps at Wisdom's gate.' Gentlemen, you have entered the gates of the Temple of Justice, and at these gates also does Suspicion lie dormant. You must not only think no ill where no ill is, but you are bound to think no ill where no ill is *proved*. And last of all, let me implore you, now that my lips are about to be closed, and the last words that can be uttered in favour of the prisoner are to fall upon your ears—let me beseech you, fearlessly, manfully, like Britons, like Scotsmen, to throw fear and suspicion away, and to return that verdict which you shall answer for to your God, and which, if it be not in favour of the prisoner, can only be pronounced when you are satisfied that it is supported by evidence leaving no rational doubt upon your minds of the guilt of this man. If you do otherwise, I conclude by repeating that a more fearful and a more tremendous slaughter than even the murder of Smith shall be committed by that judicial execution.'

The Lord Justice Clerk began his summing up at two o'clock, but by eleven P.M. he had only succeeded in revising the evidence for the prosecution, and the Court was adjourned at that late hour to meet on the following day to hear the conclusion of his address. On that day—the eighth of the trial—he resumed his address at half past ten, and completed it at half past four, thus occupying fifteen hours in its delivery. The evidence on both sides was sifted with judicial acumen, and in a style so thoroughly unbiassed that it must have weighed with the jury to a great extent. He pointed out at the very beginning of his address how important the evidence of Christie was, since no confession of the murder could be found elsewhere. But if the statements of this witness could not be believed—if he was perjured—then the whole charge of murder against M'Lean, and consequently against the other prisoners, fell to the ground. For his own part he thought that if Christie's evidence was not true, it required a most extraordinary share of invention. The witnesses adduced in support of the *alibi* were severely censured by his Lordship; and

he plainly stated that but for a doubt existing in the minds of some of his brethren on the bench, he would have rejected them entirely. Examining the charges *seriatim*, he expressed his opinion that the sending of threatening letters by M'Neil had not been proved, as *libelled*, nor had it been proved that M'Lean was hired by the other four prisoners to commit the murder of which they were accused. On the question as to whether M'Lean was the murderer, they had only the very unsatisfactory evidence of the *alibi* to rebut the charge; and though he professed grave doubts as to its admissibility, it still left some shade of uncertainty by which the prisoner should benefit.

At the conclusion of this summing-up the jury retired, and were secluded for five hours, the Court meanwhile continuing to sit. They returned their verdict at nine o'clock, in these terms:—

"The Jury, by a majority, find the charges Nos. I., II., III., and X. in the libel, against all the panels, Proven as libelled, and unanimously find the rest of the libel Not Proven."

The first three charges referred to the appointment of Guards, and to the riots at Oakbank and Mile end. The tenth charge was founded upon the hiring by the prisoners of Riddell and others to invade the dwelling of Thomas Donaghey; but as in the Criminal Letters this charge depended upon the fifth in the libel—referring to the appointment of a Secret Select Committee—which had not been found proved, the prisoners' counsel objected to the verdict as it stood, and, after debate, the objection was sustained. Lord Mackenzie then proposed that the prisoners should be sentenced to seven years' transportation, in which Lord Moncrieff concurred; and the Lord Justice Clerk accordingly pronounced sentence to this effect in a most impressive speech. The proceedings were concluded at nearly twelve o'clock on Thursday night, having occupied the jury for ninety-six hours, and forming thus one of the longest trials in the records of the Scottish Criminal Courts. The trial of Lord Provost Stewart, of Edinburgh, for complicity with the Rebels in 1745, comes most nearly up to it, having lasted for ninety-four hours.

The influence of the eloquence displayed by the prisoners' advocates will be understood when we state that despite the array of powerful evidence brought by the Crown, the accused nearly succeeded in escaping entirely from justice, the jury having found the charges proven by the narrow majority of one. On the 17th of January 1838 the prisoners were conveyed to London on board the Leith steam vessel, and sent thence to complete their sentence in exile. M'Neil had been married only a few months before his apprehension, and his wife was permitted to visit him in prison whilst he remained in this country

The interest which the country had taken in the trial of the cotton spinners did not terminate with their transportation. Indignation meetings were resumed throughout Scotland, and petitions, numerously signed, were sent to Parliament asking a total remission of the sentence. " Radical Paisley,' as it was then termed, distinguished itself specially, the petitioners holding a crowded meeting in the Low Church there, and expressing their indignation with the assistance of an instrumental band. On the 9th of February the matter was brought simultaneously before both Houses of Parliament. Lord Brougham presenting a petition for mitigating the sentence from Glasgow, and Mr Wakley laying four similar petitions before the House of Commons. Amongst the latter were one petition from the working classes of Dundee, and another from Manchester, signed by no less than eighteen thousand inhabitants. On the following Monday (February 12) Mr Wakley again laid on the table of the House of Commons seven petitions upon the subject from Edinburgh, Leith, Islington, Cumnock, Dalkeith, and Dublin, and on the day after he brought up other five petitions asking remission of the sentence.

Lord Brougham, in presenting the petition to the House of Lords, had animadverted severely upon the conduct alike of Crown officers and Judges in this case, pointing out, with more rhetoric than reason, that the prisoners could only have been imprisoned for *three months* in England if found guilty of the same offence, but Lord Melbourne replied to this sophistical argument with temper

ance and success. When Mr Wakley presented the last lot of petitions in the other House a debate ensued, in which the Lord-Advocate defended himself from the accusations levelled against him, and Mr Daniel O'Connell warmly supported him in his courageous attempt to expose and defeat trade terrorism. Ultimately a Committee to inquire into the nature and extent of trades combinations was appointed, and sat for a protracted period taking evidence. No legislation on this subject followed, however, for many years after, and when the Royal Commissioners on Trades Unions were appointed in 1867 they found the law unaltered. Principally through their recommendations the Unions were freed from those limitations which rendered them dangerous, and they have thus been made of real value to their members. And there is much truth in these remarks of a writer in the *Glasgow Herald* of 17th September 1883—" It is probable that in future ages the period in which combination was forbidden to workmen, whilst it was fully permitted in the case of employers, will be regarded with astonishment. It is difficult to understand why one party in the association by which wealth is produced should have been prohibited from using all necessary efforts to secure for itself its full and fair share of the profits, whilst complete freedom of action was left to the other. It would, of course, be absurd to attempt any defence of the violent means by which in former years workmen strove to attain their end. Happily those days are now long gone by, and the combination of workmen to secure their rights by legal and pacific means is as natural and ordinary an event as can be conceived "

CRAIGCROOK CASTLE IN 1770 *(From an Old Print)*

THE MYSTERY OF CRAIGCROOK

PART I

"*Mephistopheles* — One thing more—
To make the matter sure I must just beg
A line or two
Faustus — How pedant! Wilt thou have
A written document? Hast never known
Man nor the word of man?
What wouldst thou evil spirit marble brass
Parchment or paper? Shall I write with pen
Graver or style? Thou hast the choice of all
Mephis — Why with such needless vehemence exert
Thy rhetoric? The smallest scrap will do
Thou wilt subscribe it with a drop of blood

—*Goethe's Faust (Professor Ferrier's translation)*

The Castle of Craigcrook stands on the eastern slope of the Corstorphine Hills, about three miles from Edinburgh, and not far from the historical mansions of Ravelston and Lauriston the seats formerly of the families of Foulis and Keith, and of Napier and Law During this century Craigcrook has attained to a literary celebrity through having been the residence for more than thirty years of Francis Jeffrey, the autocrat of British criticism, and his long and recent connection with the romantic spot has served to overshadow to some extent all its previous history

K

The place is most picturesquely situated in the centre of a sylvan landscape, embowered amid trees, and secluded from public view The towers and spires of the Scottish metropolis may be traced from the road which leads past the Castle, and far to the northward the gleaming course of the Firth of Forth is distinctly visible Though so near the city of Edinburgh as to be within easy walking distance, the spot affords retirement and seclusion, and the beauty of the scenery with which it is surrounded has been praised alike by poet and by orator

In that sweet season when the year is green
And hearts grow merry as spring groves full of birds
While life for pleasure ripples as it runs
And young Earth putteth forth the lovely things
She hath been dreaming through long winter nights
Then Craigcrook puts its budding glory on
An emerald Eden nestling in the North
To which the mariner, worn on life's salt wave
Might point his prow and find a conqueror's home
And storm tossed Love unfold his wearied wings
Warm on the bosom of mellifluous Rest

When Jeffrey came into possession of Craigcrook

Castle in 1815 it presented a very different appearance from what it does now. Writing at that time to his father in law he thus describes it:—

"Try to conceive an old narrow high house, eighteen feet wide and fifty long, with irregular projections of all sorts, three little staircases, turrets, and a large tower at one end, with multitudes of windows of all shapes and sizes, placed at the bottom of a green slope ending in a steep woody hill, which rises to the height of 300 or 400 feet on the west, and shaded with some respectable trees near the door, with an old garden stuck close on one side of the house, and surrounded with massive and aged stone walls fifteen feet high."

So many alterations were carried out by the new proprietor that the present Castle is hardly recognisable from this description, but it is the older building that is associated with the story we have now to relate, and which is still referred to as "the Mystery of Craigcrook."

The Castle is believed to be one of the most ancient inhabited houses in the rural district of Edinburgh. The history of the estate can be traced back to the middle of the fourteenth century, at which time it belonged to the family of the Grahams of Kinpunt and Dundaff, the ancestors of the present Duke of Montrose. Afterwards it came into the possession of the Adamsons, and one of this family, who was a burgess of Edinburgh, was slain at the battle of Pinkie in 1547. It is probable that he built the old Castle of Craigcrook, as its architecture belongs to this period. The estate passed through several hands afterwards, and was at length purchased in the beginning of the eighteenth century by Mr John Strachan, a Clerk to the Signet, with whose name this mystery is inseparably connected.

Besides his residence at Craigcrook Castle, Mr Strachan had a town house in the High Street of Edinburgh, which was left in charge of a housekeeper when the family was absent. In the year 1707 this office was filled by a young woman named Helen Bell, and as the members of the household seem to have been frequently from home during that year, the housekeeper had been in the habit of admitting several of her associates somewhat freely to the house. Amongst them were two tradesmen named William Thomson and John Robertson, who appear to have been on terms of close intimacy with her. There are several versions of her story extant, and it is not easy to discover precisely what relationship existed between her and them. One writer avers that Robertson had been formerly employed in the service of Mr Strachan, and this statement is not unlikely when considered in connection with after events.

On the night of Saturday, 1st November 1707 —not Hallowe'en, as stated by one narrator— these two men were in company with Helen Bell in her master's house, and she then told them that she had orders to leave Edinburgh very early on the following Monday morning, to walk to Craigcrook Castle. At the appointed time she set out upon her journey, but was destined never to complete it. Her dead body was found lying at the foot of the Castle Rock of Edinburgh, frightfully mutilated, and it was also discovered that Mr Strachan's house in the High Street had been robbed, and a large sum of money taken from it. Though there was a considerable distance between the scenes of the murder and the robbery, it was impossible to dissociate the two crimes, and in the *Edinburgh Gazette* of the following day (Nov 4) a reward of five hundred merks was offered for the discovery of the criminals who had committed the horrid deed. Several weeks elapsed, however, without any trace of the murderers being found; but suspicion having fallen upon the man Thomson, he was apprehended, and made a full confession of his crime.

Several of the writers who narrate this story diverge from each other in some of the particulars, though they all refer to Wood's "History of Cramond" as their authority. We have thought it safest, therefore, to quote the version given by the latter writer in his somewhat rare work, so that the reader may form his own conclusions regarding it:—

"A tradition exists that a murder was committed in Craigcrook House, but it appears that this is a mistake grounded on the circumstance of Mr Strachan's housekeeper, Helen Bell, having been murdered in her way out there on Monday, 3d November 1707, by William Thomson, wright in Edinburgh, and John Robertson, smith in Pleasance. These two men had been in company with the unfortunate victim in Mr Strachan's house in Edinburgh on the Saturday preceding, and she having mentioned that she was going out to Craigcrook on the Monday morning, they met her at 5 A.M. near the West Bow, and told her they were going part of her way. She gave Thomson two bottles and the key of her master's lodging to carry in order to lighten her burden, but when they came below the Castle they threw her over the steps, struck her with a hammer, and having thus despatched her, returned to the house to rob it, having opened it with the key. They lighted a candle at the kitchen fire, prized up the study door, broke open the chest where the cash was kept, out of which they took eight bags of money and a purse of gold, leaving two bags behind. Thomson carried six of the bags and the purse, and Robertson the other two bags (one containing £100) in their aprons The latter proposed to carry all the tow and lint they could find and the bed clothes to a back room and set them on fire in order to burn the house, but Thomson said he had done wickedness enough already, and was resolved not to commit more, even when Robertson threatened him for that refusal

"What is remarkable, Thomson deposed that on their return through the Grassmarket after the murder they swore to each other to give their souls and bodies to the devil if ever any of them should discover and inform against the other, even after being apprehended Robertson proposing that this engagement should be engrossed in a bond, a man started up betwixt them in the middle of the Bow, and offered to write the bond, which they had agreed to subscribe with their blood, but on Thomson's demurring the person (whom he said he had never before seen) immediately disappeared

"The perpetrators of this atrocious action remained undiscovered for some weeks, but at last suspicions arising against Thomson he was taken up, and having made a voluntary confession of the murder and robbery, both he and Robertson were executed '

Who was the mysterious visitant who had thus appeared in the very nick of time, with his offer to prepare the soul destroying bond? Could it be a delusion of Thomson's, caused by the mental tortures of remorse, or was it a deeply laid scheme on his part to awaken special interest in his case, with a view to his escape, or was it merely a chance passer by who had listened, unperceived in the darkness of that winter morning, to the dispute between the two men, and sought to play off a joke upon them?

"No contemporary, of course," writes Dr Robert Chambers, "could be at any loss to surmise who the stranger was '

Besides the account of this case given by Wood, which we have quoted, a still more marvellous tale regarding it is related by Wodrow, the credulous minister of Eastwood, which is interesting as showing how the superstitions of early times lingered almost to our own day

CRAIGCROOK IN 1884

PART II

Mercutio —   "I talk of dreams,
Which are the children of an idle brain
Begot of nothing but vain fantasy
Which is as thin a substance as the air
And more inconstant than the wind

                        —*Romeo and Juliet*

The tale which Wodrow tells with reference to the discovery of the Craigcrook mystery is alluded to by more than one of the writers who narrate the story, but we fear that few of them have taken the trouble to examine his version of it for themselves, or they would have seen that it was quite incompatible with the facts of the case. To prevent any future allusion to Wodrow as an authority in the matter, we may lay the story as he recites it in his *Analecta*—which work is not easily referred to—in his own quaint language before the reader

The minister of Eastwood is well known for his standard works upon the history of the Church in Scotland, and for his sketches of the Scottish Reformers, but besides these serious undertakings he left behind him a profusion of notes, contemporary letters, and gossiping jottings, which are valuable as showing, unconsciously on his part, the manners of the time (1679 1734) in which he flourished They were published long after his death under the title of *Analecta Scotica*, and the following *verbatim* quotation may give some idea of the style of this work, and afford a glimpse of the writer's character —

" Sept 1730 —

" Mrs Maxwell at the same time told us that shee had what folloues from the first hands at Edinburgh —About seven or eight years ago, Graycrookes, the gentleman that left his estate by a Mort fication for the support of indigent ministers' widoues, and his lady, from whom I think my informer had the account at that time, had a servant man and woman   The woman had some money scraped together, and shee was murdered in a cellar, as was violently suspected, and her chest opened and robbed   and Gray crooks (if I remember) missed some of his own money at the same time   The matter was so secretly done that ther appeared no presumptions at all against the man   However, Graycrooks parted with him very soon A year or more afterwards, one night the Lady Graycrooks dreamed that she saw the man murder the woman in the cellar and carry off her money, and put it in two old barrells filled with trash When she awakned she communicat her dream, which left a deep impression upon [her] Graycrooks was a liver and a wise man, and desired her to speak of it to nobody He made inquiry about the fellou, who was now set up for a smith, I think, some part in the suburbs of Edinburgh, and found that he had plenty of money In a feu dayes he got a warrand from the Magistrates suddainly to search his house, which was done, and in two old barrells, as his lady had dreamed, full of old iron nails and such trash, found some money, and his own baggs, which he krew on seeing them, and which had been missing at that time The fellow was apprehended, and tryed and sentenced to dye, and if I remember, confessed the murder and was execute'

A slight examination of this story will show that it is a very different tale from the true account of the Craigcrook tragedy which we have given as found in Wood's "History of Cramond," and in the newspapers of the time Wodrow, writing in 1730, alludes to the incident as having happened "about seven or eight years ago —that is to say, in 1722 The discovery of the murderer, he avers, did not take place till "a year or more afterwards"—say 1723—and the confession and execution would not likely happen, therefore, until 1724 But we find that Wood's statement of the date of the murder as "3d Nov 1707' is confirmed in an indirect but indisputable manner by the appearance of the advertisement offering a reward for the apprehension of the murderers in the *Edinburgh Gazette* for 4th Nov 1707, some fifteen years before the date assigned by Wodrow

The latter seems to wish to impart an air of accuracy to his statement by declaring that his informer had the account "from the first hands at Edinburgh," which he afterwards explains to mean, according to his supposition, the Lady Craigcrook herself We have absolute proof, however, that this statement cannot possibly be correct Mr Strachan, the Laird of Craigcrook, died in 1719, five years before the murderer was brought to justice, according to Wodrow, and there is every probability that his wife predeceased him for the following reason By a deed dated 24th September 1712 he bequeathed the whole of his property, including Craigcrook and North Clermiston, together with all his movables, with the exception of a few legacies, for a charitable purpose The fund thus provided still exists, and is known under the name of the "Craigcrook

Mortification,' its object being to assist orphans and old men and women who have been reduced in circumstances The trustees are the Presbytery of Edinburgh, the members of the Faculty of Advocates, and two members of the Society of Writers to the Signet, the beneficiaries being limited to old persons of over sixty five and orphans under twelve years of age The completeness with which Mr Strachan devised his property in 1712 suggests the idea that his wife was dead at the time since no provision is made for life renting her in the lands should she survive him If this supposition be true, Wodrow is in error to the extent of twelve years, and it is manifestly impossible that his 'informer' could have heard this marvellous tale from Lady Craigcrook's own mouth in 1730 unless we invent another miracle

The very terms of the story are different in most important particulars from that which Wood relates Thomson, instead of being a wright, is described by Wodrow as holding a situation as fellow servant with Helen Bell, and afterwards becoming a smith The murder is said to have been committed in a cellar, not on the road to Craigcrook, and the original motive suggested is the robbery of the unfortunate girl's savings, though no allusion whatever is made elsewhere to this theory For clearness and coherency Wood's narrative is certainly preferable, and it has the additional recommendation of being corroborated by the newspapers of the period And, indeed, upon its own internal evidence, we are almost forced to reject Wodrow's story as absolutely incredible

But how does it happen that we find a grave and reverend historian and divine setting down so non sensical a legend amongst matter of the most serious kind ? Was he the victim of an original joke, or merely the victim of a victim ' or had his "informer" mixed up two separate stories so thoroughly in her mind that they had fallen into inextricable confusion ? The latter, perhaps, is the most reasonable explanation and curiously enough we notice that it is precisely what has happened to the latest narrator of this Craigcrook Mystery The author of a recent history of Edinburgh when dealing with this case begins by quoting Chambers, then winders into Wood's narrative—which he has evidently never read "at first hands,' since he misquotes it—and after denouncing "the credulous Wodrow,' strangely recites the dream story of the latter as "more to the purpose" than the first version he has given ' There seems to be a fatal fascination about this Craigcrook tragedy which beguiles the clearest heads into temporary aberration of intellect, making them confess their in competence to deal with it upon rational grounds. We have endeavoured to lay the whole matter before the reader in an intelligible manner, and trust the subject has not betrayed us into similar obscurity.

Apart from the interest of the story itself, it is a curious illustration of the credulity of the age that even Wodrow was prepared to accept the dream theory as an unquestionable statement of fact. Though much maligned by his theological enemies, there can be no doubt that he was possessed of a highly cultivated mind, and was no simpleton to be easily imposed on. His faith in this dream, therefore, may be taken as exhibiting the notions of educated men at the time upon the subject. That the story was actually told him hardly admits of doubt, for Charles James Fox in his "History of James II" alludes to him as one "whose veracity is above suspicion," and he had nothing to gain by inventing such a tale merely for the pleasure of inserting it in a private note book. John Hill Burton's estimate of Wodrow is perhaps the most reasonable when he describes him as "a prejudiced, but, in a great measure, a trustworthy narrator of things within the scope of his narrow inquiries." He was credulous, but not more so than his contemporaries, and even expresses doubts of the genuineness of manifestations which were not questioned by his compeers. On the whole, therefore, we are inclined to think that the Craigcrook story did not present so many difficulties in the way of its acceptance as to lead him to doubt its credibility, and his ignorance of the original parties concerned prevented him from testing its genuineness as we have done. We trust, however, that we have sufficiently shown the absurdity of this tale, and that it will no longer be referred to either as a proof of dream revelations or as a veritable version of the mystery of Craigcrook.

The exquisite taste of Francis Jeffrey and his wife led them to transform the old castle into a rural retreat of sylvan beauty. The ancient circular tower which formerly rose, bare and forbidding, to confront the visitor, was covered by climbing ivy and clematis, which gave it at once an artistic beauty and an antique charm. Portions of the wall which surrounded the policies were set apart for the cultivation of roses, and these soon became one of the chief attractions of the place. Lord Cockburn, enumerating the delights of Craigcrook, speaks of "the flowers, not forgetting the glorious wall of roses," and Gerald Massey breaks forth into song as he contemplates them —

"Craigcrook Roses! ruby golden,
    Glowing gorgeous faint with passion,
To the sweet flower-soul unfolden,
    Wreath me in the old Greek fashion
Queen of sweetness crowned with splendour
    Every rich round bud uncloses,
Yet so meek and womanly tender
Are you royal Craigcrook Roses,
Warm and winy Craigcrook Roses."

To the latter poet do we owe the poetical yet truthful description of Craigcrook as it appeared one hundred and fifty years after its tragedy had been accomplished; and with it we shall close this "tale of the days of old" —

" 'Mid glimpsing greenery at the hill foot stands
The castle with its tiny town of towers
A smiling Martyr to the climbing strength
Of Ivy that will crown the old bald head,
And Roses that will mask him merry and young
Like an old man with children round his knees,
With cups of colour reeling Roses rise
On walls and bushes, red and yellow and white,
A dance and dazzle of Roses range all round.

The path runs down and peeps out at the lane,
That loiters on by fields of wheat and bean,
Till the white gleaming road winds city ward.
Afar in floods of sunshine blinding white,
The city lieth in its quiet pride,
With castled crown, looking on towns and shires,
And hills from which cloud highlands climb the heavens
A happy thing in glory smiles the Firth,
Its glowing azure winding like an arm
Around the warm waist of the yielding land."

REFERENCES

PETER YOUNG —Black Kalendar of Aberdeen, Chambers's Miscellany, Tract "Gypsies," Pitcairn's Criminal Trials, Blackwood's Magazine, Vol II

GRAHAM OF FINTRY —Pitcairn's Criminal Trials.

WIFE O' DENSIDE —Trial reprinted from "Dundee Courier," 1827; Broadsheet Account of Trial and Verdict, Trial, specially reported, Montrose, 1827, "Dundee Advertiser" of the following dates —1826, October 5th, 12th, December 14th, 1827, January 4th, 11th, 18th, 25th, February 15th, 22nd

BOSWELL MURDER TRIAL —Acta Parliamentorum, IV 230, VI 601, 824, X 77, Edinburgh Review, LXXV 422, LXXX 229 Report of Hist MSS Commission, IV 530, 531 Edinburgh Annual Register for 1819, page 316, for 1822, pt II, page 3 Townsend's "Modern State Trials," I 171 "Dundee Advertiser," 1821, October 5th, November 2nd, 1822, February 1st, March 28th, April 18th, 25th, June 13th, 20th, July 4th, 18th Cockburn's 'Memorials" Lockhart s "Life of Scott'

MALCOLM GILLESPIE —Report of Trial, with Life and Dying Declaration, Aberdeen, 1827, Edinburgh Review, LII 398, LV 528, Black Kalendar of Aberdeen, Cockburn's "Memorials," "Aberdeen Chronicle," 1827, November 19th

GLASGOW COTTON SPINNERS —Townsend's "Modern State Trials,' II 156, Trial of Glasgow Cotton-Spinners, reported by James Marshall, S S C, 1st and 2nd Editions, Report of Trial of Thomas Hunter, &c, by Arch Swinton, Advocate, Edinburgh Review, LXVII 244, J Hill Burton's "Political and Social Economy," Edinburgh Annual Register for 1825, p. 134, Eleventh Report of Royal Commissioners on Trades Unions (1867), Vol. I, Memo by Sir W Erle, "Glasgow Chronicle," 1837, November 24th, "Glasgow Herald," 1883, September 17th, "Dundee Advertiser," 1837, July 28th, August 11th, November 3rd, 10th, 17th, December 1st, 8th, 15th, 22nd, 1838, January 5th, 12th, 19th, 26th, February 2nd, 9th, 16th, 23rd, March 2nd, April 20th

CRAIG CROOK.—Chambers's "Domestic Annals," III 333, Grant's "Old and New Edinburgh," III 108, Wodrow's "Analecta," IV 171, Wood's "History of Cramond," p 39, Cockburn's "Life of Jeffrey," I 134, II 154

9 781275 0999